VOTES FOR WOMEN!

ALSO BY WINIFRED CONKLING

PASSENGER ON THE PEARL
The True Story of Emily Edmonson's Flight from Slavery

RADIOACTIVE!
*How Irène Curie & Lise Meitner Revolutionized Science
and Changed the World*

VOTES FOR WOMEN!

American Suffragists
and the Battle for the Ballot

WINIFRED CONKLING

ALGONQUIN 2020

Published by
Algonquin Young Readers
an imprint of Algonquin Books of Chapel Hill
Post Office Box 2225
Chapel Hill, North Carolina 27515-2225

a division of
Workman Publishing
225 Varick Street
New York, New York 10014

First paperback edition, Algonquin Young Readers, January 2020. Originally
published in hardcover by Algonquin Young Readers in February 2018.
Printed in the United States of America.
Published simultaneously in Canada by Thomas Allen & Son Limited.
Design by Carla Weise.

LIBRARY OF CONGRESS CATALOGING-IN-PUBLICATION DATA
Names: Conkling, Winifred, author.
Title: Votes for women! : American suffragists and the
battle for the ballot / Winifred Conkling.
Description: First edition. | Chapel Hill, North Carolina : Algonquin
Young Readers, 2018. | Includes bibliographical references and index.
Identifiers: LCCN 2017031132 (print) | LCCN 2017044599 (ebook) |
ISBN 9781616207694 (ebook) | ISBN 9781616207342 (hardcover : alk. paper)
Subjects: LCSH: Women—Suffrage—United States—History—Juvenile
literature. | Suffragists—United States—History—Juvenile literature. |
Women's rights—United States—History—Juvenile literature. | CYAC:
Women—Suffrage—United States—History. | Suffragists—United States—
History. | Women's rights—United States—History.
Classification: LCC JK1898 (ebook) | LCC JK1898.C656 2018 (print) |
DDC 324.6/23/0973—dc23
LC record available at https://lccn.loc.gov/2017031132

ISBN 978-1-61620-988-9 (PB)

10 9 8 7 6 5 4 3 2 1
First Paperback Edition

We all know how the story ends:
For nearly a hundred years, American women have had
the right to vote in our country's elections.

Many of us know how the story began:
A group of women gathered to discuss starting
a movement for women's rights at a meeting
in Seneca Falls, New York, in 1848.

But a lot happened in between,
and far too few of us know those stories.

This book is dedicated to my daughters—
Hannah, Ella, and Gwendolyn—
and every other reader who
wants to know the whole story.

CONTENTS

PREFACE

"AYE"

Everyone expected Harry T. Burn to vote against the Nineteenth Amendment, which gave women the right to vote. The twenty-four-year-old first-term member of the Tennessee House of Representatives was from Niota, Tennessee, a conservative area in the mountains. It was August 1920. Burn was running for reelection in the fall, and most of his constituents were opposed to female suffrage. If he wanted to win, surely, they thought, he would vote against the bill.

But Burn hadn't made up his mind.

Tennessee governor Albert H. Roberts had called the state legislature into special session to consider whether to support the Nineteenth Amendment. The year before, the United States Congress had passed legislation giving women the right to vote, but before it could become the law of the land, three-fourths of the forty-eight states needed to ratify or approve it.

Thirty-five states had voted in favor of the amendment. One

more was needed to make it law. Would Tennessee be that state?

From the moment Burn and his fellow legislators arrived in Nashville, women on both sides of the issue had been pressuring them for their votes. Carrie Chapman Catt, president of the National American Woman Suffrage Association, organized the pro-suffrage side. Josephine Anderson Pearson, head of the Tennessee State Association Opposed to Woman Suffrage, worked against ratification of the amendment.

Both women stayed at the elegant Hermitage Hotel, which became ground zero in the suffrage fight. Pearson took over the hotel mezzanine and decorated the room with American flags, red roses, and a sign that read ANTI-RATIFICATION HEADQUARTERS. She passed out propaganda arguing that women didn't need the vote because they were already represented by their husbands, fathers, and brothers.

Catt kept a lower profile. To downplay accusations of being an outside agitator, she ran her operation out of her hotel room, offering direction to state and local suffragists. She left the lobbying to a group of young, beautiful pro-suffrage Tennessee wives and mothers, whose presence undermined the argument of the "antis"—those who did not support women's right to vote—who said that the suffrage movement was run by outsiders and bitter, ugly old spinsters.

Both sides invited the legislators to receptions and dinners at the fashionable Hermitage, which was just down the street from the Tennessee State Capitol. As soon as politicians entered the building, women on both sides of the issue would approach the men. In what became known as the War of the Roses, the antis slipped red roses into the legislators' lapels. The suffragists, who supported women's right to vote, passed out yellow roses.

On the morning of August 18, a stiflingly hot day even by Nashville standards, elected officials gathered at the statehouse. The

Tennessee Senate had passed the suffrage measure five days before. It was up to the House of Representatives to decide the issue.

Women crowded the second-floor galleries of the statehouse, waiting to see history made. A suffragist had attached a yellow sunflower to the golden eagle statue perched at the front of the chamber. Some tried to count flowers to determine which side was going to win, but the room seemed evenly divided between those wearing red and yellow roses.

Catt waited back at the hotel, sitting next to the window and listening to the noisy crowds at the statehouse.

At 10:30 a.m., Seth Walker, Speaker of the House and a dedicated anti, gaveled the meeting to order.

He called for a vote to set aside the decision until the fall, which would mean women would not be able to vote in that year's election.

The roll call vote on that question ended in a tie, 48 to 48.

The Speaker called for a second vote. The result was the same.

In that moment, Walker changed his strategy. Since the suffragists didn't appear to have enough votes to win, he decided to call for an immediate vote on the question.

The legislature debated the issue for an hour, but the arguments had all been heard before. It seemed that the legislators had made up their minds.

"The hour has come!" Walker said.

Harry Burn, the youngest member of the state legislature, wore a red anti-suffrage rose on his lapel. He had voted with the antis to delay the decision, but this was a vote on the main question.

The roll call began.

"Anderson," the clerk said.

"Aye."

Sweat trickled down Burn's face, a combination of a hot day, a crowded room, and nerves.

Blackman. Bond. Boyd. One by one, he heard the names of his colleagues called in alphabetical order. His name was seventh on the list. It all came down to this: a single man, a single vote, a single question. Yes or no. Should American women have the right to vote?

His heart pounded. What was he going to do?

"Burn," the clerk said. Burn had to make a choice, take a stand.

"Aye," he said in a weak voice. Yes.

Burn had changed his mind.

Every outward sign had indicated that Burn would vote against suffrage. What no one but Burn knew was that earlier that morning he had received an important letter that made him question his position. He had that letter in his pocket when he cast his vote.

The scene in the Tennessee State Capitol as the clerk tallied the votes on the suffrage question

A Confederate veteran of the American Civil War sits between Josephine Anderson Pearson (left, with flag) and Mrs. James Pinkard, president of the Southern Women's League for the Rejection of the Susan B. Anthony Amendment, at the Hermitage Hotel in Nashville, Tennessee.

With that single vote, that single syllable, the all-male Tennessee legislature had changed the United States Constitution and given women nationwide the right to vote.

The question seemed to come down to this single moment, but this vote, this turning point in history, had actually been more than seventy years in the making. Women had been working for the right to vote since Elizabeth Cady Stanton and a group of reformers first called for female suffrage in 1848.

In the middle of the nineteenth century, most Americans considered female suffrage a ludicrous idea, a radical position first suggested by a radical woman. But why was Elizabeth Cady Stanton willing to make such an unusual demand? What made her a rebel willing to challenge law and custom and risk scorn and rejection to take a stand for women's right to vote? The story of women's suffrage ended with Henry Burn's vote in the Tennessee statehouse in 1920, but it began almost a century earlier with Elizabeth Cady, a young girl in Johnstown, New York, in 1826.

1 "OH, MY DAUGHTER, I WISH YOU WERE A BOY!"

Before Seneca Falls

Johnstown, New York, 1826

ELIZABETH CADY LISTENED TO HER OLDER BROTHER'S barking cough echo down the upstairs hallway. She watched her father pace back and forth, straining to hear his son's next wheezing breath. Hour after hour, Elizabeth heard the rhythmic gasping, the silence growing longer between each lungful of air, until, finally, the breathing stopped.

It happened quickly: Eleazar, just twenty years old, had recently graduated from Union College and returned to the family estate forty miles northwest of Albany, planning to study law under his father. He had been perfectly healthy until that morning, when he woke with a fever and croupy cough. Twelve hours later he was dead.

In the days after the unexpected loss, the family mourned, but Elizabeth's father, Judge Daniel Cady, was inconsolable. He had already lost four sons to childhood illnesses, and he had expected

Eleazar—the last surviving male heir—to be the one who would inherit his wealth and follow in his footsteps.

"A young man of great talent and promise, [Eleazar] was the pride of my father's heart," Elizabeth remembered, acknowledging that "this son filled a larger place in our father's affections and future plans than the five daughters together."

Her brother's death was a turning point in Elizabeth's life. Decades later, she still vividly remembered entering the darkened parlor in their home and finding the mirrors and pictures draped in white, a mourning custom of the time. Her father sat next to her brother's casket.

Elizabeth didn't want to leave her father alone with his grief, so she entered the room and climbed onto his lap. He mechanically put his arms around his eleven-year-old daughter, and she rested her head against his heart. They sat for several minutes in silence as Elizabeth tried to think of something to say or do to ease her father's pain.

Eventually, her father sighed and told her, "Oh, my daughter, I wish you were a boy!"

In response, Elizabeth threw her arms around her father's neck and said, "I will try to be all my brother was." It was a mission that would motivate and frustrate her all her life. "Then and there," she later wrote in her autobiography, "I resolved that I would not give so much time as heretofore to play, but would study and strive to be at the head of all my classes and thus delight my father's heart."

Elizabeth began thinking about how she could live up to her promise. "All that day and far into the night I pondered the problem of boyhood," she wrote. "I thought that the chief thing to be done in order to equal boys was to be learned and courageous."

In the morning, Elizabeth went outside and greeted her neighbor, the Reverend Simon Hosack, who was working in his garden. She asked him, "Which do you like best, boys or girls?"

"Why, girls, to be sure," he said, undoubtedly sensing her need for support. "I would not give you for all the boys in Christendom."

"My father prefers boys," Elizabeth said.

She asked her neighbor for help studying Greek, a subject most often studied by boys. Reverend Hosack agreed to help. He lent her the textbook he had studied while attending the University of Glasgow, and she completed her first Greek grammar lesson before breakfast.

She also set out to prove her courage and physical strength. Elizabeth became a skilled equestrian and learned how to jump ditches and four-foot fences on horseback. At first, she was frightened, but soon she learned to ride as boldly as any boy she knew.

In addition to trying to earn her father's respect for her accomplishments, Elizabeth also stood by her father's side emotionally. She became her father's companion on his daily visits to the cemetery to visit her brother's grave.

"For months afterward, at the twilight hour, I went with my father to the new-made grave," she wrote. "Near it stood two tall poplar trees, against one of which I leaned, while my father threw himself on the grave, with outstretched arms, as if to embrace his child." This painful ritual went on week after week, until "at last the frosts and storms of November came and threw a chilling barrier between the living and the dead, and we went there no more."

Elizabeth longed for her father's approval, but he was stingy with his praise. Still, she kept up with her study of Greek and made rapid progress. When their neighbor, Reverend Hosack, would visit the house, Elizabeth would whisper in his ear, "Tell my father how fast I get on."

Eager to oblige, Reverend Hosack would boast about how bright Elizabeth was and how well she was doing, but her father would only sigh.

"I taxed every power," Elizabeth remembered, "hoping some

day to hear my father say: 'Well, a girl is as good as a boy, after all.' But he never said it."

Determined to prove she was her brother's equal, in addition to Greek, Elizabeth began to study Latin and mathematics with a class of older boys at the Johnstown Academy. Several years later, two prizes were presented for the top Greek students in the school. Elizabeth took second. "Now, my father will be satisfied with me," she thought.

Overjoyed, she ran down the hill, rushed breathlessly into her father's office, and placed her prize, a book written in Greek, on the table. "There, I got it!" she said.

Her father thumbed through the book and asked Elizabeth a few questions about the class, then handed the prize back to her.

She waited for him to say something about her achievement.

"You should have been a boy!" he said finally, and Elizabeth wilted. She knew her father loved her, but that was not the point. The one thing she could not do—be a boy—seemed to be the only thing that would improve her status in his eyes. She realized that she could never satisfy her father in this way no matter how hard she tried.

Daniel Cady (1773–1859) was a lawyer and judge in upstate New York. He was elected to the state legislature in 1808, and he served until 1814, when he was elected to Congress. He was defeated after one term and returned to Johnstown to practice law. In 1847, he became an associate justice of the New York State Supreme Court for the Fourth District and served until he was eighty-two years old. Elizabeth Cady Stanton described her father as "a conservative's conservative." She wrote, "Though gentle and tender, he had such a dignified repose and reserve of manner that, as children, we regarded him with fear rather than affection."

"GIRLS WERE CONSIDERED AN INFERIOR ORDER OF BEINGS"

Elizabeth Cady began to notice other ways that most people favored boys over girls. She thought back to one of her earliest memories, when she was four years old and her sister Catherine was born. Elizabeth noticed that when a boy was born, a family received congratulations, while disappointment often followed the delivery of a girl. "I heard so many friends remark, 'What a pity it is she's a girl!' that I felt a kind of compassion for the little baby," she wrote years later. "I did not understand at that time that girls were considered an inferior order of beings."

Elizabeth learned more about the second-class status of women when she overheard the female clients who came to beg for help at her father's law office, which adjoined the main house. One afternoon, Elizabeth listened to a widow named Flora Campbell tearfully explain that, without her consent, her husband had mortgaged the farm that had been in her family for years. Creditors now claimed the land, and Campbell didn't know what to do.

Surely, her father would come up with a clever legal solution, Elizabeth had assumed. Instead, she stood dumbstruck as her father explained that as a wife, Campbell had no legal right to challenge her husband: He had the freedom to do as he pleased with the land, and she could not stop him.

It wasn't fair.

After the meeting, Elizabeth went up to Campbell and offered to help. She said that she was going to get a pair of scissors and go through her father's legal books, cutting out the passages that were unfair to women, as if she could eliminate the laws by slicing them out of the legal texts.

Elizabeth's father found out about his daughter's plot and explained that the only way she could change the law was to go the capital of New York and convince the legislators to vote for new laws.

"When you are grown up, and able to prepare a speech, you must go down to Albany and talk to the legislators; tell them all you have seen in this office," her father said. "If you can persuade them to pass new laws, the old ones will be a dead letter."

So instead of cutting up her father's law books, Elizabeth read them and made notes in the margins of the sections that affected women. The more she learned about the law, the more unfair to women it seemed.

In the early nineteenth century, women had few legal rights. Married women had even fewer rights than single women. When they were young and single, girls were legally bound to do whatever their fathers said; when they married, women had to obey their husbands. Legally, a married woman suffered "civil death." In other words, she and her husband became one person—and that one was the husband.

Women did not have the right to own property.

Women could not enter into contracts or sign legal documents.

Women could not keep their wages; if a woman worked, her pay belonged to her husband or her father.

Women who did work had few job options, and they were always paid significantly less than men for the same work. Teaching was the most common female profession at the time, and schools typically paid women 20 to 50 percent less than they paid men.

A woman could not have custody of her children if she divorced her husband for any reason; her children—like all of her property—belonged to her husband.

Women could be beaten by their husbands and fathers, as long as the men used a whip no thicker than a thumb.

Women could not attend college; higher education was considered unnecessary for women, who were expected to manage the home.

Women could not serve on juries or testify in court.

Women needed male escorts when they traveled.

Women were expected to remain quiet in public. Addressing a "promiscuous" audience—a group of women and men—was considered scandalous.

Women did not have the right to vote.

Of all of these injustices, Elizabeth considered suffrage, the right to vote, most important. If women had the right to vote, she believed, they would have the power to change all the other laws that kept them unequal to men.

SPEAKING OUT FOR WOMEN'S RIGHTS

By the time she was a teenager, Elizabeth Cady had become outspoken in her support of women's rights. At any given time, two or three law students studied under her father, and many of them delighted in teasing Elizabeth about her passion for equality.

One Christmas, Elizabeth showed one of the law students a new coral necklace and bracelets she had been given. The law student taunted her, saying that if at some point in the future she should become his wife, then the jewelry would be his. "I could take them and lock them up, and you could never wear them except with my permission," he said. "I could even exchange them for a box of cigars, and you could watch them evaporate in smoke."

Elizabeth had no rebuttal. He was right. It was not fair, but it was the law.

Elizabeth enjoyed sparring with the young apprentices. She appreciated the fact that they took her seriously. "Nothing pleased me better than a long argument with them on woman's equality," she remembered. "I confess that I did not study so much for a love of the truth or my own development, in these days, as to make those young men recognize my equality."

When not debating the law, she challenged the law students to chess and other board games. Her intelligence and take-no-prisoners approach to playing made her a formidable opponent. "I soon noticed that, after losing a few games of chess, my opponent talked less of masculine superiority," she wrote in her autobiography.

As Elizabeth grew older, Judge Cady may have become concerned about his daughter's feminist philosophy. Behavior that had seemed clever and precocious in childhood would have been considered uncouth in a young woman. He believed that women should have no public role outside the home. So after Elizabeth finished high school, her father encouraged her to enjoy her social life and learn "how to keep house and make puddings." He imagined a future for her as a wife and mother, defined by her sex and limited to her proper place—in the "domestic sphere."

Elizabeth envisioned a different future for herself. She wanted to continue her education. Her brother-in-law Edward Bayard defended her ambition. He urged her father to allow Elizabeth to attend Troy Female Seminary, a secondary school founded by Emma Willard in 1821. Bayard argued that Elizabeth's curiosity and intellect demanded additional education. Eventually, Judge Cady gave in.

However, Elizabeth was disappointed at the prospect of attending an all-girls' seminary instead of Union College. "The thought of a school without boys, who had been to me such a stimulus both in study and play, seemed to my imagination dreary and profitless," Elizabeth later wrote.

When she arrived on campus, Elizabeth discovered that she had already mastered most of the academic curriculum offered at the school. "I had already studied everything that was taught there except French, music, and dancing," she wrote, "so I devoted myself to these accomplishments."

She settled in and began to thrive. "The large house, the society of so many girls, the walks about the city, the novelty of everything made the new life more enjoyable than I had anticipated," Elizabeth recalled.

Elizabeth's confidence vanished later that year, however, when she and some of the other girls at school attended a six-week series of religious revival meetings led by the Reverend Charles Grandison Finney, a dynamic evangelical minister, whom Elizabeth later called "a terrifier of human souls."

Reverend Finney was tall and intimidating: His voice boomed, his face grimaced and frowned, and his eyes stared, piercing and cold. He lectured about the personal choice between salvation and

Troy Female Seminary, established in 1821 by Emma Willard, was the first secondary school in the country to provide women with an education equal to that offered to men.

damnation, and although Elizabeth tried to remain on the side of righteousness, she was haunted by the prospect of hellfire and eternal damnation.

"Fear of the judgment seized my soul," she wrote. "Visions of the lost haunted my dreams." She became sick and had to return home, but she didn't feel safe, even in the security of her childhood bedroom. She had trouble falling asleep, and her nights were interrupted by vivid nightmares. "I often at night roused my father from his slumbers to pray for me," she wrote, "lest I should be cast into the bottomless pit."

It took weeks for her to sleep through the night. Rather than strengthening her faith, Elizabeth's traumatic experience with Reverend Finney made her skeptical of organized religion, a doubt that continued for the rest of her life.

Ultimately, it was the comfort offered by her brother-in-law Edward Bayard that calmed her. He encouraged her to read science texts to improve her understanding of the world around her. "Religious superstition gave place to rational ideas based on scientific facts," she wrote, "and . . . as I looked at everything from a new standpoint, I grew more and more happy." Elizabeth's faith in science made her less anxious. She returned to school and finished her education, and she never again attended a revival meeting.

VISITING PETERBORO

After graduating from Troy Female Seminary in 1832, Elizabeth returned home. For a time, she fulfilled her father's expectation of living a frivolous, carefree life; she loved riding horses, singing, dancing, socializing, and flirting with the law students who studied with her father. She might have married and settled on a more

Gerrit Smith (1797–1874) was one of the richest men in the United States, heir to a vast fortune acquired through fur trapping and land speculation. He used his fortune to finance liberal causes, including abolition, temperance, and women's rights.

conventional path if she had not spent several weeks each summer visiting her cousin Gerrit Smith in Peterboro, New York.

Smith was an eccentric rebel who surrounded himself with people interested in the progressive issues of the day, and Elizabeth found the environment at his home a thrilling contrast to her father's safe, conservative household. "Here one was sure to meet scholars, philosophers, philanthropists, judges, bishops, clergymen, and statesmen," Elizabeth wrote. She loved the spirited discussions and provocative debates. "The rousing arguments of Peterboro," Elizabeth wrote, "made social life [at home] seem tame and profitless."

She often stayed at her cousin's estate for weeks at a time, enjoying "an atmosphere of love and peace, of freedom and good cheer." It was there that she underwent a radical education that changed her worldview and altered the course of her life.

One day, Elizabeth was in the parlor of her cousin's Peterboro home chatting with relatives when Cousin Gerrit came in.

"I have a most important secret to tell you," he said, "which you must keep to yourselves religiously for twenty-four hours."

Intrigued, Elizabeth and the others promised. At his request, the young women followed him upstairs to the third floor. Gerrit opened the door to a large room, where a mixed-race girl, about eighteen years old, sat in silence.

"Harriet," Smith said, "I have brought all my young cousins to see you. I want you to make good abolitionists of them by telling them the history of your life."

Smith told the women that Harriet Powell was a slave from Mississippi who had recently escaped while in Syracuse with the slaveholder. "She will start [for Canada] this evening and you may never have another opportunity of seeing a slave girl face to face," he said, "so ask her all you care to know of the system of slavery."

For two hours, Harriet recounted the story of how she was torn from her family and sold "for her beauty" in the New Orleans market when she was fourteen years old. "The details of her story I need not repeat," Elizabeth wrote. "The fate of such girls is too well known to need rehearsal." Suffice it to say, Elizabeth and the others learned the truth about how young African American girls were raped and sexually molested by those who held them in slavery.

Elizabeth wept as she heard Harriet's story. "We needed no further education to make us earnest abolitionists," she wrote.

That night, Elizabeth watched as Harriet dressed in the plain gray dress and bonnet typically worn by Quaker women, then left with one of Gerrit Smith's clerks in a carriage bound for Oswego, New York, where they planned to cross the lake to freedom in Canada.

The next day, Elizabeth trembled when the slaveholder and marshals from Syracuse arrived at the Smith home. They had managed to track Harriet to the house, but they did not know if she was still there. Elizabeth admired her cousin's cleverness and courage as he welcomed the men and gave them permission to search the house and grounds.

He also invited the men to stay for dinner.

It was then that Elizabeth realized what Cousin Gerrit was doing: The longer he delayed the men in their search, the more time Harriet had to get away.

Over dinner, the men politely discussed the problem of slavery. At the end of the evening, they shook hands. By the time the slave owner had resumed his search, Harriet had made her way safely to freedom.

"WHAT THEN CAN WOMAN DO FOR THE SLAVE, WHEN SHE HERSELF IS UNDER THE FEET OF MAN AND SHAMED INTO SILENCE?"

After hearing Harriet's story, Elizabeth's respect for abolitionists grew. At Peterboro, she met other abolitionists, including the Grimké sisters, Sarah and Angelina, daughters of a South Carolina slaveholding family. Elizabeth learned that the sisters had grown up witnessing the horrors of slavery. When they were young adults, the Grimkés had moved to Philadelphia, Pennsylvania, and become Quakers. Angelina had recently written a pamphlet titled *An Appeal to the Christian Women of the South*. A few months later, Sarah published *An Epistle to the Clergy of the Southern States*. These pamphlets were widely read by abolitionists in the North, but they were confiscated and burned in the South.

Elizabeth admired the Grimkés' courage to publish their work, but she was even more intrigued with their role as public speakers, because at the time, it was considered scandalous for women to speak in public.

At first, the Grimké sisters were invited by the American Anti-Slavery Society to discuss their experiences with slavery with small groups of women in private parlors. When the parlors became too crowded, they moved to church halls, and it was not long before hundreds of people attended their speeches. They drew large crowds both because they offered a unique perspective as Southerners who had witnessed slavery firsthand, and because Angelina was an effective and engaging speaker.

The Grimké sisters continued to ignore convention when they set off on an extensive lecture tour across Massachusetts in 1837. The fact that they drew large crowds infuriated a group of prominent clergymen, who called their behavior "intolerably offensive and disgusting." A pastoral letter from the General Association of Congregational Ministers of Massachusetts denounced the sisters

Sarah (1792–1873), left, and Angelina Grimké (1805–1879) were abolitionists, feminists, and writers. In February 1838, Angelina addressed the Massachusetts state legislature, becoming the first American woman to speak before a legislative body. She spoke against slavery and for women's right to become more politically active.

as unwomanly and unchristian, arguing that they would fall in "shame and dishonor in the dust."

Unrepentant, the Grimkés continued with their work. Sarah wrote a pamphlet titled *Letters on the Equality of the Sexes, and the Condition of Woman*. In it she denied any biblical justification for the inferior position of woman. "I ask no favors for my sex," Grimké wrote. "I surrender not our claim to equality. All I ask of our brethren is, that they will take their feet from off our necks and permit us to stand upright on that ground which God designed us to occupy." Angelina wrote a series of letters about women's role in society that were published in the *Liberator*, an abolitionist newspaper.

Elizabeth marveled at the Grimké sisters' boldness and bravery. Other abolitionists at Peterboro begged the sisters to lower their profile, fearful that the controversy around women's rights would detract from the main cause, ending slavery.

Angelina stood firm. "Why, my dear brothers can you not see the deep laid scheme of the clergy against us as lecturers?" she wrote in a letter to two abolitionist leaders. "If we surrender the right to *speak* in public this year, we must surrender the right to petition next year, and the right to *write* the years after, and so on. What *then* can *woman* do for the slave, when she herself is under the feet of man and shamed into *silence*?"

In her autobiography, Elizabeth described the discussions of abolition and women's rights at Peterboro as "white hot." "I had become interested in the anti-slavery and temperance questions, and was deeply impressed with the appeals and arguments," she wrote. "I felt a new inspiration in life and was enthused with new ideas of individual rights and the basic principles of government." The world seemed open to new ideas and new possibilities for women, and Elizabeth was trying to figure out where she fit in.

MARRYING HENRY STANTON

While visiting Peterboro in the fall of 1839, twenty-four-year-old Elizabeth was introduced to Henry Brewster Stanton. He was tall and handsome, charismatic, and, in Elizabeth's words, "the most eloquent and impassioned orator on the anti-slavery platform." In other words, he was the type of man she knew she would fall for, except that she had been told he was already engaged to another woman.

Because she did not see the possibility of starting a relationship with him, Elizabeth felt at ease around Henry. She felt free to be herself—opinionated, witty, and playful—and, of course, the two hit it off right away. Elizabeth heard Henry speak at a series of anti-slavery conventions in the area. "As I had a passion for oratory, I was deeply impressed with his power," she wrote. "He could make his audience both laugh and cry."

Elizabeth hadn't met a man like Henry before, and she was smitten. Not long after they began to get to know one another, she discovered that he did not have a girlfriend after all. By that point, they were already mutually infatuated.

They shared stories of their pasts. When Elizabeth confided her terror after hearing the sermons of the Reverend Charles Finney, Henry told her that he had heard those same words but that they had left a very different impression on him. Henry explained that he had started a career as a journalist, but after hearing Reverend Finney's remarks, he was inspired to leave journalism and enroll at Lane Seminary in Ohio. This was a turning point in his life: Henry told Elizabeth that it was then that he became a dedicated abolitionist, who brought the topic of slavery up in almost every discussion. His passion and commitment frustrated others at the seminary, and the trustees at the school told him he had to stop talking about the slavery issue. Henry refused to compromise; he left school, abandoned his plans to become a clergyman, and took a job as an agent of the American Anti-Slavery Society.

Elizabeth became intoxicated with the promise of social reform and her possible role in all of it. "The enthusiasm of the people in these great meetings, the thrilling oratory, and lucid arguments of the speakers, all conspired to make these days memorable as among the most charming in my life," Elizabeth wrote. "It seemed to me that I never had so much happiness crowded into one short month."

Elizabeth didn't want these exciting days to end; neither did Henry. On a clear October morning, Henry asked Elizabeth to join him after breakfast.

"What do you say to a ride on horseback this morning?" he asked.

She accepted. After a refreshing ride through the country-side, they stopped to admire the scenery. "When walking slowly through a beautiful grove," she remembered, "he laid his hand on the horn of the saddle and, to my surprise, made one of those charming revelations of human feeling which brave knights have always found eloquent words to utter, and to which fair ladies have always listened with mingled emotions of pleasure and astonishment."

Henry asked Elizabeth to marry him. She accepted his proposal.

Cousin Gerrit warned Elizabeth that her father would never consent to her marrying an abolitionist.

Elizabeth knew he was right, so she decided to tell her father the news in writing. "It was better to announce my engagement by letter than to wait until I returned home, as thus I might draw the hottest fire while still in safe harbor," she wrote in her autobiography.

Judge Cady told his daughter that Henry might be a fine person but he was not necessarily a suitable husband. Specifically,

Elizabeth's father didn't think Henry would be able to support a family. "Mr. Stanton's present business cannot be regarded as a business for life," Judge Cady said. "If the object of the Abolitionists be soon accomplished he must be thrown out of business—and if success does not crown their efforts—the rank and file will not much longer consent to pay salaries."

Edward Bayard opposed the marriage as well. He appealed to Elizabeth's knowledge of the law: As a married woman she would become subject to the same restrictive and unfair laws that she had wanted to cut out of the law books when she was a young girl.

Bayard may have also had selfish reasons for opposing the marriage. According to a story told by several members of the Stanton family over the years, Bayard was in love with Elizabeth. Bayard, who was married to Elizabeth's sister Tryphena, had been very close to his sister-in-law; they had enjoyed spending time together, reading novels, riding horses, and discussing philosophy and law.

In her autobiography, Elizabeth described Bayard as "a tall, fully developed man, remarkably fine looking, with cultivated literary taste and a profound knowledge of human nature." He was older—he had been a classmate of her brother Eleazar's—and he became part of the family after her brother died. "He was soon a great favorite in the family, and gradually filled the void made in all our hearts by the loss of the brother and son."

Bayard offered to divorce his wife and marry Elizabeth, according to family lore. It's not clear whether Elizabeth shared his romantic interest or if she loved him like a brother. In any case, Elizabeth refused to hurt her sister this way. She turned Bayard down, and they were never again alone together.

Elizabeth agonized over her future. She felt torn between living up to the expectations of her father and her fiancé, both important men in her life. She wanted to please them both, but this seemed impossible. She called this period of her life "a season of doubt and conflict" and broke off the engagement with Henry. "Heretofore my apprehensions had all been of death and eternity," she wrote. "Now life itself was filled with fears and anxiety as to the possibilities of the future."

Henry Stanton didn't give up. He wrote letters begging her to reconsider his proposal. She loved him, but she still wasn't sure what to do. Then in the winter of 1840, Henry wrote that he had been elected as a delegate to the World Anti-Slavery Convention, in London, and he would be abroad for about eight months. He asked her to marry him and join him on the journey.

The two were married in Johnstown, New York, on May 1, 1840. "We did not wish the ocean to roll between us," Elizabeth wrote.

Even so, she insisted on two changes to the traditional wedding ceremony: She removed the word "obey" from their vows—she was pledging herself to a marriage between equals—and she insisted on using her own name. Instead of being known as Mrs. Henry Stanton, as would have been customary at the time, she demanded that she be referred to as Elizabeth Cady Stanton.

"HUMILIATION AND CHAGRIN" IN LONDON

On May 12, 1840, the newlyweds boarded the ship *Montreal*, bound for England. Once they arrived, they spent several weeks sightseeing before they were joined by some of the others in the American delegation to the World Anti-Slavery Convention.

As soon as the group gathered, the delegates began to debate whether women should be allowed to participate.

The issue had already caused a split within the American Anti-Slavery Society. Just before the delegates left for the convention, some of the members, who didn't think that women should be delegates, had resigned and formed an all-male group, the American and Foreign Anti-Slavery Society.

When the conference leaders in England learned that the American Anti-Slavery Society had elected several female delegates, they wrote to discourage the group from bringing the women to the convention. They argued that allowing women to participate would distract from the key issue: abolition.

The society ignored the recommendation. In any case, Lucretia Mott, one of the female delegates, had declared that she had no intention of staying home. She was a Quaker, and like other members of her religion, she believed that an "Inner Light" existed within every person, regardless of sex, race, or class. By the time of the convention, she was a legendary Quaker preacher and radical activist who had spent decades working for abolition, temperance (outlawing consumption of alcoholic beverages), Native American rights, prison reform, and women's rights. She believed that men and women were equal before God and that it was her obligation to work to make the world a better place. For her, that meant working to end slavery and to promote equality, including attending the World Anti-Slavery Convention.

Many of the men who objected to including women argued that the presence of women would violate God's will and bring ridicule to the convention. While in England, one of the male delegates confronted Mott and urged her not to attend the conference, explaining that women were "constitutionally unfit for public meetings with men."

"It's interesting that thou should put it that way," Mott replied. (It was customary for Quakers to use "thou" and "thy" when speaking and writing.) "Hast thou ever heard slaveowners talk? They use that phrase to say the colored men are constitutionally unfit to mingle with whites." This was a scathing criticism for a

LUCRETIA COFFIN MOTT (1793–1880) *was a gifted public speaker who became an ordained Quaker minister at age twenty-eight. The taboo against women speaking in public did not apply in Quaker meetings, where women were encouraged to speak freely. Mott attended the first meeting of the American Anti-Slavery Society in 1833. She sat at the back of the hall, listening and knitting, until during a debate over the wording of a declaration, she blurted out, "Friends, I suggest—" Mott had forgotten that outside of a Quaker gathering she was expected to remain silent in public. A man in the front row turned and frowned, aghast that a woman had dared to speak. But the chairman encouraged her to continue. "We shall all be glad to hear you," he said. She offered a change of wording, which strengthened the text, and later made several other contributions during the discussion.*

Before adjourning, the chairman encouraged her to invite "the ladies of the land" to form their own anti-slavery societies. At the time, there were no formal women's organizations in the United States. Three days later, Mott had spoken with eighteen women and they had formed the Philadelphia Female Anti-Slavery Society. She saw both abolition and women's rights as causes destined to make the world more just. By 1839, the women's organization ended, because the American Anti-Slavery Society voted to invite "all persons opposed to slavery"— including women—to join.

man who had just traveled three thousand miles to attend an abolitionist convention.

Stunned and defenseless, the male delegate turned and walked away.

When the session opened on June 12, Mott and her husband, James, entered the building together. One of the event organizers guided James, a delegate from the Pennsylvania Anti-Slavery Society, to a seat on the convention floor, while Lucretia Mott, also a duly elected delegate, was ushered to another section of the auditorium.

When Elizabeth Cady Stanton and the other women entered the hall, they too were directed to the special section. The women were expected to sit silently, separated from the men by a bar and low curtain.

The first order of business at the conference was a motion to admit the female delegates. Some delegates, including Henry Stanton, spoke in favor of including the women. A British lawyer pointed out that it was "ridiculous to call it a World Convention and then exclude half the world."

After hours of debate, a vote was taken and the motion to include the women was overwhelmingly defeated. In fact, many of the men considered themselves generous to allow the women to remain in "the ladies' portion of the hall."

Several days after the convention began, prominent abolitionist William Lloyd Garrison arrived. When he learned about the vote to exclude the women, he said, "After battling so many long years for the liberties of African slaves, I can take no part in a convention that strikes down the most sacred rights of all women." For the remainder of the conference, he sat in silence with the rejected women in order to prove his point.

Elizabeth Cady Stanton was not a delegate to the World Anti-Slavery Convention, but she sat with the wives of delegates

The World Anti-Slavery Convention met in London in June 1840. The female delegates and spectators were seated separately from the men and were not permitted to participate in the proceedings.

and shared the female delegates' "humiliation and chagrin." She later wrote: "It struck me as very remarkable that abolitionists, who felt so keenly the wrongs of the slave, should be so oblivious to the equal wrongs of their own mothers, wives, and sisters. . . . To me there was no question so important as the emancipation of women from the dogmas of the past."

While she was in London, Stanton visited with Angelina and Sarah Grimké, her abolitionist friends from New York, but she was most impressed by Lucretia Mott and the work she did as an activist. "Mrs. Mott was to me an entire new revelation of womanhood," Stanton wrote. "I embraced every opportunity to talk with her."

Stanton also admired the marriage of this forty-seven-year-old mother of six. Mott believed that "independence of the husband and wife is equal, their dependence mutual, and their obligations reciprocal." That was the kind of relationship Stanton wanted to have with her husband, too. "I sought every opportunity to be at her side, and continually plied her with questions. I had never heard a woman talk what . . . I had scarcely dared to think."

Mott encouraged Stanton to trust her opinions and speak her mind, and Stanton found a role model in the uncompromising middle-aged activist. Stanton later wrote that when she was around Mott she "felt a new born sense of dignity and freedom." To her, Mott "seemed like a being from some larger planet."

When not attending meetings, Stanton and Mott spent time together, wandering through the city and visiting the sights. On one occasion, they joined a group touring the British Museum. They sat on a marble bench near the front door and told the group to start the tour without them; they planned to catch up in a few minutes. Three hours later, they were still engrossed in conversation.

Near the end of the convention, Stanton and Mott decided to take a stand. On the last day, the two women made a pledge to one another. "As Mrs. Mott and I walked home, arm in arm, commenting on the incidents of the day," Stanton recalled, "we resolved to hold a convention as soon as we returned home, and form a society to advocate the rights of women." That decision would change their lives and eventually the life of every woman across the United States.

2 "ALL MEN AND WOMEN ARE CREATED EQUAL"

Seneca Falls Convention, 1848

WHEN ELIZABETH CADY STANTON RETURNED TO THE United States, her friends and family asked what had impressed her most about her honeymoon tour of Great Britain and France. Buckingham Palace? Stonehenge? Notre Dame?

Stanton responded, "Lucretia Mott." While her travels and sightseeing had been exciting, Stanton had discovered in Lucretia Mott a true mentor and friend, one who challenged her to imagine a world with greater freedom and opportunities for women.

Although the two women exchanged letters, it took eight years for them to follow through on the promise they had made in London to hold a women's rights convention.

After the World Anti-Slavery Convention, Elizabeth and Henry Stanton moved to Johnstown, New York, where they stayed for several years while Henry trained to be a lawyer under the supervision of Elizabeth's father, Judge Daniel Cady. During that time, Elizabeth became involved in the temperance movement. In 1841, she made her first public speech, lecturing on temperance with a "dose" of women's rights, as she reported in a letter to Mott.

Stanton scaled back her work on temperance reform after 1842, when she gave birth to her first child, a boy, named Daniel Cady Stanton. Elizabeth may not have been able to be the son her father wanted, but she could name her son in his honor.

Like many new parents, Stanton prepared for motherhood by reading dozens of books and consulting doctors for advice. Unlike many new parents, she had faith in her own abilities. She listened to what the doctors recommended, but on many occasions she ignored their guidance and relied on a combination of maternal instinct and common sense. When her son damaged his collarbone, the doctor bandaged the injury so tightly that the child's fingers turned blue. Stanton removed the bandage and wrapped it her own way.

"I trusted neither men nor books absolutely after this . . . ," Stanton wrote in her autobiography, "but continued to use my 'mother's instinct,' if 'reason' is too dignified a term to apply to woman's thoughts."

After the baby was born, Henry joined a law firm in Boston, and Elizabeth alternated between living there with her husband and in New York with her parents. In 1844, she gave birth to a second son, Henry Brewster Stanton Jr., and decided that she and her husband needed to settle the family in a home of their own.

At the time, Henry didn't earn enough money to buy a house for his family, so Judge Cady bought them one in Chelsea, Massachusetts, with a view of the Boston Harbor. There, the Stantons' third son, Gerrit Smith Stanton, was born in 1845. With the assistance of two servants, Stanton devoted herself to raising her children and running the household while Henry began a career in antislavery politics.

Elizabeth Cady Stanton thrived. "I had never lived in such an enthusiastically literary and reform latitude before," she later wrote, "and my mental powers were kept at the highest tension." She enjoyed cultural events and "all sorts and sizes of meetings and lectures" on temperance, abolition, and other social reform movements. She never missed an antislavery convention, and she became friends with writers and other social reformers, including Nathaniel Hawthorne, Ralph Waldo Emerson, and Frederick Douglass.

She also read extensively about women's rights, including *A Vindication of the Rights of Woman*. The author, Mary Wollstonecraft, argued that women weren't naturally inferior to men but lacked educational opportunities that allowed them to achieve equality.

However, Boston didn't suit Henry. He was forced to leave the law firm where he worked when he refused on principle to represent a liquor dealer in court. He had spent a great deal of time working with the Liberty Party, an antislavery political party, but he was never able to launch his own political career. He also suffered from chronic headaches, which he blamed on the harsh New England weather. After a few years in Boston, he wanted to start his career over in a new town.

So in 1847, the Stantons moved to Seneca Falls, a small mill town in the Finger Lakes region of upstate New York, where

Mary Wollstonecraft (1759–1797), an English activist, philosopher, and writer, published A Vindication of the Rights of Woman *in 1792. Wollstonecraft's argument was radical in the late eighteenth century.*

Elizabeth Cady Stanton moved into this home in Seneca Falls, New York, in 1847.

Elizabeth's sister Tryphena and brother-in-law Edward Bayard lived. Judge Cady owned property in the area, and he gave Elizabeth and Henry a run-down house on a two-acre lot at 32 Washington Street, as well as the money necessary to fix it up.

Stanton recalled her father telling her, "You believe in woman's capacity to do and dare; now go ahead and put your place in order."

Eager to prove herself, Stanton acted as general contractor for the project. Within a few months, the family moved into a refurbished house with a completely renovated kitchen.

It didn't take long for Elizabeth Cady Stanton to realize that she despised small-town life. She missed her activist friends and the cultural stimulation of the city. Henry wasn't around much, because he spent most of his time working and trying to launch a political career. Her children, ages five, three, and almost two, exhausted her, and she felt isolated and unhappy. Her older boys always seemed to find trouble—throwing stones at the pigs, falling out of trees, or tormenting the baby. This was not the life she had imagined.

She recalled these difficult times with clarity: "To keep a house and grounds in good order, purchase every article for daily use, keep the wardrobes of half a dozen human beings in proper trim, take the children to dentists, shoemakers, and different schools, or find teachers at home altogether made sufficient work to keep one brain busy as well as all the hands I could impress into the service. . . . I suffered with mental hunger, which, like an empty stomach, is very depressing."

Her domestic struggles made Stanton sympathize with the concerns facing other women of her time. She reported that she "fully understood the practical difficulties most women had to contend with . . . the chaotic conditions into which everything fell without her constant supervision, and the wearied, anxious look of the majority of women."

Frustrated and suffocated by the confines of the domestic sphere, Stanton joyfully accepted an invitation to tea with friends in a nearby town. She needed a break, and she was thrilled to learn that Lucretia Mott would be joining them. Both of the women were eager for a reunion: Stanton and Mott had not seen one another since their time in London eight years before.

TALK OF TEA AND REVOLUTION

On the afternoon of July 13, 1848, five women—Elizabeth Cady Stanton, Lucretia Mott, Mary Ann McClintock, Martha Coffin Wright, and Jane Hunt—sat down to tea in Waterloo, New York. Mott had traveled to the area from Philadelphia to attend a yearly Quaker meeting and to visit Martha, her sister, who was expecting a baby. By all appearances, they were an unlikely group of revolutionaries—they were married mothers or grandmothers, ranging in age from thirty-two to fifty-four years old—but what happened that afternoon became a pivotal moment in the movement to secure women's voting rights in the United States.

While sipping tea and nibbling on cakes, the women complained about the injustices of their daily lives. Stanton spoke freely about her own situation, griping about the challenges of raising children and running a household. "I poured out . . . the torrent of my long-accumulating discontent, with such vehemence and indignation that I stirred myself as well as the rest of the party to do and dare anything," she later wrote. The other women echoed her concerns.

Stanton and Mott had not forgotten their plans to hold a women's rights convention. Inspired by one another, the women decided to take action: They planned to gather women together to "discuss the social, civil and religious condition and rights of Woman." They made arrangements for a notice to be published the following day in the local newspaper, the *Seneca County Courier*. It read:

WOMAN'S RIGHTS CONVENTION
A convention to discuss the social, civil, and religious condition and rights of women will be held in the Wesleyan Chapel, Seneca Falls, N.Y., on Wednesday and Thursday, the 19th and 20th of July current; commencing at 10 o'clock A.M. During the first day the meeting will be exclusively for women, who are earnestly invited to attend. The public generally are invited to be present on the second day, when Lucretia Mott, of Philadelphia, and other ladies and gentlemen, will address the convention.

The women did not realize the significance of what they were doing: planning the first women's convention ever held in the United States.

THE DECLARATION OF SENTIMENTS

The Sunday morning before the convention, four of the five women gathered around a circular mahogany table in McClintock's parlor to plan the program. (Jane Hunt wasn't at the planning session.) They had only three days to prepare for the meeting, and they weren't sure where to start.

For years, the women had worked on abolition, temperance, and other social reforms, but they had no experience organizing a meeting of their own. They wanted to prepare a "Declaration of Sentiments" similar to those they had read at other reform movement meetings they had attended, so they began by reviewing papers from other meetings. None of the examples seemed quite right.

What they wanted to do was truly revolutionary: They wanted to redefine the status of women in society. They wanted to promote equality between the sexes by granting women property rights, access to education, opportunities for employment, and, most importantly, by giving them the right to vote.

In a flash of inspiration, Stanton suggested using the Declaration of Independence as a model for their Declaration of Sentiments. Everyone agreed that it was an ideal choice. While all of the women expressed their opinions and made suggestions, Stanton was left to draft the document that would summarize their concerns. In her rewrite of the Declaration of Independence, Stanton replaced the phrase "all men are created equal" with the words "all men and women are created equal."

In addition to its statement of purpose, the Declaration of Sentiments listed twelve resolutions intended to promote female equality. It called on reforms in education, employment, property rights, religion, and, most notably, suffrage. The ninth resolution read: "Resolved, that it is the duty of the women of this country to secure to themselves their sacred right to the elective franchise." (Both "suffrage" and "franchise" refer to the right to vote. "Suffrage" comes from the Latin word *suffragium*, meaning "approval" and "the right to vote"; "franchise" comes from the French word *franche*, meaning "free.")

When Stanton shared the first draft of the document with the other women, even Mott balked at the suffrage resolution.

"Thou will make us ridiculous," Mott warned. "We must go slowly."

Mott knew that at the time, no nation on earth recognized women's right to vote. She also may have felt ambivalent about the suffrage issue because she was a Quaker; many Quakers refused to vote because they did not want to participate in a government that waged war.

Stanton stood firm. She insisted that voting rights were the key to making other social changes. Without the vote, women would not have the power to change unfair laws.

When Stanton shared the Declaration of Sentiments with her husband, Henry, he told her that demanding suffrage would make the entire convention a "farce." He worried that his wife's taking such a radical stand could harm his political future, so he encouraged Elizabeth to drop the proposal and threatened to leave town if she read the resolution.

She refused to back down, and Henry did, in fact, leave Seneca Falls during the meeting to avoid any association with what he considered an outrageous idea.

While Stanton accepted her husband's right to his own opinion, his lack of support felt like a personal rejection. "Henry sides with my friends who oppose me in all that is dearest in my heart," she wrote.

The women worried that no one would show up to the meeting. The notice had appeared in the local newspaper only once, less than a week before the event. Mott wrote to Stanton, urging her to keep her expectations low: "The convention will not be as large as it otherwise might be, owing to the busy time with the farmers, harvest, etc." It was "haying season," the busiest part of the year, and farmers would have very little free time. "But," Mott wrote, "it will be a beginning, and we hope it will be followed in due time by one of a more general character."

The women had no idea how many others were ready to join their revolution.

"WE ARE ASSEMBLED ... TO DECLARE OUR RIGHT TO BE AS FREE AS MAN IS FREE"

On Wednesday morning, July 19, 1848, Elizabeth Cady Stanton and the four other organizers of the convention gathered at the Wesleyan Chapel. To their surprise, when they got there they found dozens of people already waiting outside, as well as a steady stream of horses and wagons arriving. The demands of haying season had not kept the crowds away.

But when the women went to open the front door of the church, they found that it was locked. In fact, every entrance was shut tight.

Next, they tested the windows. Finally, they found a single unsecured widow at the side of the building and opened it as far as it would go. A young man—some accounts say that it was Elizabeth Cady Stanton's nephew, while others report that it was a young professor from Yale College—was lifted and then pulled himself up and through the opening. He unlocked the front door, and dozens of people flooded into the small building.

By the time the meeting began, more than three hundred people had crowded into the church. Some had come from as far as fifty miles away, a journey that would have taken a full day.

The Wesleyan Chapel, site of the first women's rights convention, was built in 1843. It is now maintained by the National Park Service.

Charlotte Woodward, a nineteen-year-old farmer's daughter, wanted to work as a typesetter in a print shop. She supported women's rights because she wanted to keep her own wages. When Charlotte read the notice in the newspaper, she hurried from neighbor to neighbor, encouraging others to join her at the convention. Some of the people she spoke with shared her enthusiasm; others did not. On the morning of the meeting, Charlotte set off with six friends in a wagon pulled by farm horses. When she arrived at the meeting, she sat in the back of the chapel and listened.

Although the notice had advertised that the first day of the convention was for women only, about forty men were mixed in with the crowd. Many of them had hitched up the horses and driven their wives to the meeting, and now they wanted to come inside and take part.

Should they be allowed to attend? Stanton and the other organizers whispered to one another in an impromptu conference and decided to allow the men to stay. With that decision, the Seneca Falls leaders established that it was a person's attitude about female equality and not their sex that should determine who was, in fact, a feminist.

Once inside the building, Stanton and the other organizers were overwhelmed by the size of the crowd. They felt nervous about speaking in front of so many people, and they lacked confidence about how to run a meeting. Again, they huddled together to decide what to do.

Eventually, they turned to Lucretia Mott's husband, James, and asked him if he would preside over the meeting. Stanton later recalled that when it came to running the meeting, she and her friends "felt as helpless and hopeless as if they had been suddenly asked to construct a steam engine." James Mott accepted, so it was a man, not a woman, who called to order the first women's rights convention ever held in the United States.

The woman most confident addressing the crowd was Lucretia Mott, with her long history of speaking within her Quaker meetings. After her husband opened the convention, she explained the purpose of the gathering and offered a brief overview of the status of women around the world. One by one, the organizers stood and read the speeches they had prepared. There was no amplification, however, and many of the women were so tense and inexperienced at addressing a crowd that it was difficult to hear what they were saying. The audience repeatedly cried out for them to speak louder.

Finally, it was Stanton's turn. Her voice started out weak, but her words gained power and energy as she gained confidence. "I should feel exceedingly diffident to appear before you at this time," she began, "having never before spoken in public, were I not nerved by a sense of right and duty, did I not feel that the time had come for the question of woman's wrongs to be laid before the public, did I not believe that woman herself must do this work; for woman alone can understand the height, the depth, the length, and the breadth of her degradation."

Stanton continued: "We are assembled . . . to declare our right to be as free as man is free, to be represented in the government which we are taxed to support." She went on to read the Declaration of Sentiments, which was the cornerstone of the entire meeting.

For hours, the audience listened to speeches and debates about women's rights. Those in attendance supported most of the ideas outlined in the document, and when it was passed around the room for those in attendance to sign, eleven of the resolutions passed unanimously.

The only resolution that did not pass so easily was the suffrage amendment. A significant number of the people in attendance had been shocked by the proposal that women should have the right to vote.

Stanton held firm and pointed out that "the power to choose rulers and make laws, was the right by which all others could be secured." She told the listeners: "Strange as it may seem to many, we now demand our right to vote according to the declaration of the government under which we live. . . . The pens, the tongues, the fortunes, the indomitable wills of many women are already pledged to secure this right."

It was then that Frederick Douglass, a civil rights leader who had escaped from slavery ten years before, asked to address the crowd. He stood more than six feet tall and was a captivating lecturer. He explained that without the vote, women would be unable to change the laws that treated them unfairly.

The words he spoke that day were not written down, but several days later he wrote an editorial in his newspaper, the *North Star*, which is believed to be a summary of his remarks at the convention. Douglass wrote: "All that distinguishes man as an intelligent and accountable being is equally true of woman; and if that government only is just which governs by the free consent of the governed, there can be no reason in the world for denying to woman the exercise of

FREDERICK DOUGLASS (1818–1895) *was an abolitionist and reformer who escaped from slavery in 1838. He was the only African American to attend the Seneca Falls convention.*

the elective franchise, or a hand in making and administering the laws of the land. Our doctrine is that 'right is of no sex.'"

Douglass's speech stirred the audience. After eighteen hours of discussion and debate over a two-day period, the suffrage resolution passed by a narrow margin.

By the time the convention closed, one-third of the three hundred participants—sixty-eight women and thirty-two men—had signed the Declaration of Sentiments. Others in attendance likely sympathized with the cause but were unwilling to sign their names. The list of signers included Charlotte Woodward, the only person at that meeting who would live long enough to see female suffrage become the law of the land.

Whether they knew it or not, the women and men at the convention were making history. When the Seneca Falls Woman's Rights Convention ended, the women's suffrage movement had officially begun.

3 "THE RIGHT IS OURS"

Creating a National Suffrage Movement

THE SENECA FALLS CONVENTION MADE HEADLINES across the country. In the weeks following it, newspapers wrote about the gathering—most, critically. Some called the meeting "The Hen Convention," and those who had planned it were described as "divorced wives, childless women, and some old maids." (At best this was sloppy reporting: In fact, the women who organized the meeting were married mothers and grandmothers.)

Editors at many newspapers tried to convince women that they didn't need any additional rights. In September of 1848, the editors of the *Philadelphia Public Ledger and Daily Transcript* wrote, "A woman is nobody. A wife is everything. A pretty girl is equal to ten thousand men, and a mother is, next to God, all powerful. . . . The ladies of Philadelphia, therefore, under the influence of the most serious, sober second thoughts, are resolved to maintain their rights as Wives, Belles, Virgins and Mothers, and not as Women."

"All the journals from Maine to Texas seemed to strive with each other to see which could make our movement appear the most ridiculous," Elizabeth Cady Stanton wrote in her autobiography.

The disparaging reports caused some of those who had signed the Declaration of Sentiments to have second thoughts. Some even asked to have their names removed from the document. "So pronounced was the popular voice against us, in the parlor, press, and pulpit, that most of the ladies who had attended the convention and signed the declaration, one by one, withdrew their names and influence and joined our persecutors," Stanton wrote. "Our friends gave us the cold shoulder."

While the storm of negative reports may have made some of the leaders second-guess their plans, it did not prevent them from planning a second convention two weeks later.

A SECOND CONVENTION

According to Elizabeth Cady Stanton, the Seneca Falls Convention "set the ball in motion." Less than two weeks after the gathering—on August 2, 1848—a second women's rights convention, organized by Amy Post, a prominent Quaker abolitionist, took place at the Unitarian church in Rochester, New York. Again, the pews were overflowing with people interested in learning more.

Stanton attended, although she worried about the hostile press. "If I had had the slightest premonition of all that was to follow that [first] convention, I fear I should not have had the courage to risk it," she recalled, "and I must confess that it was with fear and trembling that I consented to attend another."

When the meeting opened, Stanton and Lucretia Mott sat with the other leaders on the stage. Stanton became nervous when Post nominated her friend, activist Abigail Bush, to serve as president. Wary of more bad press, Stanton wanted James Mott or Frederick

In the decade following the first women's rights convention, other meetings were held throughout the North and West. On June 11, 1859, HARPER'S WEEKLY published a wood engraving mocking such conventions.

Douglass to preside. She worried that Bush lacked experience and that having a woman run the meeting would only give their critics one more reason not to take their cause seriously.

Post, however, favored a female president, and the crowd backed her.

In an expression of disagreement, Stanton and Mott left the stage and sat in the audience.

Unlike at the Seneca Falls meeting, which focused on legal and intellectual ideas of women's rights, the second convention emphasized practical pocketbook issues. The women discussed inheritance rights of widows, property rights, and control of their wages. They stated that the lack of control over finances left women "almost to the condition of a slave."

Bush proved to be a capable president, and the women successfully managed the meeting on their own.

When the meeting adjourned, Mott hugged Bush and thanked her for taking the lead, and Stanton realized she had been wrong to underestimate the female leadership.

Embarrassed, Stanton went home and wrote an apology to

Post, telling her she regretted her "foolish conduct." She explained that she was still not familiar with seeing women "act in a public capacity." This was not a mistake she would make again.

From the Rochester convention forward, Stanton no longer feared bad press. Instead, she embraced all publicity. "It will start women thinking, and men, too," Stanton wrote to Mott, "and when men and women think . . . the first step is taken. The great fault of mankind is that it will not think."

"WHAT ARE WE NEXT TO DO?"

The Rochester meeting sparked nationwide interest in women's rights. Other conventions followed in Ohio, Indiana, Massachusetts, Pennsylvania, and New York. Increasing family responsibilities often kept Elizabeth Cady Stanton from traveling to meetings. Instead, she wrote articles and letters to the editor of various newspapers, collected signatures on women's rights petitions, and began her career as a public speaker at events closer to home. She often asked, "What are we next to do?"

Stanton gave her first major speech on women's rights at a Quaker meetinghouse in Waterloo, New York. She spoke out in favor of women's suffrage, saying, "The right is ours. Have it we must. Use it we will."

Stanton regularly wrote for the *Lily*, a women's temperance movement newspaper published by Amelia Bloomer, who worked as the deputy postmistress of Seneca Falls. At first, Stanton signed her articles with a pseudonym, "Sunflower," and later she used her initials, E. C. S.

Bloomer had attended the Seneca Falls Convention, but she had not signed the Declaration of Sentiments, because she had been there as a reporter, not a participant, and she worked to be

Amelia Jenks Bloomer (1818– 1894) began her temperance newspaper, the Lily, *in January 1849. It was first national women's newspaper in the United States. Bloomer's husband owned the* Seneca County Courier, *and she wrote for that publication before launching the* Lily.

objective in her journalism. Stanton didn't challenge Bloomer to take a stronger stand on women's rights in the *Lily*, but she did try to work feminist ideas into her articles. In an article about sewing, she wrote, "It will be a glorious day . . . when men and boys make their own clothes, and women make theirs in the plainest possible manner."

When Stanton could not attend women's rights conferences, she often wrote letters that could be read to the audience during the meetings there. In April 1850, the organizers of the first Ohio Women's Convention, in Salem, invited Stanton to speak. It promised to be an important meeting, because Ohio legislators were gathering at the same time to revise the state constitution, but Stanton didn't feel she could leave her three young boys behind at home.

In her letter to the Ohio Women's Convention, Stanton emphasized the central importance of female suffrage: "Depend upon it," she wrote, "this is the point to attack the stronghold of the fortress—*the one* women will find the most difficult to take, *the one* man will most reluctantly give up." Only with the vote, Stanton wrote, would all other change be possible for women.

This convention differed from previous women's rights conventions in that men could not address the audience. The demand that they remain silent made them that much more eager to speak.

"Not a man was allowed to sit on the platform, to speak or vote," recalled one participant. "They implored just to say one word; but no; the President was inflexible—no man should be heard. If one meekly arose to make a suggestion, he was at once ruled out of order. For the first time in the world's history, men learned how it felt to sit in silence when questions in which they were interested were under discussion."

The women in attendance adopted an "Address to the Women of Ohio," in which they outlined the rights of women. It declared, in part: "The legal theory is, marriage makes the husband and wife one person, and that person is the husband. . . . Women of Ohio! . . . Slaves we are, politically and legally. . . . If men would be men worthy of the name, they must cease to disfranchise and rob their wives and mothers, they must forbear to consign to political and legal slavery their sisters and daughters. And we women . . . must cease to submit to such tyranny."

After the convention, the leadership presented this declaration, plus a petition with eight thousand signatures supporting women's suffrage, to the Ohio lawmakers revising the state's constitution.

They were ignored. Once again, women were denied the right to vote.

"AIN'T I A WOMAN?"

Despite setbacks, the women's movement was gaining momentum. The convention in Salem was followed by an even larger women's rights meeting in Akron, Ohio, in May 1851.

One person, Sojourner Truth, didn't look like the other women at the convention. She was African American, stood almost six feet tall, and wore a white turban on her head and a gray dress. She marched deliberately into the church, walked "with the air of a queen" up the aisle, and sat on the steps to the pulpit. The church buzzed with whispers of concern, and some said the meeting was about to become "an abolition affair."

Frances Dana Barker Gage, the president of the convention, restored order and the meeting continued. Truth sat quietly throughout.

During an intermission, some of the women attending the conference urged Gage not to let Truth address the convention. "Don't let her speak," one of them said. "It will ruin us. Every newspaper in the land will have our cause mixed up with abolition . . . and we shall be utterly denounced."

"We shall see when the time comes," Gage responded.

On the second day of the convention, Truth returned to the same spot. A group of Methodist, Baptist, Episcopal, Presbyterian, and Universalist ministers—all men—dominated the discussion that day, challenging the women's rights resolutions that had been presented. One claimed that men were more intelligent than women; another claimed that men were superior because Christ was male.

The women in attendance were appalled, but no one dared to challenge or contradict the religious leaders.

And then Sojourner Truth stood. She moved slowly and solemnly toward the podium, placed an old sunbonnet at her feet, and turned toward Gage for permission to speak.

Gage rose and announced, "Sojourner Truth."

The room fell silent. Truth spoke in a deep voice, loud enough to reach "every ear in the house and away through the throng at the doors and windows," according to Gage.

"Well, children," Truth said, "where there is so much racket there must be something out of kilter. I think that 'twixt the negroes of the South and the women at the North, all talking about rights, the white men will be in a fix pretty soon. But what's all this here talking about?

"That man over there says that women need to be helped into carriages, and lifted over ditches, and to have the best place everywhere. Nobody ever helps me into carriages, or over mud-puddles, or gives me any best place! And ain't I a woman?"

Truth bared her right arm to the shoulder and flexed her muscles to show her strength. "Look at me! Look at my arm!" she said. "I have ploughed and planted, and gathered into barns, and no man could head me! And ain't I a woman?

"I could work as much and eat as much as a man—when I could get it—and bear the lash as well! And ain't I a woman?"

She reminded those in the audience that there was another reason she was not like them: She had been enslaved. "I have borne thirteen children, and seen most all sold off to slavery, and when I cried out with my mother's grief, none but Jesus heard me! And ain't I a woman?"

Truth did not back down when it came to religion. "Then that little man in black there," she said, pointing toward one of the men in the audience, "he says women can't have as much rights as men, 'cause Christ wasn't a woman! Where did your Christ come from?" Raising her voice louder, she said, "From God and a woman! Man had nothing to do with Him."

The crowd cheered.

"If the first woman God ever made was strong enough to turn the world upside down all alone, these women together"—she pointed to the women in the audience—"ought to be able to turn it back, and get it right side up again! And now they is asking to do it, the men better let them."

Applause echoed in the chamber. "Obliged to you for hearing me," Truth concluded. "And now old Sojourner ain't got nothing more to say."

At this point, even some of the clergymen were clapping. She

SOJOURNER TRUTH (1797–1883) *was born into slavery in New York State. She was originally called Isabella Baumfree, but she changed her name in 1843. As a child she was owned by a Dutch-speaking family, who did not teach her English. She suffered severe beatings when she was sold, because she did not understand what her English-speaking owner was saying. She escaped to freedom with her infant daughter in 1826 and gained legal freedom a year later when a New York law freed slaves under age forty. She attended another women's rights convention in New York City in 1853, where a number of men in the audience tried to disrupt the speakers by shouting and hissing. Truth put the protesters in their place by saying: "Some of you have got the spirit of a goose, and some have got the spirit of a snake. We'll have our rights. You may hiss as much as you like, but it is coming."*

left "more than one of us with streaming eyes, and hearts beating with gratitude," Gage recalled. "She had taken us up in her strong arms and carried us. I have never in my life seen anything like her magical influence."

With that single speech, Truth established herself as a celebrity suffragist, one of the most effective advocates for women's rights. She also showed that she understood the important link between women's rights and the rights of enslaved people.

AN IMPORTANT INTRODUCTION

The same month Sojourner Truth made her speech, a history-making feminist friendship was forged between Elizabeth Cady Stanton and Susan B. Anthony. Stanton had attended a lecture in Seneca Falls given by her friend William Lloyd Garrison. After the lecture, she met with Amelia Bloomer, who wanted to introduce Stanton to Anthony.

Years later, Stanton vividly recalled her first impression of Anthony. "There she stood," Stanton wrote, "with her good, earnest face and genial smile . . . I like her thoroughly." Stanton would have invited Anthony and Bloomer over for dinner, she wrote, but she didn't know what kind of mischief her children had been up to in her absence.

In reflecting on their first meeting, Anthony also remembered that there was an "intense attraction" between them. They complemented one another: Stanton, the thinker, was burdened with family responsibilities; Anthony, the organizer, was a master at the logistics of executing petition campaigns and planning events. They almost intuitively realized that together they would make a great team.

Anthony was an unmarried thirty-one-year-old headmistress and temperance worker; Stanton was now thirty-five and the mother

Susan Brownell Anthony (1820–1906) was raised as a Quaker in Adams, Massachusetts. Throughout her life, Anthony was self-conscious about the fact that her right eye turned outward slightly (a condition known as strabismus), so she usually asked to be photographed from the left side or looking away from the camera.

of four boys, ages three months to nine years old. While the women shared an interest in abolition, Anthony did not have much interest in women's rights or suffrage. (Anthony was quite surprised after the fact to learn that her father, mother, and youngest sister, Mary, had attended the 1848 Rochester women's rights convention and signed the resolutions, including the call for suffrage.)

As a Quaker, Anthony had been raised with the understanding that men and women were equal, a point of view she almost took for granted. Of course, she had experienced inequalities; she knew that when she was a teacher, she was paid less than men doing the same job. She also knew that her mother's name did not appear on the deed for the family farm, even though she had provided the money for the down payment. But Anthony had not experienced many of the frustrations and inequities that married women had to endure.

Anthony's Quaker upbringing also had discouraged interest in partisan politics and women's suffrage, so she focused on working with the temperance movement. As pacifists, many Quaker men refused to vote, as a protest against government engagement in war. In fact, Anthony's father did not vote in a presidential election until 1860, when he cast a ballot for

Abraham Lincoln after concluding that slavery could only be abolished by force.

In the middle of the nineteenth century, the rate of alcoholism was high in the United States, and with the high rates of drinking came violence, much of it targeting women in their own homes. Anthony had joined the Daughters of Temperance in Canajoharie, the central New York town where she was a school headmistress.

Anthony gave her first public speech to two hundred people at a Daughters of Temperance meeting on March 2, 1849. "All that is needed to produce a complete Temperance and Social reform in this age of Moral Suasion, is for our Sex to cast their United influences into the balance," she wrote for her speech. "Ladies! There is no Neutral position for us to assume."

FOUNDING THE WOMAN'S NEW YORK STATE TEMPERANCE SOCIETY

Susan B. Anthony's first major wake-up call about the need for women's equality came in January 1852 when the Sons of Temperance invited Anthony to a statewide meeting in Albany, New York. She accepted as a representative of the Daughters of Temperance, the women's affiliate group.

During the meeting, Anthony stood up to speak.

She was immediately chastised. "The sisters were not invited here to speak, but to listen and learn," she was told.

Anthony objected. No one had worked harder than she to gather signatures on petitions and contact state legislators; she had a right to have her opinions heard.

When no one came to her defense, Anthony walked out. A couple of other women joined her, but for the most part the women stayed silent and seated.

Unwilling to back down, Anthony went from the convention hall to the *Albany Evening Journal*, where she persuaded an editor to cover the story of her being shut out of the meeting. She also urged interested citizens to come hear her speak the next day at the local Presbyterian church.

It was at the meeting there that Anthony organized a new group, the Woman's State Temperance Society.

Anthony wrote hundreds of letters of invitation to prospective members, and almost single-handedly raised the money, hired the hall, and organized the speakers for the group's first meeting. One of the people she contacted was her new friend Elizabeth Cady Stanton, whom she recruited to serve as president and to write a speech for Anthony to present.

"I will gladly do all in my power to aid you," Stanton responded.

This 1846 lithograph by Currier & Ives shows the nine steps of "the drunkards progress"—from having "a glass with a friend" to the decline into criminal activity and "death by suicide." A weeping woman with a child waits under the archway.

"Come & stay with me . . . and I will write you the best lecture I can." Stanton also offered practical advice: "I have no doubt a little practice will make you an admirable lecturer. Dress loose, take a great deal of exercise & be particular about your diet, & sleep enough, the body has great influence upon the mind. In your meetings if attacked be good-natured & cool, for if you are simple & truth loving no sophistry can confound you."

Regarding her own speech, Stanton told Anthony, "Anything from my pen is necessarily radical." She said that she would understand if Anthony wanted to dissociate herself from her opinions, that she was "ready to stand alone." She said that she did not "write to please any one . . . but to proclaim [her] highest convictions of truth."

Anthony respected Stanton's wisdom and wanted to work with her.

On April 20, 1852, five hundred women gathered in Rochester for the first meeting of the new organization. Men attended, too, but they were not permitted to hold office or vote. The group elected Stanton as president and Anthony as secretary.

Stanton gave a persuasive speech. As part of her temperance message, she argued that a woman should be allowed to divorce a "drunkard" and retain custody of her children.

When Stanton's father learned about his daughter's speech, he was appalled. He did not believe that women should participate in public life or make speeches about divorce. Anthony's father, on the other hand, encouraged his daughter to speak out about issues that concerned her, and he gave her money for living expenses.

Two months later, Anthony was invited to attend another Sons of Temperance meeting. She had assumed she was going to be praised for her work in Maine the previous winter, when she had collected more than one hundred thousand women's signatures in support of a prohibition law. She was mistaken.

When Anthony arrived, some of the men objected to her attendance and she was asked to leave. Some criticized her for joining the lofty cause of temperance with what they considered to be vulgar appeals for women's rights. One angry minister said that women's rights advocates were "a hybrid species, half man and half woman, belonging to neither sex."

Disgusted, Anthony left the meeting.

That fall, she attended her first women's rights convention, finally embracing the central importance of suffrage. Without the right to vote, women could not change unjust laws or initiate political change. Anthony continued with her temperance and abolition work, but her focus shifted to women's rights.

"A CHAMPION OF THE CAUSE IS BORN"

While Susan B. Anthony was becoming energized to begin working for women's rights, Elizabeth Cady Stanton had less time for reform work as her family demands increased. On October 20, 1852, Stanton gave birth to her fifth child, a girl.

Whenever Stanton had a baby, a flag was raised outside her house—a red flag for a boy, white for a girl. She delighted in her first white-flag baby, named Margaret Livingston Stanton, after Margaret Livingston Cady, her mother.

"I am at length the happy mother of a daughter," Stanton wrote to her friend Lucretia Mott. "Rejoice with me all Womanhood, for lo! a champion of the cause is born. I have dedicated her to this work from the beginning. May she . . . leave her impress on the world for goodness and truth."

With a fifth child in the house, Stanton had little time for suffrage work, or anything else but changing diapers and managing the household. She strived to maintain a link with outside reform work to avoid being "wholly absorbed in a narrow family selfishness."

Anthony remained devoted to her friend and encouraged her to remain engaged with the temperance and suffrage movements.

"WOMAN CAN NEVER DEVELOP IN HER PRESENT DRAPERY"

One of the small ways Stanton showed solidarity with her feminist friends was to wear "bloomers," the controversial new fashion, a below-the-knee skirt worn over loosely fitting pants. Stanton's cousin, Elizabeth Smith Miller, had designed the outfit in 1851, but after Amelia Bloomer published an article about "Turkish trousers" in the *Lily*, the "costume" was popularly referred to as "bloomers."

Stanton found the outfit comfortable and emancipating. "Like a captive set free from his ball and chain," she wrote in her autobiography, "I was always ready for a brisk walk through sleet and snow and rain, to climb a mountain, jump over a fence, work in the garden."

Henry Stanton was horrified to see his wife wearing baggy pants under what was considered to be a short dress (even though it ended four inches below the knee). He worried that when the women sat onstage their legs would be exposed, even though they were wearing pants. Stanton's husband told her that men in the audience could tell "whether their lady friends have round and plump legs, or lean and scrawny ones." Stanton wrote to Lucretia Mott: "Woman can never develop in her present drapery. She is a slave to her rags."

The style never became mainstream. "People would stare," Stanton wrote. "Some men and women make rude remarks; boys follow in crowds, or shout from behind fences." Stanton's father told her she was not welcome in his home wearing bloomers. Her

ELIZABETH SMITH MILLER (1822–1911), *Elizabeth Cady Stanton's cousin and daughter of Gerrit Smith, developed bloomers to wear when gardening. Stanton and her neighbor, Amelia Bloomer, copied the design. Bloomer published an article about the dress in her temperance newspaper, the* Lily, *and before long it was known as the "bloomer outfit." When Bloomer wore it, people accused her of "mannishness." Bloomer replied: "I feel no more like a man now than I did in long skirts, unless it be that enjoying more freedom and cutting off the fetters [chains] is to be like a man."*

sons begged her to wear a conventional dress when she visited them at boarding school.

Stanton wrote to one of her sons and asked him to imagine that they were walking in a field and a bull began chasing them. While her son could run away fast, she would not be able to because she would be weighed down with heavy petticoats. "Then you in your agony, when you saw the bull gaining on me, would say: 'Oh! How I wish mother could use her legs as I can.' Now why do you wish me to wear what is uncomfortable, inconvenient, and many times dangerous? I'll tell you why. You want me to be like other people.

You do not like to have me laughed at. You must learn not to care for what foolish people say."

For the time being, however, the critics won. The physical freedom, Stanton later said, "did not compensate for the persistent persecution and petty annoyances suffered at every turn." By early 1854, most women who wore bloomers gave up their pants to avoid harassment. In the end, Stanton even pushed Anthony to return to more traditional clothing.

"The cup of ridicule is greater than you can bear," she said. "It is not wise, Susan, to use up so much energy that way."

"BIGGER FISH TO FRY"

In June 1853, Elizabeth Cady Stanton and Susan B. Anthony attended the second annual convention of the Women's State Temperance Society. Anthony had worked to build the membership, and the group now numbered more than two thousand.

Stanton addressed the crowd on the issue of women's rights, arguing that the topic was relevant at a temperance meeting because many people in the audience still questioned whether women should be permitted to speak. She also discussed the need for divorce reform so that women married to alcoholic men could escape difficult, dangerous marriages.

This time the men in the audience were ready. The conservatives in the organization did not want the temperance group to have any link to suffrage, women's rights, or the divorce issue. A motion was made from the floor to change the organization's constitution and allow men to be elected as officers.

Both Stanton and Anthony backed the resolution, believing that the men "would modestly permit women to continue the work she had so successfully begun."

Instead, the men in the organization staged a coup. First, Stanton was defeated in her reelection bid for president. And when the newly elected male president offered her the vice presidency, she turned him down. In a show of solidarity, Anthony refused to run for reelection as secretary, letting go of control of the organization she had founded two years before.

As a final insult, the group voted to change its name from the Women's State Temperance Society to the People's League.

"Do you see, at last?" Stanton asked Anthony, trying to persuade her that they should work on women's rights issues before temperance and other reforms. Stanton had joined the temperance organization out of her allegiance to Anthony; her heart belonged to the suffrage movement.

"At last, I see," Anthony replied.

Stanton did not wait long to refocus her energy. When she returned to Seneca Falls, she wrote Anthony a letter. "You ask me if I am not plunged in grief at my defeat at the recent convention for the presidency of our society. Not at all. I am only too happy in the relief I feel from this additional care. I accomplished all I desired by having the divorce question brought up. . . . Now, Susan, I beg of you to let the past be past, and to waste no powder on the Woman's State Temperance Society. We have other and bigger fish to fry."

4 "IN THOUGHT AND SYMPATHY WE WERE ONE"

A Feminist Friendship

Susan B. Anthony became an unapologetic femi-
nist. Although she remained active in other reform activities,
she fully embraced the women's rights agenda. In August 1853,
several months after her betrayal by the men in the temperance
movement, Anthony attended the New York teachers' convention
in Rochester, New York. Those in attendance paid one dollar to
participate in the meeting.

On the first day, Anthony listened.

On the second day, the group discussed the question of "why
the profession of teacher is not as much respected as that of lawyer,
doctor, or minister." Anthony stood to address the convention.
"Mr. President," she said.

"What will the lady have?" the president asked.

"I wish to speak to the question under discussion," Anthony
said.

"What is the pleasure of the convention?" he asked the crowd.

Anthony remained standing while the men debated whether to

allow her to express her opinion. She knew that if she sat down, the men would assume she had given up and agreed to remain silent. After a half-hour discussion, she was permitted to speak.

"It seems to me you fail to comprehend the cause of the disrespect of which you complain," Anthony said. "Do you not see that so long as society says woman has not brains enough to be a doctor, lawyer or minister, but has plenty to be a teacher, every man of you who condescends to teach, tacitly admits . . . that he has no more brains than a woman?"

There were about five hundred people in attendance—and about three hundred of them were women—but no one applauded. Embarrassed silenced followed and then whispers: "Did you ever see such a disgraceful performance?" people said. And, "I was never so ashamed of my sex."

Anthony later said that she was filled with "grief and indignation" when she looked at the faces of the female teachers at the conference and realized "that by far the larger proportion were perfectly satisfied with the position assigned to them."

A small group of women did take a stand for women's rights, by introducing two resolutions: one that gave women the right to speak and fully participate in the organization and a second that supported equal pay for female teachers. Much to the surprise of the men running the meeting, both resolutions passed.

Anthony didn't back down. She had found her voice and she planned to continue to use it. In the months that followed, she returned to the temperance organizations that she had helped to organize just a few years before, but she found that many of the groups had disbanded. When she investigated further, she discovered that the groups had failed because they did not have the money necessary to continue their work. The women involved may have wanted to support temperance and other reform movements, but ultimately men controlled the finances.

"Woman must have a purse of her own," Anthony concluded. Once she identified the problem, Anthony knew what to do: She would go to the New York State Legislature and change the law.

SPEAKING TO THE NEW YORK STATE LEGISLATURE

At first, Susan B. Anthony focused her campaign on two issues: a married woman's right to keep her own wages and a mother's right to share equal guardianship of her children. She organized a group of sixty women who canvassed the state of New York, collecting ten thousand signatures on petitions. She planned to present the signatures to the New York State Legislature in Albany in February 1854.

Anthony asked Elizabeth Cady Stanton to be the spokesperson for the effort and to address a joint session of the Judiciary Committee of the New York Legislature. The topic of the speech would be injustice in the laws facing women.

Stanton wasn't sure she wanted to do it. Her daughter Margaret was only sixteen months old. But after putting up some resistance, she told Anthony, "I find there is no use saying 'no' to you." Stanton asked Anthony to put her in touch with a lawyer who might help her identify eight of the "most atrocious" laws affecting women.

Anthony's friend Judge William Hay came up with thirteen laws for Stanton to include in her remarks.

On February 14, 1854, Stanton felt the swish of her black silk dress as she approached the podium. She talked about women as citizens, wives, mothers, and widows. She spoke of taxation, child custody, and inheritance laws that treated women unfairly. She set out her case for "a new code of laws." She considered her address to have been persuasive and powerful—"a great event" in her life.

After the speech, however, the chairman of the Senate Judiciary Committee, Samuel G. Foote, refused to take action. He argued that Stanton's reforms would "unsex every female in the land."

He went on to mock the speech, pointing out that most of the men in the legislature were married and had experience dealing with women. "Thus aided," he said, "they are enabled to state that the ladies always have the best place and choicest tid-bit at the table. They have the best seats on the carts, carriage and sleighs. They have their choice on which side of the bed they will lie. . . . If there is any inequality or oppression in the case, the gentlemen are the sufferers."

Then, after noting that some of the signatures on Stanton's petition included names of both husbands and wives, the chairman suggested that the legislators change the law so that "the husband may wear petticoats and the wife the breeches."

Despite the demeaning response, Stanton and Anthony considered the speech a victory: Women had spoken before the legislature. Anthony ordered fifty thousand copies of the remarks printed in pamphlet form, and she spread them around the state "like flakes of snow." She gave copies to every New York legislator and sold the others to cover the printing expenses.

On the day of the speech, only Anthony had shown up to support Stanton. Stanton's husband blamed her for embarrassing him in public. There are two very different accounts of her father's response. In her autobiography, Stanton wrote that her father beamed with pride and was "moved to tears" when he read about her speech. In another, more likely version of events, Judge Cady is said to have strongly objected to his daughter's remarks. According to an account recorded by a friend of Stanton's, her father told her, "Your first lecture will be a very expensive one," threatening to disinherit her if she went through with it.

She is said to have replied, "I intend that it shall be very profitable." (Judge Cady did write Stanton out of his will, but he changed his mind—and his will—shortly before he died so that she inherited a portion of his estate.)

"I passed through a terrible scourging when last at my father's," Stanton wrote in a letter to Anthony several months after the speech. "I cannot tell you how deeply the iron entered my soul. I never felt more keenly the degradation of my sex. To think that all in me of which my father would have felt proper pride had I been a man is deeply mortifying to him because I am a woman."

STANTON'S RETREAT

Stung by the criticism from her father and husband, Elizabeth Cady Stanton stopped accepting invitations to public events and once again focused her attention on her family.

Her heart remained with the reformers, however. "My whole soul is in the work," Stanton wrote to Anthony, "but my hands belong to my family."

In another letter to Anthony, Stanton confessed that she often wished she "were as free" as her unmarried friend so that she could "stump the State in a twinkling." She explained that her husband objected to her work and "all that is dearest" to her. He was "not willing that I should write even on the woman question," she told Anthony. "Sometimes, Susan, I struggle in deep water."

A short time later, Lucretia Mott wrote to Stanton and urged her to attend the annual National Woman's Rights Convention in Philadelphia. "Can't thou take thy baby, & come to our Woman's Convention?" Mott asked. "We shall need thee and all other *true* women."

Stanton declined.

Anthony refused to allow Stanton to be swallowed by her domestic duties. Although she was less active than she had been, Stanton did write articles and help Anthony prepare her speeches. In 1856, Anthony approached Stanton and begged for help with remarks for an upcoming conference. Stanton famously replied: "Come here and I will do what I can . . . if you will hold the baby and make the puddings."

It was undeniable: Stanton and Anthony made a dynamic team. "I forged the thunderbolts, she fired them," Stanton said.

They balanced one another. "In thought and sympathy we were one, and in the division of labor we exactly complemented each other," Stanton said. "In writing we did better work than either could do alone. While she is slow and analytic in composition I am rapid and synthetic. I am the better writer, the better critic. She supplied the facts and statistics, I the philosophy and rhetoric. . . . Our speeches may be considered the joint products of our two brains."

Stanton remained devoted to the cause of women's rights, but at least for the time being, Anthony knew she had to wait until Stanton could spare more time for the movement.

ANTHONY ALONE

As a young woman, Susan B. Anthony had considered and turned down several marriage proposals, choosing to devote herself to her work instead of family. In an interview later in her life she said, "I'm sure no man could have made me happier than I have been. . . . I never felt I could give up my life of freedom to become a man's housekeeper. When I was young, if a girl married poor, she became a housekeeper and a drudge. If she married wealth, she became a pet and a doll. Just think, had I married at twenty,

I would have been a drudge or a doll for fifty-five years. Think of it!"

While Anthony did not regret the choices she made, she was profoundly disappointed when two other leaders of the women's rights movement—Lucy Stone and Antoinette Brown—both decided to marry. Anthony didn't oppose marriage, but she did think that certain women could lead more meaningful lives as unmarried radicals than as wives and mothers. The way Anthony saw things, each time one of their leaders married, it created one more obstacle, one more distraction that would interfere with the progress of suffrage and women's rights.

She and Lucy Stone had worked together in the temperance and women's rights movements. They exchanged letters for years, each offering the other support and encouragement. "I thank God every day for you and me," Stone wrote to Anthony, praising her independence as a person "who can work on and take care of oneself."

Stone grew up on a four-hundred-acre farm in West Brookfield, Massachusetts, with an overbearing father who drank too much. "There was only one will in my family and it was my father's," Stone wrote. When she was a young woman, her father told her that he doubted she could ever find a husband because "her face was like a blacksmith's leather apron—'It keeps off the sparks'"—and he made fun of the mole on her upper lip. After her father's cruel remarks, Stone told him that she had no intention of ever marrying and that she wished she were even plainer so that no one would ever ask her.

Stone worked for nine years to save enough money to cover her tuition at Oberlin College, and she became the first woman from Massachusetts to earn a college degree, in 1847. After graduation, she became a paid lecturer in the abolitionist movement. Some who heard her speak described her as "birdlike" with a voice like a "silver flute."

Life on the lecture circuit was hard, especially for a woman. People who didn't approve of Stone's abolitionist message some-times threw trash at her as she spoke. Once, in the middle of winter, someone opened a window while she was lecturing and threw ice water on her; instead of surrendering, Stone wrapped a shawl around her shoulders and kept talking. When someone hurled raw eggs at her, she wiped away the gooey mess and said that the "seeds of truth" in her words could not be so easily removed.

In 1853, Stone met Henry Blackwell at an antislavery meeting in New York. Blackwell came from a progressive family full of strong women, including his sister Elizabeth, the first woman to earn a medical degree in the United States. For Henry Blackwell, the attraction was immediate. He asked for Stone's address and began to write her letters. "Love me if you can," he wrote. "You may forget me. . . . I shall not forget you."

The two spent time together at conventions, but Stone remained unconvinced of a future together. She changed her mind in 1854 when she learned that Blackwell had boarded a train and rescued a runaway eight-year-old slave girl who was being forced to return to the South. After his act of heroism, Blackwell was harassed, a $10,000 bounty was put on his head, and he was charged with violating the Fugitive Slave Act of 1850. But he won Stone's heart.

Blackwell, who was seven years younger than Stone, promised her that marriage did not have to involve submission of the wife to the husband. He wanted to share a marriage of equals, a relationship that would not interfere with her work on abolition and women's rights. "I would not have my wife a drudge," he wrote. "I would not even consent that my wife should stay at home to rock the baby when she ought to be addressing a meeting or organizing a society."

He seemed to know just what Stone wanted to hear. "I do so love you," she finally wrote. "My heart warms toward you all the time."

LUCY STONE (1818–1893) *was a prominent leader in the women's rights movement and the first Massachusetts woman to earn a college degree. Because she did not take her husband's name when she married in 1855, the term "Lucy Stoners" was sometimes used to describe women who refused to accept their husband's name.*

Lucy Stone with her daughter, Alice Stone Blackwell. When Lucy was born, her own mother said, "Oh dear! I am sorry it is a girl. A woman's life is so hard."

They were married May 1, 1855. As part of their unconventional wedding ceremony, Blackwell renounced his legal privileges as husband, and Stone announced that she would keep her own name. "A wife should no more take her husband's name than he should hers," she said. "My name is my identity and must not be lost."

Throughout her life, Stone had to deal with people who refused to call her by her preferred name. On many legal documents her signature would not be considered valid unless she wrote her name followed by the words "married to Henry Blackwell."

Even Susan B. Anthony chose to express her anger and disappointment at Stone's choice to marry by referring to her as Mrs. Henry Blackwell. Stone's engagement had caught Anthony by surprise, because the two women had discussed the issue and Stone had said that she planned never to marry. The two women had pledged that they would remain single and devote themselves to the fight for women's rights. Stone finally called out Anthony and asked her to use the name Lucy Stone, and Anthony relented.

Still, although Stone dedicated the rest of her life to working for women's rights, Anthony never forgave her for what she considered a personal betrayal.

To make matter worse for Anthony, Elizabeth Cady Stanton announced that she was pregnant again, with her sixth baby. The pregnancy took a toll on Stanton both physically and emotionally.

After Harriot was born in 1856, Stanton wrote to Anthony that she was "very happy, that the terrible ordeal is passed & that the result is another daughter." But a month later Stanton wrote again. "Imagine me," she said, "day in and day out, watching, bathing, dressing, nursing, and promenading the precious contents of the little crib. . . . I pace up and down these two chambers of mine like a caged lioness longing to bring nursing and house keeping cares to a close."

Anthony thought she knew just what Stanton needed: a writing project. Anthony was struggling to draft the remarks she was to present at the upcoming state teachers' convention. "For the love of me," she wrote to Stanton, "& for the saving of the *reputation of womenhood*, I beg you with one baby on your knee & another at your feet & four boys whistling buzzing hallooing *Ma Ma* set your self about the work . . . *don't* say *no*, nor *don't delay* it a moment, for I must have it done . . . Now will *you load my gun*, leaving me to pull the trigger."

Stanton invited Anthony to her home, and together they wrote a speech that scolded female teachers for accepting lower pay than their male colleagues received.

Anthony presented the speech, but it didn't go over well. Most of the women rejected the call for equal pay, because they believed it would be unladylike.

Stanton was disgusted. "What an infernal set of fools these school-marms must be!!" Stanton wrote to Anthony. "Well, if in order to please men they wish to live on air, let them. The sooner the present generation of women die out the better. We have jack-asses enough in the world now without such women propagating any more."

A RETURN TO REFORM

While her heart remained with the work of the women's movement, Susan B. Anthony needed to find a way to support herself. She joined "the lecturing corps" as an agent of the American Anti-Slavery Society, earning ten dollars a week, an amount equal to about $300 in today's dollars. As part of the job, she toured the country, speaking out against slavery.

It wasn't easy. She dealt with foul weather, inadequate food and housing, and angry crowds. Audience members—especially the men—hissed, shouted, and threw eggs at her. Three times she was hung in effigy.

The press was cruel when covering her speeches. Reporters called her "a reformatory Amazon" and "an ungainly hermaphrodite, part male, part female with an ugly face and shrill voice."

Faced with such hurtful and hostile interactions, she turned to her female friends to keep her strong. When Stanton learned about Anthony's work, she was proud. "I glory in your perseverance,"

Stanton wrote. "Oh! Susan, I will do anything to help you . . . You and I have a prospect of a good long life. We shall not be in our prime before fifty, & after that we shall be good for twenty years at least."

Stanton was ready to return to reform work when, to her surprise and dismay, she learned that at age forty-three she was pregnant with her seventh child.

Anthony was appalled. She wrote to a mutual friend: "Ah me!!! alas!! alas!!!! *Mrs. Stanton*!! . . . For a *moment's pleasure* to herself or her husband, she should thus increase the *load of cares* under which she already groans."

Robert Livingston Stanton was born in March 1859. Elizabeth Cady Stanton wrote to Anthony, "You need expect nothing from me for some time. . . . You have no idea how weak I am & I have to keep my mind in the most quiet state in order to sleep." Stanton, who had always been proud of her resilience following childbirth, complained that the baby "seemed to take up every particle of [her] vitality, soul and body."

Stanton was at home in October of that year when she learned about the bloody slave revolt that had been led by white abolitionist John Brown in Harpers Ferry, Virginia (now West Virginia). She then heard that her beloved cousin Gerrit Smith had helped to fund the raid. Facing prosecution and jail, Smith suffered a mental breakdown and briefly committed himself to an insane asylum.

Two weeks later, Stanton's father died at age eighty-six. Stanton had devoted much of her life to seeking her father's respect, but he died before they had healed the rift between them caused by her speech before the New York State Legislature several years before.

Faced with these devastating losses, she longed for comfort and support from Anthony. On December 23, she wrote: "Where are you? Since a week ago last Monday, I have looked for you every day . . . but lo! you did not come . . . The death of my father, the

worse than death of my dear Cousin Gerrit, the martyrdom of . . .
John Brown—all this conspire to make me regret more than ever
my dwarfed womanhood. In times like these, everyone should do
the work of a full-grown man."

Elizabeth Cady Stanton meant it. After her father's death, she
rediscovered her voice. She never won her father's approval, but
with his death, she was at last free of his disapproval.

In the spring of 1860, Stanton prepared a speech in defense
of married women's property rights and returned before the
Judiciary Committee of the New York State Legislature to present
it. Anthony encouraged her, telling her that the women of New
York were depending "upon her bending all her powers to move
the hearts of our law-givers at this time."

Stanton delivered a stirring speech about the "sacred right"
of women's suffrage. Earlier that spring, the legislature had voted
in favor of the Married Women's Earnings Act of 1860, which
gave married women in New York the right to own property,
collect their own wages, engage in their own business, enter into
contracts, and sue and be sued. Both Stanton and Anthony were
delighted with the achievement, but eager for the legislature to
move forward on the question of giving women the right to vote.

DISAGREEMENTS OVER DIVORCE

Elizabeth Cady Stanton was back. In May 1860, she took the stage
at the Tenth National Woman's Rights Convention at Cooper
Union in New York City. In a speech that was said to have "set
the convention on fire," she spoke in favor of allowing women to
divorce their husbands if they were violent or habitually drunk or
if they had abandoned the family.

Stanton had been away from the podium at women's rights

conventions for six years, but most people in the audience still knew her by name. Still, she shocked the crowd. She caused a scandal when she said that marriage was "nothing more than legalized prostitution. . . . There is one kind of marriage that has not been tried, and that is a contract made by equal parties to lead an equal life. . . . Thus far, we have had *man* marriage and nothing more."

Stanton's remarks infuriated a number of supporters, including abolitionist Wendell Phillips, a longtime advocate of women's rights. He argued that divorce should not be discussed at a women's rights conventions because it involved both men and women. Phillips moved to remove Stanton's entire speech from the official convention record.

Though the motion was defeated, Stanton had considered Phillips an ally, and she was hurt by his rejection. Anthony tried to explain Phillips's action by suggesting that "he is a man and can not put himself in the position of a wife; can not feel what she does under the present marriage code." Stanton said that she was pleased that she didn't know Phillips's opinion before she made her remarks because "the desire to please those we admire and respect often cripples conscience."

Another abolitionist criticized Anthony for taking a position on the issue of divorce. He told her, "You are not married, you have no business to be discussing marriage."

She responded, "You are not a slave, suppose you quit lecturing on slavery."

Stanton and Anthony refused to apologize or back down. The more their abolitionist friends challenged their positions, the more unyielding they became in their opinions about women's rights.

Several months later, they locked horns with their abolition movement colleagues again when Anthony assisted a woman who was being abused by her husband. In December 1860, Phoebe Harris Phelps and her thirteen-year-old daughter showed up at

Anthony's house late at night. Phelps explained that she had run away from an abusive and unfaithful husband, who was a prominent member of the Massachusetts state legislature.

Phelps told Anthony her story: Almost two years before, Phelps confronted her husband with proof of his extramarital affairs. Rather than admitting his infidelity, he threw her down a flight of stairs and had her committed to the McLean Lunatic Asylum, charging that she was suffering from delusions. (This was not unheard of at the time; a husband could sign his wife into an asylum simply for challenging his authority.)

A year and a half later, Phelps's brother fought for her release from the asylum and offered her a place to live. Her husband eventually allowed her to see her son and daughter. But when she asked to spend more time with her daughter, her husband refused. Even her brother told her, "The child belongs by law to the father and it is your place to submit. If you make any more trouble about it we'll send you back to the asylum."

She ran away and took her daughter with her. She first went to a Quaker family, but her husband found her. The second time she ran, she turned to Anthony for help.

After verifying Phelps's story, Anthony decided to help the woman and her child find a place to live in New York City. On Christmas Day 1860, Anthony dressed the runaways like beggars and escorted them aboard a southbound train. They arrived in the city during a snowstorm, and one hotel after another turned the three women away because they did not have a male escort. Anthony eventually arranged for Phelps and her daughter to live in Philadelphia, and Anthony returned home.

Phelps's husband learned that Anthony had helped his wife escape, and he accused her of abducting his child, but Anthony refused to give him any information about their whereabouts.

Once again, Wendell Phillips and other abolitionists told

Anthony that her behavior was compromising the antislavery cause. Phillips sent her a telegraph: "Let us urge you at once to advise and insist upon this woman's returning to her relatives."

Anthony ignored him.

At an antislavery convention, William Lloyd Garrison confronted her. "Don't you know the law of Massachusetts gives the father the entire guardianship and control of the children?" he asked.

"Yes, I know it," Anthony replied, "and does not the law of the United States give the slaveholder the ownership of the slave? And don't you break it every time you help a slave to Canada?"

"Yes, I do."

"Well, the law which gives the father the sole ownership of the children is just as wicked and I'll break it just as quickly," Anthony said. "You would die before you would deliver a slave to his master, and I will die before I give up that child to its father."

Anthony felt she had been undermined by her friends. Her father reached out to support her. "My child," he wrote, "I think you have done absolutely right, but don't put a word on paper or make a statement to any one that you are not prepared to face in court. Legally you are wrong, but morally you are right, and I will stand by you."

A year later, Phelps's daughter was abducted by agents sent by her father, while she was walking to church on a Sunday morning. The woman never saw her daughter again. Anthony was heartbroken.

PREPARING FOR WAR

In November 1860, Abraham Lincoln was elected president of the United States. As part of his candidacy, he had pledged to stop the expansion of slavery to the West. The abolitionists didn't think that position went far enough; they favored full and immediate emancipation. Anthony started a "No Compromise with Slavery" speaking tour in New York.

Tensions between slaveholders and abolitionists kept growing, and by mid-January 1861, five slaveholding states—South Carolina, Mississippi, Florida, Alabama, and Georgia—had seceded from the United States. Within weeks, Louisiana and Texas had joined them. A war between the states seemed unavoidable.

Stanton accepted the inevitability of war and saw it as the only way to end slavery. Anthony remained a pacifist and held on to the hope that slavery could be abolished without resorting to fighting.

On April 12, 1861, Southern forces attacked Fort Sumter, a military post in Charleston, South Carolina, marking the beginning of the Civil War.

Once the fighting began, most of the women who had been active in the suffrage movement suspended that work and focused their energy on the war effort. Stanton believed that the Union needed the support of all its citizens during the war, and, in time, the loyal service of the women would be rewarded with suffrage and additional rights once peace was restored.

Anthony wasn't so sure. She worried that easing up on their demands during the war would cause women to lose ground and forfeit the modest gains they had won.

Anthony had already made plans for the Eleventh National Woman's Rights Convention, set for May in New York, and she wanted to move forward with the meeting. Stanton and other speakers refused to participate.

"I have not yet seen *one good reason* for the abandonment of all our meetings," Anthony wrote to a friend. She acknowledged that she was "more and more ashamed and sad" by the turn of events. "All alike say 'Have no convention at this crisis!' . . . 'Wait until the war excitement abates.' I am sick at heart, but cannot carry the world against the wish and will of our best friends."

Despite their differences in opinion, Stanton and Anthony always made a point to present a united front. "We have indulged freely in criticism of each other when alone, and hotly contended whenever we have differed," Stanton later recalled. "To the world we always seem to agree and uniformly reflect each other. Like husband and wife, each has the feeling that we must have no differences in public."

Ultimately, Anthony was outvoted and the women's rights convention was canceled. Anthony begrudgingly accepted that the work of the suffrage movement was suspended, at least for the duration of the Civil War.

5

"YOU MUST BE TRUE ALIKE TO THE WOMEN AND THE NEGROES"

Division in the Suffrage Movement

DURING THE EARLY DAYS OF THE CIVIL WAR, SUSAN B. Anthony lived on her family's farm in Rochester, New York. As weeks turned into months and the fighting continued, she fell into a predictable routine of daily chores and abolition work. Anthony described her activities in her personal diary: "Washed every window in the house today. Quilted all day . . . stained and varnished the library bookcase today. . . . The last load of hay is in the barn. . . . Fitted out a fugitive slave for Canada with the help of Harriet Tubman."

The work at home was exhausting, and for Anthony taking a break from her reform work was agonizing. She grew increasingly restless not doing "public work." She wrote, "To forever blot out slavery is the only possible compensation for this merciless war."

In 1862, Elizabeth Cady Stanton and her family moved from Seneca Falls to New York City when her husband took a job there. After settling into her new home, Stanton focused on abolition, touring the state and trying to convince others to join the anti-slavery cause.

Like many other abolitionists, both she and Anthony considered President Lincoln too cautious in his approach to slavery. They wanted him to eliminate slavery all at once, but Lincoln preferred an incremental approach. His first priority was the preservation of the nation, and he didn't want to anger residents in the "border states"—Delaware, Maryland, Kentucky, and Missouri—because those states still allowed slavery, even though they were part of the Union.

On January 1, 1863, Lincoln issued the Emancipation Proclamation, which freed the slaves living in the eleven states that had seceded from the Union. The order left both sides unhappy: Northern abolitionists were dissatisfied because the Emancipation Proclamation did not outlaw slavery everywhere; Southern slaveholders were enraged because it freed millions of slaves living in their states.

The nation was in peril. In early 1863, the war was going badly in the North and it was not clear that the Thirteenth Amendment to the US Constitution—which abolished slavery—would pass Congress and be ratified by the states. Elizabeth Cady Stanton's husband, Henry, encouraged his wife and her friend Susan B. Anthony to lead work in support of the amendment. In a letter to Anthony, he wrote, "The country was never so badly off as at this moment . . . You have no idea how dark the cloud is which hangs over us. . . . Here then is work for you. Susan, put on your armor and go forth."

Stanton and Anthony wasted no time. In March 1863, they published a notice in the *New York Tribune* calling for a meeting of "The Loyal Women of the Nation." Interested women were invited to a gathering at the Church of the Puritans in New York City on May 14. The notice read, in part: "At this hour the

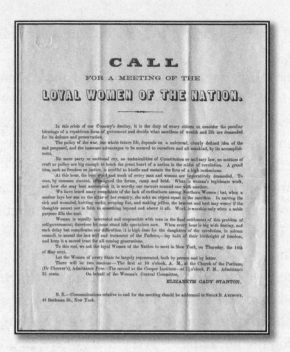

This notice urged women to become involved in what became known as the Women's Loyal National League, devoted to passage of the Thirteenth Amendment. It was the first national women's political organization in the United States. The Loyal League disbanded in August 1864, when it became clear that the amendment would pass.

best word and work of every man and woman are imperatively demanded. . . . Woman is equally interested and responsible with man in the settlement of this final problem of self-government; therefore let none stand idle spectators now."

Women came from as far away as Maine and California to form the new organization, the Women's Loyal National League, which would work to abolish slavery and preserve the nation. Many of the women knew one another from their earlier women's rights work, but some were new to reform efforts.

Anthony called the first meeting to order, and Stanton was elected to serve as president. The group promptly passed several resolutions, including one that endorsed the abolition of slavery and another that offered support to the federal government. In addition, the women pledged to collect one million signatures on a petition supporting the Thirteenth Amendment.

After some discussion, Anthony introduced another resolution, which read, "There can never be a true peace in this Republic until the civil and political rights of all citizens of African descent and all women are practically established."

This statement was too radical for some of the women at the meeting, who wanted nothing to do with the women's rights agenda.

A woman from Wisconsin objected. "There are ladies here who have come hundreds of miles to attend a business meeting of the Loyal League of the North," she said. "We all know that Woman's Rights . . . has not been received with the entire favor by the women of the country, and . . . women will not go into any movement of this kind if this idea is made prominent." These women wanted to join a "Loyal League" that supported the country and President Lincoln, nothing more.

Still, some of the women's rights advocates refused to give up so easily. They pointed out the link between the oppression of women and the oppression of enslaved people. The experienced abolitionist and women's rights advocate Angelina Grimké said, "I rejoice exceedingly that the resolution should combine us with the negro. . . . True, we have not felt the slave-holder's lash . . . but our *hearts* have been crushed."

Lucy Stone thought the group should support the rights of both African Americans and women. She recognized that at the close of the war the nation would face an opportunity for radical change; she argued against compromise, citing the example of war-weary leaders at the end of the American Revolutionary War who begrudgingly accepted slavery, rather than dealing with the issue at the time. Stone gave an impassioned plea:

> [The Founding Fathers] said nothing about slavery, and let the wretched monster live.
>
> To-day, over all our land, the unburied bones of our fathers and sons and brothers tell the sad mistake that those men made when long ago they left this one great wrong. They could not accomplish good by passing over a wrong. . . .
>
> All over this land women have no political existence. . . . We come to-day to say to . . . our Government . . . "do not forget that you must be true alike to the women and the negroes."

In the end, the group chose to pass a resolution so unambitious that almost everyone in attendance was willing to sign on. They pledged themselves "one to another in a Loyal League, to give support to the Government in so far as it makes the war for freedom."

Even so, Stanton saw the resolution as an important beginning. "Many women spoke ably and eloquently," she said. "Women who had never before heard their own voices in a public meeting discussed points of law and constitution in a manner that would have done credit to any legislative assembly." Stanton recognized their participation as a feminist act, even if the language in the resolutions was tamer than she had wanted.

After the meeting, a network of two thousand women set off on a nationwide mission to collect signatures on a petition urging Congress to pass the Thirteenth Amendment, abolishing slavery. Their goal was to "go to the rich, the poor, the high, the low, the soldier, the civilian, the white, the black—gather up the names of all who hate slavery, all who love liberty, and would have it the law of the land, and lay them at the feet of Congress."

In the first year, the women collected more than one hundred thousand signatures. One woman who circulated the petition in Wisconsin had already lost her husband and all four of her sons in the Civil War. She walked more than one hundred miles collecting two thousand signatures in an effort to help end slavery and give meaning to her family's sacrifice.

Members of the Loyal League divided the petitions by state, sewed the pages together, and decorated the scrolls with colored ribbons. On February 9, 1864, two African American men carried large bundles of petition rolls into the Senate chamber.

"These petitions are signed by 100,000 men and women, who . . . ask nothing less than universal emancipation," said Senator Charles Sumner of Massachusetts, who presented the

A page of the petition circulated by the Women's Loyal National League. The group collected four hundred thousand signatures from women who supported the Thirteenth Amendment, abolishing slavery.

petitions on behalf of the Loyal League. Although it was a particularly hot and humid summer, the women of the Loyal League continued their campaign and collected three hundred thousand more names.

The Civil War ended in April 1865. By the end of the year, the Thirteenth Amendment had been ratified and added to the Constitution. The Women's Loyal National League had successfully completed its mission, and many people believed that women had earned the right to vote through this work.

"When the war-cry was heard in 1861, the advance-guard of the Woman's Rights party cried 'halt!' And for five years we have stood waiting. . . . Not as idle spectators, but as the busiest and most unwearied actors," wrote suffragist Frances Dana Barker Gage in a letter to the *Anti-Slavery Standard*, an abolitionist newspaper. "We have . . . fought half the battle . . . [yet] seventeen millions of women . . . are proclaimed a disfranchised class."

"THIS IS THE NEGRO'S HOUR"

In May 1866, more than a year after the war ended, a group gathered in New York City for the final meeting of the American Anti-Slavery Society, which was planning to disband because it had met its ultimate objective, ending slavery.

Wendell Phillips argued that the group, instead of dissolving, should continue to work until all freed slaves and other African Americans had the right to vote. The society was reorganized under a new name—the American Equal Rights Association—with a goal of universal suffrage.

Susan B. Anthony was pleased that the goal included female suffrage. "We can no longer . . . work in two separate movements to get the ballot for the two disfranchised classes—the negro and woman," she said, "since to do so must be at double cost of time, energy and money."

The new association included both new faces and veteran organizers. Lucretia Mott, now seventy-three years old, was elected president. She protested, arguing that "feebleness unfitted her," but she reluctantly agreed to serve with support from her vice president, Elizabeth Cady Stanton.

At a follow-up meeting in Boston a few weeks later, the women's rights advocates were distraught to learn that many abolitionists planned to focus only on winning the vote for black men. Stanton had assumed that the American Equal Rights Association would be dedicated to winning universal suffrage—voting rights for all. But Wendell Phillips said that it would be too difficult to win the vote for both groups at the same time.

"As Abraham Lincoln said, 'One war at a time'; so I say, 'One question at a time,'" Phillips told the group. "This is the negro's hour."

Stanton thought it was wrong to ask women to wait. She saw it as an issue of natural rights. To give voting rights to African Americans over women was to endorse what Stanton called the "aristocracy of sex." Stanton felt that if women did not win the right to vote at this time, it could be decades before they would have another chance.

For years to come, women would hear the refrain "This is the negro's hour" to justify why they should set aside their demands for their own rights. Phillips and other Republican leaders encouraged women to be patient and wait until African American men secured their right to vote. They didn't oppose female suffrage, but it wasn't their first priority, and they didn't want to press for universal suffrage if it would make black suffrage less likely.

The movement was dividing into two groups—one that made voting rights for black men the priority and another that demanded that female suffrage also be considered—and this disagreement changed the relationships among advocates. For years, Anthony had been able to publish notices of women's rights meetings in the *Anti-Slavery Standard*, an abolitionist newspaper, at a discount. Suddenly, Anthony was charged the full amount, and the paper stopped publishing Stanton's letters and articles.

"The gate is shut, wholly," Anthony said. The women's suffrage advocates were on their own.

Stanton and Anthony wrote articles and letters, held meetings, and circulated petitions demanding that Congress "extend the right of suffrage to woman." When Stanton encountered women who refused to sign petitions for women's suffrage, she told them that their rejection "would have been a wet blanket to Susan [B. Anthony] and me were we not sure that we were right."

She followed up with a personal assault. "When your granddaughters hear that . . . you made no protest," she said, "they will blush for their ancestry."

When Stanton asked Lucretia Mott to sign the petition for female suffrage, she refused. Mott said that she believed it was, in fact, the Negro's hour.

Stanton challenged her, arguing that the "negro's hour was decidedly the fitting time for woman to slip in."

Mott considered Stanton's position and changed her mind. She signed.

"WOMAN'S CAUSE IS IN DEEP WATER"

While there was consensus within the women's rights movement about support for the Thirteenth Amendment to end slavery, there was disagreement over endorsement of the Fourteenth

Amendment, which ensured citizenship and civil rights for former slaves. It also introduced the word "male" to the Constitution for the first time. The amendment established that basic rights of citizenship—including suffrage—would be granted to *male* former slaves, and by specifying the sex it explicitly denied those rights to women.

Some women accepted the Fourteenth Amendment as a step toward democracy for African American men, assuming that women's rights would follow. Others asked themselves, if not now, when? And they objected to making discrimination against women part of the Constitution, fearful that it would make it more difficult for women to establish their rights at a later date.

As the nation spent much of 1866 and 1867 debating the issues surrounding the Fourteenth Amendment, tensions grew within the women's rights movement. Elizabeth Cady Stanton was outraged by the amendment. "If that word 'male' be inserted as now proposed . . . it will take us a century at least to get it out again," she wrote to Gerrit Smith at his home. "Oh! my cousin! Heal my bleeding heart with one trumpet note of manly indignation."

Smith let Stanton down. He wrote back, "I think such a mixture would lose for the Negro far more than we should gain for the woman."

Stanton realized that opposing the Fourteenth Amendment would be a difficult fight; many of her closest friends and former allies disagreed with her position. She then wrote to Susan B. Anthony. "Woman's cause is in deep water," she said. "Come back and help. . . . I seem to stand alone."

Anthony was equally disgusted with the wording of the Fourteenth Amendment, and she pledged that she would work against its ratification. "I would sooner cut off my right hand than ask the ballot for the black man and not the woman," she wrote to abolitionist Wendell Phillips. Anthony didn't see the amendment as progress for African American men; she saw it as "an outrage against women."

When the American Equal Rights Association met in 1867, the group debated whether to support the Fourteenth Amendment.

Sojourner Truth, who saw the issue from the point of view of both a woman and an African American citizen, summed up her position in one line: "If I am responsible for my deeds the same as the white male citizen is, I have a right to all the rights he has."

Women's rights advocate Frances Dana Barker Gage worried about the status of African American women. She said that she had spoken with African American women in the South who told her, "You give us a nominal freedom, but you leave us under the heel of our husbands, who are tyrants almost equal to our masters." She argued that women—black and white, Southern and Northern—needed suffrage and all the rights and protections of citizenship.

Charles Lenox Remond, an African American activist from Massachusetts, spoke out at the meeting in favor of the women. He said that he objected to the "negro's hour" strategy: "I repudiate the idea of expediency. All I ask for myself, I claim for my wife and sister. Let our action be based on everlasting principle. No class of citizens in this county can be deprived of the ballot without injuring every other class."

So rather than choosing between the rights of women and the rights of African Americans, the American Equal Rights Association adopted a memorial favoring a position of gender and racial unity. Stanton and Anthony organized a petition drive in New York in support of female suffrage. The group sent a statement to Congress.

"HOLD YOUR CLAIMS . . . UNTIL THE NEGRO IS SAFE"

Once the debate was framed as an issue of women's rights versus African American rights, the arguments used by some female suffragists became increasingly elitist. Elizabeth Cady Stanton initially favored universal suffrage—voting rights for all—but when it became clear that expanded voting rights for both African Americans and women would not be considered, she changed her position and supported "educated suffrage," the idea that the vote should be given only to people who were educated, regardless of sex or race. In an attempt to support their new position for educated women's rights, both Stanton and Susan B. Anthony began to use divisive and racist arguments. When Stanton met with Horace Greeley, the editor of the *New York Tribune*, he told her, "hold your claims . . . until the negro is safe, and your turn will come next."

But Stanton was tired of waiting, and she launched into a racist rant. She demanded that Greeley consider how he would feel if he were disenfranchised. She asked him what he would think if editorials supported suffrage for uneducated immigrants while he was asked to wait patiently. She said that women had "stood with the black man for half a century" and should get the vote at the same time. "Enfranchise him and we are left outside with lunatics, idiots, and criminals for another twenty years."

Appalled, Greeley ended the meeting, but not before he warned that if Stanton and Anthony continued to push for female suffrage ahead of African American suffrage, then they could "depend on no further help from [him] or the *Tribune*."

Stanton and Anthony stood fast as the battleground for suffrage shifted to the West. In a speech in Missouri in 1867, Anthony argued, "When you propose to elevate the lowest and most degraded classes of men to an even platform with white men . . . it is certainly time for you to begin to think at least whether it might not be proper to lift the wives, daughters, and mothers of your State to an even pedestal."

Women in Kansas already had the right to vote in school elections, and many women's rights leaders thought that there was a real possibility that full suffrage could be won there. Many westerners believed that the pioneering women who had moved west and endured significant hardship now deserved the right to participate in government through the vote.

A dozen Kansas women organized a women's rights society to advocate for full female suffrage, and Lucy Stone and Henry Blackwell went to Kansas to work on the campaign. They spoke in churches, schools, and courthouses. Stone wrote to friends back east with stories of a woman who "carried petitions all through the town for female suffrage, and not one woman refused to sign."

In September 1867, Stanton and Anthony traveled to Atchison, Kansas, to assist with the campaign. But when they arrived, they found that they were considered meddlesome outsiders. One woman who had offered to host Stanton in her home was distraught to discover that Anthony would be staying with her instead. She had heard such unpleasant things about Anthony that she was quite surprised when she "met a dignified, quaker looking lady." Confused and embarrassed, the woman reluctantly invited Anthony in for tea, and while she prepared it, "Aunt Susan" so charmed her family that she remained there for six weeks.

Stanton spoke at rallies and lectured wherever she could. Anthony organized events and sold pamphlets about suffrage. She found it easier to sell printed material in the West than in the East because, she reported, "reading matter is so very scarce that everybody clutches at a book of any kind." By the time she and

Stanton left Kansas, Anthony said, "there was scarcely a log cabin in the State that could not boast one or more of these [suffrage] documents."

GEORGE FRANCIS TRAIN AND THE *REVOLUTION*

George Francis Train was a wealthy eccentric who was an outspoken advocate for women's suffrage. He was well-known for his unusual dress—he wore purple vests, lavender gloves, and pastel waistcoats—and for his racist words. Although Train was infamous for making hateful remarks about African Americans, during the Kansas campaign some suffragists, including Susan B. Anthony and Elizabeth Cady Stanton, were so eager to rally support for their cause that they were willing to overlook his bigoted fearmongering and forge an alliance with him.

In October 1867, a group of suffragists, Stanton and Anthony among them, found out that Train was in Nebraska, so they sent a telegram: COME TO KANSAS AND STUMP THE STATE FOR EQUAL RIGHTS AND FEMALE SUFFRAGE.

Train accepted the invitation. But in his speeches, he tried to convince audiences that giving African Americans the rights of citizenship would undermine white society and safety. "Carry negro suffrage," he said, "and we shall see some

George Francis Train
(1829–1904)

white woman in a case of negro rape being tried by 12 negro jurymen."

On the ballot in November 1867, the men in Kansas faced two referendums, one that deleted the word "white" from the description of voters and a second that deleted the word "male." In other words, voters could grant suffrage to African American men, to white women, to neither group, or to both groups, which would include African American women. Kansas voters did not face a choice between voting rights for black men or white women; both groups could have won the right to vote.

Instead of working together, however, those working on behalf of each group undermined one another. The end result: Both proposals failed by roughly three-to-one margins. Neither African American men nor white women were granted the right to vote.

During the Kansas campaign, Stanton and Anthony spent weeks with Train, and at one point, Train asked Stanton why she and the other suffragists didn't have a newspaper of their own.

She explained that the women's movement didn't have the money to buy one.

"I will give it to you," Train said.

Stanton and Anthony were eager to replace the connection to the press that they had lost in the split with Horace Greeley and the *New York Tribune*, so they accepted his offer.

When word got around that Stanton and Anthony were working with Train, their friends begged them to reconsider. Lucy Stone was among those shocked at the alliance between the suffragists and the bigoted Train. "It seems to me that [Anthony] is hardly less crazy than he is," Stone said.

The duo ignored the warnings. "So long as Mr. Train speaks nobly for the woman," Anthony wrote, "why should we repudiate his services?"

Stanton agreed. "All there is about [Train] is that he has made it possible for us to establish a paper," she said. "If the Devil him-self had come up and said ladies I will help you establish a paper I should have said Amen!"

Train came through with the initial funding, and in January 1868 Stanton and Anthony turned their backs on twenty years of work in the abolition movement to begin publishing the *Revolution*. Its motto, printed on the masthead, was: PRINCIPLE, NOT POLICY; JUSTICE, NOT FAVORS. After the first edition, another line was added: MEN, THEIR RIGHTS, AND NOTHING MORE; WOMEN, THEIR RIGHTS, AND NOTHING LESS.

The sixteen-page weekly paper set up its office in New York City in the same building where the Women's Loyal National League had once rented space. Anthony managed the business side while Stanton—with assistance from coeditor Parker Pillsbury, a former editor of the *National Anti-Slavery Standard*—handled the editorial content.

Stanton and Anthony prided themselves on publishing arti-cles on topics not covered in conventional newspapers, such as the eight-hour workday, employment discrimination, divorce, abortion, infanticide, prostitution, and, of course, the injustice of the Fourteenth Amendment's exclusion of women. Many former friends thought the paper was too radical or too embarrassing, and they refused to subscribe.

Some suffragists and potential contributors found the publica-tion's name—the *Revolution*—off-putting. Harriet Beecher Stowe, the renowned best-selling American author of *Uncle Tom's Cabin*, offered to write for Stanton, but only if the paper would consider a less provocative name.

Other women who had an interest in the newspaper decided not to subscribe because they didn't want to associate with Train.

Stanton refused to make changes to accommodate criticism. She further offended other suffragists by advocating for "educated

The Revolution.

PRINCIPLE, NOT POLICY: JUSTICE, NOT FAVORS.

VOL. I.—NO. 1.   NEW YORK, WEDNESDAY, JANUARY 8, 1868. $2.00 A YEAR.

The Revolution;

THE ORGAN OF THE

NATIONAL PARTY OF NEW AMERICA.

PRINCIPLE, NOT POLICY—INDIVIDUAL RIGHTS AND RESPONSIBILITIES.

THE REVOLUTION WILL ADVOCATE:

1. IN POLITICS—Educated Suffrage, Irrespective of Sex or Color; Equal Pay to Women for Equal Work; Eight Hours Labor; Abolition of Standing Armies and Part; Despotisms. Down with Politicians—Up with the People!

2. IN RELIGION—Deeper Thought; Broader Idea; Science not Superstition; Personal Purity; Love to Man as well as God.

3. IN SOCIAL LIFE—Morality and Reform; Practical Education, not Theoretical; Facts not Fiction; Virtue not Vice; Cold Water not Alcoholic Drinks or Medicines. It will indulge in no Gross Personalities and insert no Quack or Immoral Advertisements, so common even in Religious Newspapers.

4. THE REVOLUTION proposes a new Commercial and Financial Policy. America no longer led by Europe. Gold like our Cotton and Corn for sale. Greenbacks for money. An American System of Finance. American Products and Labor Free. Foreign Manufacturers Prohibited. Open doors to Artisans and Immigrants. Atlantic and Pacific Oceans for American Steamships and Shipping; or American goods in American bottoms. New York the Financial Centre of the World. Wall Street emancipated from Bank of England, or American Cash for American Bills. The Credit Foncier and Credit Mobilier System, or Capital Mobilized to Reconstitute the South and our Mining Interests, and to People the Country from Ocean to Ocean, from Omaha to San Francisco. More organized Labor, more Cotton, more Gold and Silver Bullion to sell foreigners at the highest prices. Ten millions of Naturalized Citizens Demand a Penny Ocean Postage, to Strengthen the Brotherhood of Labor; and if Congress Vote One Hundred and Twenty-five Millions for a Standing Army and Freedman's Bureau, cannot they spare One Million to Educate Europe and to keep bright the chain of acquaintance and friendship between those millions and their fatherlands?

Send in your Subscription. THE REVOLUTION, published weekly, will be the Great Organ of the Age.

TERMS.—Two dollars a year, in advance. Ten names ($20) entitle the sender to one copy free.

ELIZABETH CADY STANTON, } Eds.
PARKER PILLSBURY, }

SUSAN B. ANTHONY,
Proprietor and Manager.
37 Park Row (Room 17), New York City.
To whom address all business letters.

KANSAS.

THE question of the enfranchisement of woman has already passed the court of moral discussion, and is now fairly ushered into the arena of politics, where it must remain a fixed element of debate, until party necessity shall compel its success.

With 9,000 votes in Kansas, one-third the entire vote, every politician must see that the friends of "woman's suffrage" hold the balance of power in that State to-day. And these 9,000 votes represent a principle deep in the hearts of the people, for this triumph was secured without money, without a press, without a party. With these instrumentalities now fast coming to us on all sides, the victory in Kansas is but the herald of greater victories in every State of the Union. Kansas already leads the world in her legislation for woman on questions of property, education, wages, marriage and divorce. Her best universities are open alike to boys and girls. In fact woman has a voice in the legislation of that State. She votes on all school questions and is eligible to the office of trustee. She has a voice in temperance too; no license is granted without the consent of a majority of the adult citizens, male and female, black and white. The consequence is, some school houses are voted up in every part of the State, and rum voted down. Many of the ablest men in that State are champions of woman's cause, Governors, judges, lawyers and clergymen. Two-thirds of the press and pulpits advocate the idea, in spite of the opposition of politicians. The first Governor of Kansas, twice chosen to that office, Charles Robinson, went all through the State, speaking every day for two months in favor of woman's suffrage. In the organization of the State government, he proposed that the words "white male" should not be inserted in the Kansas constitution. All this shows that giving political rights to women is no new idea in that State. Who that has listened with tearful eyes to the deep experiences of those Kansas women, through the darkest hours of their history, does not feel that such bravery and self denial as they have shown alike in war and peace, have richly earned for them the crown of citizenship.

Opposed to this moral sentiment of the liberal minds of the State, many adverse influences were brought to bear through the entire campaign.

The action of the New York Constitutional Convention; the silence of eastern journals on the question; the opposition of abolitionists lost a demand for woman's suffrage should defeat negro suffrage; the hostility everywhere of black men themselves; some even stumping the State against woman's suffrage; the official action of both the leading parties in their conventions in Leavenworth against the proposition, with every organized Republican influ-

ence outside as well as inside the State, all combined might have made our vote comparatively a small one, had not George Francis Train gone into the State two weeks before the election and galvanized the Democrats into their duty, thus securing 9,000 votes for woman's suffrage. Some claim that we are indebted to the Republicans for this vote; but the fact that the most radical republican district, Douglass County, gave the largest vote against woman's suffrage, while Leavenworth, the Democratic district, gave the largest vote for it, fully settles that question.

In saying that Mr. Train helped to swell our vote takes nothing from the credit due all those who labored faithfully for months in that State. All praise to Olympia Brown, Lucy Stone, Susan B. Anthony, Henry B. Blackwell, and Judge Wood, who welcomed, for an idea, the hardships of travelling in a new State, fording streams, scaling rocky brinks, sleeping on the ground and eating hard tack, with the fatigue of constant speaking, in school-houses, barns, mills, depots and the open air; and especially, all praise to the glorious Hutchinson family—John, his son Henry and daughter, Viola—who, with their own horses and carriage, made the entire circuit of the state, singing Woman's Suffrage into souls that logic could never penetrate. Having shared with them the hardships, with them I rejoice in our success.

E. C. S.

THE BALLOT—BREAD, VIRTUE, POWER.

THE REVOLUTION will contain a series of articles, beginning next week, to prove the power of the ballot in elevating the character and condition of woman. We shall show that the ballot will secure for woman equal place and equal wages in the world of work; that it will open to her the schools, colleges, professions and all the opportunities and advantages of life; that in her hand it will be a moral power to stay the tide of vice and crime and misery on every side. In the words of Bishop Simpson:

"We believe that the great vices in our large cities will never be conquered until the ballot is put in the hands of woman. If the question of the danger of their sons being drawn away into drinking saloons was brought up, if the mothers had the power, they would close them; if the sisters had the power, and they saw their brothers going away to haunts of infamy, they would close those places. You may get men to trifle with purity, with virtue, with righteousness; but, thank God, the hearts of the women of our land—the mothers, wives and daughters—are too pure to make a compromise either with intemperance or licentiousness."

Thus, too, shall we purge our constitutions and statute laws from all invidious distinctions among the citizens of the State, and secure the same civil and moral code for man and woman. We will show the hundred thousand female teachers, and the millions of laboring women, that their complaints, petitions, strikes and protective unions are of no avail until they hold the ballot in their own hands; for it is the first step toward social, religious and political equality.

The first page of the first issue of the REVOLUTION, *January 8, 1868. Elizabeth Cady Stanton sometimes joked that they published "weekly, not weakly." Even with the support of George Francis Train, in order to buy the paper Stanton and Susan B. Anthony had to borrow some money. Anthony had to sign all the loan documents; Stanton was not allowed to sign contracts because she was a married woman.*

suffrage, irrespective of color or sex." Both Stanton and Anthony strongly objected to illiterate black men getting the vote before educated white women. In addition to describing the possibility as personally insulting, they wrote in the pages of the *Revolution* that poorly educated voters would be vulnerable to machine politics, which in the long run would make it even more difficult for women to win the right to vote.

Despite repeated appeals in the pages of the *Revolution* for state legislators to vote no, the Fourteenth Amendment was ratified in July 1868 when South Carolina became the twenty-eighth state to vote yes, giving the amendment the necessary approval of three-fourths of the states.

VICTORY, AT LAST

In 1869, the women's suffrage movement experienced its first victory: The territory of Wyoming became the first US jurisdiction to grant women the right to vote. Life on the frontier was difficult for both women and men, and communities in the West attempted to lure women there with the promise of political equality.

In Wyoming, a group of the wives of elected officials had worked behind the scenes to convince their husbands to support female suffrage. It began when Julia Bright asked her husband, William, the president of the territorial council, to introduce a suffrage bill. William Bright said that he had never been to school a day in his life, but he "venerated" his well-informed wife and willingly "submitted to her judgment and influence."

On December 10, 1869, the men in Wyoming granted women there the right to vote. Other women's rights legislation followed: Wyoming women were soon given the right to sue and be sued, to serve on juries, and to enter contracts. Next came legislation that guaranteed equal pay for equal work in public employment.

In September 1870, the women of Wyoming voted for the first time. "The morning of the election came, but did not bring out the usual scenes around the polls," a circuit judge said. In previous elections, there had been drinking and rowdiness around the polling places, but on this day everything was calm.

A Baptist minister from Vermont who had come to Wyoming two weeks before the election said that he believed he had witnessed a miracle. Typically, men openly sold their votes for alcohol, but he had noticed that it didn't happen when the women were nearby. "No one thought of trying to buy up the women, nor was it ever supposed that a woman's vote could be secured with whiskey and cigars!" he said.

The election in Wyoming demonstrated that women could vote and the world would go on.

THE SPLIT OVER THE FIFTEENTH AMENDMENT

The division within the women's rights movement continued as the nation considered the Fifteenth Amendment, which prohibited state and federal governments from denying male citizens the right to vote based on race, color, or previous condition of servitude. The amendment didn't mention sex; it didn't have to, because the Fourteenth Amendment had already excluded women from the rights of citizenship, which included voting. Male advocates who had once been their allies told the women to support the Fifteenth Amendment and wait until African American men secured their rights.

Elizabeth Cady Stanton and Susan B. Anthony refused to support the amendment. "Not for what it is, but for what it is not," Stanton wrote. "Not because it enfranchises black men, but because it does not enfranchise all women, black and white."

"I cannot forgive nor forget the listless do nothingness of the men we had always believed our best friends," Anthony wrote. "But no matter. We will still work on, even with greater vigor than ever . . . *Now* is the accepted time."

Congress passed the Fifteenth Amendment in February 1869, and it went to the states for ratification.

Eventually, Stanton went so far as to ask her readers to work *against* the proposed constitutional amendment, with an editorial in the October 21, 1869, edition of the *Revolution*:

> *All wise women should oppose the Fifteenth Amendment for two reasons: 1st. Because it is invidious to their sex . . . it reflects the old idea of woman's inferiority. . . . 2d. We should oppose the measure because men have no right to pass it without our consent. . . . If women understood this . . . there would be an overwhelming vote against the admission of another man to the ruling power. . . . It is licking the hand that forges a new chain.*

Many in the women's movement were appalled by Stanton's stand. They believed that Stanton and Anthony didn't need to work to *pass* the amendment, but they shouldn't work to *oppose* it. Other women's rights leaders, including Lucy Stone, advocated for the passage of a separate amendment that would ensure female suffrage. But Stanton and Anthony didn't back down.

Several months before the controversial piece in the *Revolution*, they were at the center of another bitter debate on the issue. In May 1869, the leadership of the American Equal Rights Association gathered at its annual meeting in New York City. Stanton went, hoping to promote unity within the movement, but things had already gone too far.

The members pushed into the crowded hall, eager to speak their minds. Stephen Foster, a representative of the Massachusetts delegation who had worked with Stanton for almost twenty years, stood and called for her resignation. "I can not shoulder the responsibility of electing officers who publicly repudiate the principles of the society," Foster said. "If you choose to put officers here that ridicule the negro, and pronounce the [Fifteenth] Amendment infamous, I must retire, I cannot work with you." He criticized Stanton for collaborating with the racist George Francis Train, and he charged that Stanton's positions were not consistent with the values of the association.

Foster was not alone in his view. Stanton called for a vote of confidence, and she got it, but the debate was just getting started. From that point forward, there was a great divide between Stanton, Anthony, and others who backed educated suffrage, and those who supported working for African American suffrage first and female suffrage afterward.

Still, Stanton and Anthony were unyielding in their position. "If you will not give the whole loaf of suffrage . . . ," Anthony said, "give it to the most intelligent first."

Stanton backed the same point, but in bluntly racist language: "Shall American statesmen . . . make their wives and mothers the political inferiors of unlettered and unwashed ditch-diggers [and] boot-blacks . . . fresh from the slave plantations of the South[?]" She asked the group to consider the uneducated new citizens "who do not know the difference between a monarchy and a republic, who can not read the Declaration of Independence or Webster's spelling-book, making laws."

African American abolitionist and civil rights leader Frederick Douglass had heard enough. He stood to challenge Stanton. First, he criticized her use of racist language. Then he laid out his case:

I must say that I do not see how any one can pretend that there is the same urgency in giving the ballot to woman as to the negro. With us, the matter is a question of life and death, at least in fifteen States of the Union. When women, because they are women, are hunted down through the cities of New York and New Orleans; when they are dragged from their houses and hung upon lamp-posts; when their children are torn from their arms, and their brains dashed out upon the pavement; when they are objects of insult and outrage at every turn; when they are in danger of having their homes burnt down over their heads; when their children are not allowed to enter schools; then they will have an urgency to obtain the ballot equal to our own.

The crowd applauded.

"Is that not all true about black women?" a voice called out.

"Yes, yes, yes," Douglass said. "It is true of the black woman, but not because she is a woman, but because she is black."

The audience cheered again.

To soften the effect of his speech, Douglass offered some kind words about Stanton. "Let me tell you that when there were few houses in which the black man could have put his head, this wooly head of mine found refuge in the house of Mrs. Elizabeth Cady Stanton," he said, "and if I had been blacker than sixteen midnights, without a single star, it would have been the same. There is no name greater than [hers] in the matter of woman's rights and equal rights."

It was Anthony who responded. "If Mr. Douglass had noticed who applauded when he said 'black men first and white women afterwards,'" she said, "he would have seen that it was only the men. When he tells us that the case of black men is so perilous, I tell him that even outraged as they are by the hateful prejudice against color, he himself would not today exchange his sex and color with Elizabeth Cady Stanton."

Douglass smiled and asked whether granting women the right to vote would change the nature of man and woman.

Anthony didn't hesitate to respond. "It will change the nature of one thing very much," she said, "[and] that is the pecuniary position of woman. It will place her in a position in which she can earn her own bread, so that she can go out into the world on equal competition in the struggle for life."

Lucy Stone tried to make peace. "Mrs. Stanton will, of course, advocate the precedence for her sex," she said, "and Mr. Douglass will strive for the first position for his. . . . [We] are lost if we turn away from the middle principle and argue for one class. . . . I thank God for the Fifteenth Amendment, and hope that it will be adopted in every State. I will be thankful in my soul if *any* body can get out of the terrible pit."

Stanton remained unwilling to compromise. She said that she "did not believe in allowing ignorant negroes and foreigners to make laws for her to obey."

The discussion went back to white women or black men. Neither side spoke of the interests of the doubly disenfranchised bloc of black women, who could have become advocates of universal suffrage.

By the end of the evening, Stanton and Anthony were defeated. The membership voted against supporting the principle of educated suffrage.

The meeting adjourned with tempers still hot and both sides feeling absolute in the rightness of their position.

THE NATIONAL AND THE AMERICAN

Elizabeth Cady Stanton and Susan B. Anthony had no intention of changing their position. The morning after the two-day

American Equal Rights Association meeting adjourned, Stanton and Anthony called friends of women's suffrage to a follow-up meeting at the Brooklyn Academy of Music. There, the National Woman Suffrage Association was born.

"There had been so much trouble with men in the Equal Rights Society, that it was thought best to keep the absolute control henceforth in the hands of women," said Stanton, who was elected president of the all-female advocacy group. "Woman must lead the way to her own salvation."

The National Woman Suffrage Association was dedicated to opposing the Fifteenth Amendment, promoting a sixteenth amendment establishing female suffrage, supporting divorce reform, and advocating for other women's rights issues.

Lucy Stone did not attend the meeting, and she objected to excluding men from the organization, arguing that her husband had worked as hard as anyone else for women's suffrage in Kansas. She, in turn, decided to start a competing group, one that would allow men to join.

"I think we need two national associations for woman suffrage," Stone said, "so that those who do not oppose the Fifteenth Amendment, or take the tone of the *Revolution*, may yet have an organization with which they can work in harmony."

After the groups split, she said, "I hope that you will see it as I do, that with two societies, each in harmony with itself . . . we shall secure the hearty active cooperation of *all* the friends better than either could do alone."

The two groups became known as the National Woman Suffrage Association (Stanton and Anthony's group) and the American Woman Suffrage Association (Stone's group). While both organizations advocated for voting rights for women, the National favored a federal amendment, while the American worked to pass women's voting rights at the state level, state by state. Stone argued that a federal amendment would be easier to obtain once women showed that they could manage the vote on a state level.

The groups also differed in leadership style and philosophy. The National was more radical; the American, more conservative. The National objected to the passage of the Fifteenth Amendment and favored educated female suffrage; the American supported female suffrage and did not oppose voting rights for any African Americans. The National became involved in women's rights issues more broadly, while the American focused narrowly on the question of a woman's right to vote. Not only were men welcome at the American, the group elected a man, the Reverend Henry Ward Beecher, to be its first president.

The division between the groups was also personal. When Stone founded a separate suffrage group, Anthony considered it another betrayal. They were no longer suffrage sisters; Stone and Anthony were outright rivals. Anthony called Stone "Saint Lucy" and criticized her as lazy, because she didn't like to work on petition drives. Stone called Anthony selfish and egotistical.

Stone was going through a difficult time in her personal life as the women's movement was fracturing into separate organizations in 1869. In addition to feeling at odds with Stanton, Anthony, and other women in the suffrage movement, she had recently learned that her husband was involved with another woman, a famous singer who was eleven years younger than she was. Stone, who had had reservations about getting married in the first place, now faced the public humiliation of dealing with an unfaithful husband.

When the American held its first national meeting in November, Anthony crashed the gathering. Stone did not invite Anthony to sit on the platform, and she criticized the approach of the National.

Some women in the suffrage movement felt compelled to choose between the National and the American; others joined both organizations. One woman in Kansas subscribed to every women's rights publication she could find. She read each issue and shared them with friends. "When I gave away *The Revolution*," she explained, "my husband said, 'Wife, that is a very talented paper; I should think you would preserve that.' I replied: 'They will continue to come until our cause is won, and I must make them do all the good they can.'"

It was not long before Lucy Stone and the American Woman Suffrage Association began publishing its own weekly newspaper, the *Woman's Journal*. The first issue came out on January 8, 1870, exactly two years after the *Revolution* published its first issue. A number of well-respected authors, such as Harriet Beecher Stowe (*Uncle Tom's Cabin*), Julia Ward Howe ("Battle Hymn of the Republic"), and Louisa May Alcott (*Little Women*), wrote for the *Woman's Journal*, which was better financed and more moderate in tone and content than the *Revolution*.

The *Revolution* could not compete. In fact, from its earliest days, it had struggled financially. Soon after the first issue was printed, the *Revolution*'s benefactor, George Francis Train, went to England and ended up in a British jail with a one-year sentence for speaking out in favor of Irish rebels. Stanton and Anthony were left without the financial support he had promised.

Anthony borrowed money from friends and family, spent all of her savings, and raised subscription rates, but the newspaper still ended up $10,000 in debt, an amount equal to about $175,000 today. Three years after launching their paper, Anthony and Stanton sold it for one dollar, and it was turned into a literary journal.

Friends urged Anthony to declare bankruptcy, but she refused. "My pride for women, to say nothing of my conscience, says no," she said.

Stanton did not share Anthony's conscientiousness. She refused to help pay off the expenses, since she had not signed for any of the loans.

In the end, Anthony went back on the lecture circuit to raise money to pay off the debt. It took six years, but she paid her creditors every cent she owed.

Anthony described the sale of the *Revolution* as being "like signing [her] own death warrant." She wrote in her diary, "I feel a great calm sadness, like that of a mother binding out a dear child that she could not support."

Stanton wasn't upset by the sale of the newspaper. "You know when I drop anything, I drop it absolutely," she wrote to Anthony. "You cannot imagine what a deep gulf lies between me and the past."

What did upset Stanton was the ratification of the Fifteenth Amendment in February 1870. Suffrage for African American men had become the law of the land. But despite the tireless efforts of the National Woman Suffrage Association and the outspoken arguments of the *Revolution*, women still could not vote.

6 "MADAM, YOU ARE NOT A CITIZEN"

---✳---

Victoria Woodhull
Speaks to Congress

IN 1870, MOST PEOPLE BELIEVED THAT THE WORD "MALE" in the Fourteenth Amendment explicitly excluded women from voting, but others read the law differently. In a movement known as the New Departure, some women's rights advocates interpreted the new amendment in a way that actually *allowed* female suffrage. One of the most famous—or infamous—of these New Departure feminists was Victoria Claflin Woodhull.

WHO WAS VICTORIA WOODHULL?

Victoria Claflin Woodhull was a complicated woman, to say the least. Clever and beautiful, she was known as a champion of women's rights, a stockbroker on Wall Street, owner and editor of the newspaper *Woodhull & Claflin's Weekly*, and a candidate for president of the United States in 1872, forty-eight years before women had the right to vote. She was also an advocate for "free love," a

VICTORIA CLAFLIN WOODHULL (1838–1927)
ran for president on a progressive platform that included an eight-hour workday, graduated income tax, and reformed divorce laws.

blackmailer, an accused bigamist, possibly a prostitute, and a spiritualist who claimed she channeled the spirit of Demosthenes, a statesman from ancient Greece.

Born in 1838 to a hard-drinking con man and a mentally unstable woman in Homer, Ohio, Victoria was the seventh of ten children. Her parents named her for Great Britain's Queen Victoria, who had taken the throne the year before.

Victoria had a difficult childhood: She said she was "worked like a slave" and "whipped like a convict." She attended school for only three years, from ages eight to eleven, but she was said to have a photographic memory and a great deal of innate intelligence. As an adult, she said that from her father she learned to rely on no one but herself, and from her mother she learned how to tell fortunes as a tent-show spiritualist.

In the mid-nineteenth century, many people were interested in communicating with the "spirit world." At that time, early death was commonplace: Families often lost children to disease, and thousands of people wanted to reach out to loved ones who had died in the Civil War.

Victoria told people that her power was discovered when she was a young girl and her mother left her to tend to her baby sister, who had a high fever. While on watch, Victoria fell asleep. When her mother woke her, angry that she had dozed off, Victoria claimed that angels had come and put her in a sleeping trance, then fanned the baby to cool the fever. When her mother checked the baby, her fever had broken. Victoria's mother concluded that Victoria must have been endowed with mystical powers.

Money was tight, so Victoria worked with her mother as a clairvoyant for a several years. In 1853, at age fifteen, Victoria married a twenty-eight-year-old physician, Canning Woodhull, thinking he would be her ticket to a better life. Unfortunately, he turned out to be an alcoholic and an adulterer, as well as a poor doctor. (At the time there were no standards in the medical profession; he declared himself a doctor after reading medical texts for a few months.) As her fiancé, Woodhull said that he was part of a wealthy family back east; they were already married by the time she found out that he was an outcast from the family and he had almost no money of his own.

Before she turned twenty-three, Victoria Woodhull was the mother of two children. Her firstborn, a son, was disabled—he would never speak or be able to care for himself—and she blamed herself for his condition. She named her second child, a daughter, Zula Maud.

In 1864, Woodhull divorced her husband, who had abandoned her, and married Colonel James Blood, a wounded Civil War veteran. Blood and Woodhull met when he visited her in an attempt to communicate with the soldiers who had died under his direction as a regimental commander. According to an account by Blood, while in a trance she told the attractive colonel that his destiny was to become her husband. He divorced his wife and married Victoria, who did not change her name.

Woodhull and Blood had an unusual marriage. Blood allowed Woodhull to pursue her interests, and he often assisted with her schemes. He followed her in 1868 when she and her younger sister, Tennessee Claflin, moved to New York City to work as spiritualist healers.

In New York, the sisters arranged a magnetic healing session with multimillionaire financier and railroad magnate Cornelius Vanderbilt. Vanderbilt longed to connect with his mother and one of his sons, both of whom had died. Woodhull had studied the Vanderbilt family, and she collected additional information about them from a friend, Josie Mansfield, who was the girlfriend of one of Vanderbilt's competitors.

Pretending to be in a trance, Woodhull passed along inside information to Vanderbilt about the business plans of his rivals, based on gossip she had heard from Mansfield. As a result of the scam, Woodhull tricked the seventy-four-year-old tycoon into believing she and her sister had mystical powers. In addition, her sister Tennessee began a romantic relationship with the wealthy widower.

To show his appreciation, Vanderbilt set up a brokerage firm, Woodhull, Claflin & Co., the first female firm on Wall Street. Blood managed the accounting and worked as Woodhull's secretary, often writing documents for her, because she had never learned elegant penmanship or proper punctuation.

Newspapers ran stories about "the Bewitching Brokers," and businessmen tolerated their presence in the all-male world of finance because they had Vanderbilt's backing. It was not long before the sisters made a fortune speculating in the gold market.

The sisters used their money to publish a newspaper, *Woodhull & Claflin's Weekly*, without worrying about whom they might offend. Articles in the paper covered feminism, suffrage, sex education, legalized prostitution, vegetarianism, women in the military, and spiritualism.

But it was in the pages of the *New York Herald*, on April 2, 1870, that Woodhull announced her candidacy for president of

WOODHULL & CLAFLIN'S WEEKLY.

PROGRESS! FREE THOUGHT! UNTRAMMELED LIVES!

BREAKING THE WAY FOR FUTURE GENERATIONS.

VOL. 2.—No. 23.—WHOLE No. 49. NEW YORK, APRIL 22, 1871. PRICE TEN CENTS.

VICTORIA C. WOODHULL & TENNIE C. CLAFLIN
EDITORS AND PROPRIETORS.

THE Cosmo-Political Party.

NOMINATION FOR PRESIDENT OF THE U. S., In 1872.

VICTORIA C. WOODHULL

SUBJECT TO

RATIFICATION BY THE NATIONAL CONVENTION.

THE FIRST WOMAN BALLOT.

The Fourteenth Amendment has Begun its Work.

WHO WILL STOP IT?

WEDDING PRESENTS OF THE PRINCESS LOUISE.

EMERALDS AND DIAMONDS IN PROFUSION.

THE BRIDEGROOM'S PRESENTS.

HER TROUSSEAU.

In 1870, *Victoria Woodhull and her sister Tennessee Claflin used the money they had made on Wall Street to publish the newspaper* WOODHULL & CLAFLIN'S WEEKLY. *They were the first to publish the English translation of* THE COMMUNIST MANIFESTO, *written by German philosophers Karl Marx and Friedrich Engels. The newspaper stayed in business for six years.*

the United States. She didn't think she would win, but she did think she could use the election as a way to start a conversation about topics she considered important, including female suffrage. Woodhull noted that the Constitution didn't prohibit women from running for president, although they did not yet have the right to vote. At times she signed her name "Future Presidentess."

"While others argued the equality of woman with man, I proved it by successful engaging in business," Woodhull was quoted in the *New York Herald*. "I boldly entered . . . politics and business and exercised the rights I already possessed. I therefore claim the right to speak for the . . . women of the country . . . and I now announce myself as a candidate for the Presidency."

"MADAM, YOU ARE NOT A CITIZEN"

Also in 1870, Victoria Woodhull moved to Washington, DC, and began working as a lobbyist for women's suffrage. She made a point to meet Representative Benjamin Butler, an influential Republican congressman from Massachusetts, who hoped to lead his party to victory in the elections based on the expansion of women's suffrage. The two hit it off, and some people said they became lovers as well as political allies.

Woodhull's relationship with Butler breathed new life into the women's suffrage movement. He taught Woodhull the arguments behind the New Departure, the controversial interpretation of the Fourteenth Amendment that asserted it gave women the right to vote. The amendment declared that "all persons born or naturalized in the United States . . . are citizens of the United States." New Departure advocates argued that women who met those conditions were citizens, so they should have all the rights of citizenship, including the right to vote.

Butler arranged for Woodhull to speak before the House Judiciary Committee, making her the first woman to ever address a committee of the United States Congress. He helped prepare Woodhull's remarks, but she was a quick study and she soon embraced the arguments as her own.

On January 11, 1871, Woodhull, now thirty-two years old, took a seat in the House chamber, waiting for her chance to speak. The National Woman Suffrage Association's annual meeting was taking place down the street, so the women decided to suspend their morning events in order to listen to Woodhull make her presentation. Many of the congressmen arrived late, but Butler had invited members of the press, so the meeting room was crowded.

After being introduced, Woodhull stood and looked at the crowd, her face flushed and her fingers quivering. "Women constitute a majority of the country," she began, her voice trembling. "They hold vast portions of the nation's wealth and pay a proportionate share of the taxes." As she spoke, she calmed herself and her words came more easily.

Woodhull pointed out that the Fourteenth Amendment used the word "persons" and that the Founding Fathers had also used the word "persons" rather than distinguish between men and women when they drafted the Constitution. She argued that since women were considered persons for the purpose of taxation, then they should be considered persons for voting, too.

Woodhull said that because the first section of the Fourteenth Amendment made no reference to sex, then women also enjoyed the "privileges and immunities" of national citizenship, including the right to vote. She also pointed out that the federal rights established by the Fourteenth Amendment took precedence over states' rights, arguing that the states could not prohibit women from voting.

Furthermore, she said that the Fifteenth Amendment bolstered her case. While the Fifteenth Amendment did not mention sex, she said that because it specifically prohibited disenfranchisement by race, women were included, arguing that "a race comprises all the people, male and female."

Woodhull asked Congress to issue a declaratory act to clarify the right of all women to vote under the authority of the Fourteenth Amendment. She knew that the law could also be clarified through lawsuits brought before the courts, but she didn't want to have to wait for the courts to decide.

When she finished her remarks, she smiled and bowed.

Impressed, one representative said Woodhull presented her case "in as good style as any congressman could have done."

The *New York Tribune* also praised her, writing, "All the past efforts of Miss Anthony and Mrs. Stanton sink to insignificance beside the ingenious lobbying of the new leader and her daring declaration."

No one in the suffrage movement knew Woodhull well before she spoke, but she immediately became the woman to watch.

However, none of this meant that the congressmen agreed with her position. During the discussion period after Woodhull's speech, the chairman of the House Judiciary Committee, Representative John Bingham, a Republican from Ohio, told Woodhull: "Madam, you are not a citizen." He didn't think the Fourteenth Amendment applied to women, and he had been one of the authors of the amendment.

Undeterred, Woodhull quoted his own words back to him: "All persons born or naturalized . . . are citizens."

Bingham put on his glasses and read the words again. He conceded the point, but did not change his interpretation of the amendment's meaning.

Several weeks later, on January 30, 1871, the House Judiciary Committee issued a report in response to Woodhull's petition. The

Victoria Woodhull arguing before the House Judiciary Committee that Congress should pass a declaratory act confirming women's right to vote as a provision of the Fourteenth Amendment

majority report, written by Bingham, rejected Woodhull's claims and declared that women were not citizens, but "members of the state." Bingham also denied that the Fourteenth Amendment gave women any new rights. He said it was up to the states to decide whether to allow female suffrage.

Several weeks after that, a pro-suffrage minority report, signed by Woodhull's main supporter, Butler, and Representative William Loughridge, from Iowa, supported the petition. The minority report argued that the Fourteenth Amendment was intended "to secure the natural rights of citizens as well as their equal capacities before the law." While the majority report rejected Woodhull's argument that the Fifteenth Amendment shifted responsibility for suffrage from the state level to the national level, the minority report agreed that the Fifteenth Amendment "clearly recognizes the right to vote, as one of the rights of a citizen of the United States."

Neither report had any lasting significance on the question of women's right to vote. The most important outcome of these hearings was the introduction of Victoria Woodhull as one of the new voices of the women's suffrage movement.

"WE ARE PLOTTING A REVOLUTION"

At the conclusion of Victoria Woodhull's testimony before the House Judiciary Committee, Susan B. Anthony invited her to attend the National Woman Suffrage Association convention the following day. Woodhull's successful speech before Congress, coupled with her pledge of $10,000 to the organization, made Woodhull welcome among the suffrage leaders—most of them, anyway.

Elizabeth Cady Stanton had reservations. And when Stanton learned that Anthony was planning to include Woodhull in a state suffrage convention in New York City in May of that year, she urged her not to "have another Train affair with Mrs. Woodhull." Ignoring her old friend's warning, Anthony asked Woodhull to speak at the meeting.

Woodhull accepted and made an impassioned speech intended to stir up the suffragists. "We mean treason," Woodhull said. "We mean secession, and on a scale a thousand times greater than was that of the South. We are plotting a revolution."

Woodhull embraced a broad women's rights agenda. "I have asked for equality, nothing more," she said. "Sexual freedom means the abolition of prostitution both in and out of marriage, [it] means the emancipation of woman from sexual slavery and her coming into ownership and control of her own body, [it] means the end of her pecuniary dependence on man. . . . Rise and declare yourself free."

After hearing Woodhull speak at the meeting, Stanton changed her mind about this new ally. She found Woodhull's fiery language honest and invigorating. Stanton called her "a grand, brave woman, radical alike in political, religious, and social principles."

And then, things began to go wrong.

THE FREE-LOVE FIASCO

It was not long before some opponents of female suffrage deliberately used Victoria Woodhull's other prominent positions to divert public attention from the Fourteenth and Fifteenth Amendments. Newspapers accused Woodhull of bigamy and support of "free love"—a term that was used to characterize everything from support for divorce reform to unbounded promiscuity. Suffrage leaders who stood with Woodhull were accused of sharing her free-love sentiments.

The attacks against her quickly became personal. In part, people accused her of impropriety because she shared her home with both her husband and her ex-husband. At first, she tried to ignore the accusations and implications, but she refused to allow herself to be characterized as a bigamist.

Woodhull's first husband was not well; he was an alcoholic and a morphine addict. So she wrote to the *New York Times*, attempting to set the record straight. "Dr. Woodhull being sick, ailing and incapable of self-support, I felt it my duty to myself and to human nature that he should be cared for," she said. "My present husband, Colonel Blood, not only approves of this charity, but co-operates in it. I esteem it one of the most virtuous acts of my life."

Woodhull was also criticized for her belief that women should have control over their reproductive and sexual lives.

Once, when she was presenting a speech in New York, a heckler taunted her by calling her a "free lover."

"Yes," she responded. "I am a free lover. I have an *inalienable*, *constitutional* and *natural* right to love whom I may . . . to *change* that love *every day* if I please, and it is your *duty* not only to *accord* [me my right] but, as a community, to see that I am protected in it."

This idea was radical at the time. Even in feminist circles, many women in the nineteenth century believed that female sexuality should be suppressed and controlled.

Elizabeth Cady Stanton was a notable exception. Rather than shunning Woodhull, Stanton respected her candor and courage. In a speech of her own, Stanton said that she wanted "unlimited freedom of divorce, freedom to institute at the option of the parties new amatory relationships, love put above marriage, and in a word the obnoxious doctrine of Free Love." She went on to say, "We are one and all free lovers at heart."

An editorial cartoon by Thomas Nast in HARPER'S WEEKLY *on February 17, 1872, shows Victoria Woodhull as a devil, trying to lure a woman burdened with an intoxicated husband down the path of free love and independence.*

Stanton was getting tired of women turning against one another. "We have had women enough sacrificed to this sentimental, hypocritical prating about purity," she wrote to her friend Lucretia Mott. "This is one of man's most effective engines for our division and subjugation. He creates the public sentiment, builds the gallows, and then makes us hangman for our sex. . . . If Victoria Woodhull must be crucified, let men drive the spikes and plait the crown of thorns."

SHOWDOWN AT THE NATIONAL CONVENTION

Despite her sympathy for Woodhull, Stanton remained cautious. She may have respected Woodhull, but she also realized that tensions were rising and the debate was dividing the women's movement and weakening the National Woman Suffrage Association.

It seemed that the more outspoken Victoria Woodhull became, the more the National Woman Suffrage Association paid the price. The organization's membership dropped dramatically after what became known as the "Woodhull Convention." State and local affiliates dissociated from the National and formed new groups. New York members established the New York Central Woman Suffrage Association, and the Connecticut Woman Suffrage Association declared its independence from the National, resolving to work "*only* for the elective franchise." To make matters worse, by the end of 1871 fourteen out of fifteen state suffrage groups had left the National and joined the American Woman Suffrage Association.

The anti-Woodhull backlash also led to the formation of organizations dedicated to *fighting* female suffrage. In Boston in 1871, an anti-suffrage committee formed to lobby against women's right to vote. The committee leadership argued that women belonged as queens of the domestic domain, rather than equals who had a role in the world at large.

Even Susan B. Anthony had started to have reservations about Woodhull. And she became positively irate when she found out that Woodhull planned to use the National's membership as the basis of a political party that would nominate her for president.

A month before the National's annual meeting in May 1872, Anthony's name appeared in *Woodhull & Claflin's Weekly* in a call to form a new party at the annual National Woman Suffrage Association convention in New York City. Anthony hadn't given her permission to do so, so she cut short a lecture tour and returned to New York to try to stop Woodhull.

Anthony reached out to Stanton for support. "I do not believe in any of us women, the majority of whom do not even own our own bodies to say nothing of our purses—forming a *political party*," she wrote. Anthony was not interested in becoming a "mere sail-hoister" for Woodhull. She believed that if Woodhull wanted to start a political party, she should hire her own hall and call her own meeting.

On this point, Stanton thought Anthony was being unreasonable, and the two friends quarreled. In the end, Stanton refused to attend the meeting, leaving Anthony to run it on her own.

On the first day of the convention, Woodhull tried to address the audience. Anthony stepped in front of her and ruled her out of order. When Woodhull's supporters objected, Anthony told them to leave the hall if they didn't like it.

The following day, while Anthony stood on the stage, Woodhull entered through a side door and walked across to the center of the stage.

Again, Anthony ruled Woodhull out of order.

Woodhull then grabbed the podium, shouted out a motion

*In addition to suffrage, Victoria Woodhull's political platform
called for labor reform, nationalizing railroads, prison reform,
and rewriting the tax code.*

to adjourn, and urged everyone to go to the Apollo Hall the next
morning for a meeting of a new political party.

In an attempt to silence her, Anthony went backstage and
ordered the janitor to cut off the gaslights, leaving Woodhull and
the entire membership in the dark.

Bewildered, the delegates stumbled and groped their way
out of the meeting. Woodhull had made her announcement, but
Anthony had also made *her* point: She was still in charge.

Stanton was appalled when she heard about the fiasco. She
accused Anthony of being narrow-minded and unfair.

"There was never such a foolish muddle," Anthony wrote in her
diary in response. "I never was so hurt by the folly of Stanton. . . .
Our movement as such is so demoralized by the letting go of the

helm of the ship to Woodhull—though we rescued it—it was by a hair breadth escape."

The following morning, more than 650 Woodhull supporters—including several dozen women who defected from Anthony's suffrage convention—showed up at Apollo Hall. When Woodhull took the stage, the crowd roared for more than five minutes, waving handkerchiefs and cheering.

At the meeting, Woodhull established the Equal Rights Party, which then nominated her as its candidate for president of the United States. The party's stated goal: the same rights for all of humankind. In addition to female suffrage, they advocated for an eight-hour workday, free education for all children, no limits on free speech, and changes to the Constitution, such as limiting the president to one term with a permanent seat in the Senate afterward. Without his consent, they also nominated Frederick Douglass for vice president. He disavowed the nomination.

After her speech, Woodhull stepped off the stage and listened from the wings to Judge A.G.W. Carter. "The time for words has passed. We want action . . . ," he said. "I propose the name Victoria C. Woodhull to be nominated president of the United States."

The crowd cheered: "Victoria! Victoria!"

Victoria Woodhull was nominated for the presidency by the Equal Rights Party in New York City on May 10, 1872.

THE HENRY WARD BEECHER SCANDAL

Victoria Woodhull wanted respect, both as a suffragist and as a candidate for president of the United States. She may have had the support of those at the convention, but many others had serious reservations about her ability to lead.

Woodhull was tired of dealing with hypocrites within the suffrage movement who she said "preach against free love openly [but] practice it secretly." Specifically, she had grown weary of having "free love" criticized by the pious Reverend Henry Ward Beecher, whom she knew to have been involved in extramarital affairs with several women in his congregation.

Woodhull warned Beecher that she was going to go public with the story of his affairs if he did not agree to introduce her before a speech in which she would talk about free love.

Beecher didn't think she'd go through with the threat.

He was wrong.

The October 28, 1872, edition of *Woodhull & Claflin's Weekly* featured an article with the title "The Beecher-Tilton Scandal Case, the Detailed Statement of the Whole Matter." The article accused the married preacher, who was not only president of the American Woman Suffrage Association but also one of the most well-known and respected clergymen in the nation, of having had inappropriate relationships with a number of his parishioners. It said Beecher had seduced Elizabeth Tilton, a prominent suffragist, Sunday school teacher, and wife of Theodore Tilton, editor of the religious weekly newspaper the *Independent*.

Woodhull's article criticized Beecher's hypocrisy, not his infidelity.

The Beecher-Tilton story was based on gossip spread in part by Elizabeth Cady Stanton and Susan B. Anthony. Stanton had heard about the affair from Theodore Tilton; Anthony had

Henry Ward Beecher
(1813–1887)

heard about it from Elizabeth Tilton. Stanton had shared the information with Woodhull.

Within minutes, the first printing of ten thousand copies of the newspaper sold out. Demand was so great that the price skyrocketed from ten cents to two dollars and fifty cents per copy in New York City. Some people even rented out their papers, for a dollar a day; one copy sold for an astounding forty dollars. Carriages surrounded newsboys on lower Broad Street to the point that the street was in gridlock as people waited for the release of the second edition. In addition to the article about Beecher, the paper also included a story about the sexual misconduct of Luther Challis, a wealthy Brooklyn stockbroker.

Two days after publication, Victoria Woodhull and her sister Tennessee Claflin were distributing three thousand copies of the paper around town when US marshals stopped them. The officers seized the unsold newspapers and arrested Woodhull and Claflin, charging them with sending obscenity through the mail. Postal inspector Anthony Comstock had requested a copy of the paper, and he had insisted that it be mailed to him. Congress had recently passed a law that prohibited mailing obscene material.

After their arrest, Woodhull and Claflin were held in New York's Ludlow Street Jail, also known as "the Tombs." Bail was set at $8,000 for each of them. While the sisters were incarcerated, the police raided the *Weekly*'s office and destroyed their presses.

Elizabeth Cady Stanton defended Woodhull, even telling

Isabella Beecher Hooker—Reverend Beecher's sister—that she knew Woodhull was in the right. "I have not a shadow of doubt of the truth," Stanton wrote to Hooker. "There is too much money locked up in Beecher's success for him to be sacrificed. The public, especially those who have a financial interest in this matter, would rather see every woman in the nation sacrificed than one of their idols of gold."

On November 5, 1872—Election Day—Woodhull was still in jail. Her name wasn't on the ballot; she hadn't been able to pay the necessary fees. In addition, she was too young to run; the US Constitution requires that the president be at least thirty-five years old, and she would still have been thirty-four on Inauguration Day.

Two supporters bailed the sisters out after a month in jail. But they were immediately rearrested, this time charged with obscenity involving the articles published about Luther Challis in the same issue. They were ultimately released, only to be arrested a third time, charged with sending obscene materials across state lines.

Woodhull and Claflin were never charged with libel, a charge that involves writing false information about a person that hurts his or her reputation.

All in all, the sisters spent almost eight months in jail. They went to trial in June 1873, and they were found not guilty.

SCANDAL AND THE SUFFRAGE MOVEMENT

Two years after publication of the article about his wife and Henry Ward Beecher, Theodore Tilton sued Beecher for adultery and the "alienation of affections" within his marriage. The sensational Beecher-Tilton trial proved to be the longest and most publicized trial of its time. For more than six months, newspapers across the country featured front-page articles describing the

This 1875 lithograph depicts the scandalous adultery trial of the Reverend Henry Ward Beecher. The central sketch shows Elizabeth Tilton sitting on Beecher's lap.

testimony from witnesses, recounting every shocking and scintillating detail.

In July 1875, an all-male jury failed to convict Beecher, by a vote of nine to three. The trial ended with a hung jury, so Beecher faced no legal consequences.

After her release from jail, Victoria Woodhull continued to spend time with her sister Tennessee Claflin and Cornelius Vanderbilt. When Vanderbilt died a few years later, his family offered the sisters $100,000 if they would leave the country. Woodhull divorced Colonel Blood in 1876, and the sisters took the money and moved to Europe the following year. Woodhull married a wealthy English banker and lived comfortably the rest of her life; Tennessee Claflin married Francis Cook, a member of the British nobility, and became Lady Cook.

Theodore Tilton was fired from the *Independent*, so he moved to Europe, where he was offered a job at the *Golden Age*, a new magazine funded by his nemesis Henry Ward Beecher.

Beecher kept his position at Plymouth Congregational Church and continued his life as a celebrity preacher.

Only Elizabeth Tilton took a serious hit. She was excommunicated from the church and left disgraced and impoverished.

The damage to the women's rights movement was also serious. Across the country, suffrage opponents successfully—if unfairly—linked women's rights with lax morals and sexual scandal. Women resigned from suffrage organizations, and prospective recruits refused to join. A suffragist in Ohio said, "'Free love' (whatever it may mean) is the most efficient agent employed to frighten people from our ranks." Churches and gathering places refused to rent their halls to suffrage organizations. Legislators who were sympathetic to the cause told women that in the "current free-love storm," it would be best to table women's suffrage legislation, at least for the time being.

By the time Woodhull's name disappeared from newspaper accounts and gossipy conversations, she was widely criticized for having set back the suffrage movement by at least twenty years.

7 "I HAVE BEEN & GONE & DONE IT!!"

✦

Susan B. Anthony
Votes for President

On November 1, 1872, Susan B. Anthony opened a copy of the *Rochester Democrat & Chronicle*. "Register Now," the headline on the front page urged. It was the last day for citizens to get their names on the voter rolls in time to cast their ballots in the presidential election to be held the following week.

Anthony was ready. For three years, she had heard Victoria Woodhull and other suffragists argue that the Fourteenth Amendment gave *all* citizens—including women—the right to vote. The amendment said, in part, "All persons born or naturalized in the United States, and subject to the jurisdiction thereof, are citizens of the United States and of the state wherein they reside. No state shall make or enforce any law which shall abridge the privileges or immunities of citizens of the United States." Surely, Anthony reasoned, one of those privileges was voting.

Anthony was willing, even eager, to face a court battle over the matter. She believed that the issue of female suffrage would not be settled until a woman was arrested for voting and a test case was brought before the courts. This was a daring strategy—one that could involve jail time—but a court ruling in their favor would clarify the meaning of the law and effectively give women the right to vote without waiting for Congress to give it to them.

There was another benefit to notoriety: A well-publicized lawsuit would help Anthony reclaim her position of leadership within the women's movement. Elizabeth Cady Stanton had often stolen the spotlight when she and Anthony shared the stage. And in recent years, Anthony had been overshadowed by Victoria Woodhull's headline-stealing theatrics. Anthony was eager to steer the suffrage movement back to what she considered its more respectable roots.

REGISTERING TO VOTE

In the months before the election, in her speeches and at public appearances, Susan B. Anthony had encouraged women nationwide to "seize their rights to go to the polls and vote." Some of them did: Across the country, hundreds of suffragists tried to register to vote, but most were turned away. In her hometown of Rochester, Anthony had convinced a group of fourteen women, including three of her sisters, to join her in registering to vote. The women were modest middle-aged and elderly housewives, not flamboyant attention-seekers.

On November 1, the Friday before the election and the last day to register to vote, the women gathered to walk over to the barbershop that was serving as the local polling place for the Eighth Ward. Wearing long dresses and wrapped in shawls, they could have been mistaken for a group of grandmothers on a garden tour.

Led by Anthony, the women entered the barbershop. They asked the three young men working as election officials to register them to vote.

The men politely explained that women were not allowed to vote.

Anthony was prepared: With a copy of the US Constitution in hand, she read the Fourteenth Amendment aloud to the election officials. She also cited the section of the New York Constitution that pertained to voting, which said nothing about sex qualification. She went on to explain that because she was a US citizen, she had the right to vote.

The election officials dismissed the women again.

But Anthony knew how to capture their attention. She told them if they were to refuse her rights as a citizen, she would bring charges against them in criminal court and she would "sue each of [them] personally for large, exemplary damages!"

The men took her seriously.

"I know I can win," Anthony insisted. "I have Judge Selden as a lawyer."

The election officials knew Henry Selden, a retired New York judge and Anthony's ally in the abolition movement, by reputation, and they didn't know what to do. They were afraid to face criminal charges, either for registering the women or failing to register them. So they contacted the supervisor of elections, Daniel Warner.

"Do you know the penalty of law if you refuse to register these names?" Warner asked.

He then suggested that they could avoid fines and jail time if they asked the women to take an oath so that the women would assume responsibility for their actions.

For the next hour, Anthony and the election officials debated the issue. Finally, Anthony and fourteen other women took the oath and had their names added to the official voter rolls.

By afternoon, word had spread that a group of women had

registered to vote, and many people disagreed with the election officials' actions. The editors of the *Rochester Union and Advertiser* wrote, "Citizenship no more carries the right to vote than it carries the power to fly to the moon. . . . If these women in the Eighth Ward offer to vote, they should be challenged, and if they take the oaths and the Inspectors receive and deposit their ballots, they should all be prosecuted to the full extent of the law."

ELECTION DAY

Four days later, on Election Day, Anthony opened her newspaper and read another article intended to intimidate her and the other women. The article warned that "illegal voters" would be subject to a $500 fine and as much as three years in prison. Anthony wasn't discouraged.

At 7 a.m., Anthony and seven of the other women who had registered went to the polling place. (The other seven registered women planned to vote later in the afternoon.) The inspectors gave each of the women ballots for local, state, and federal offices.

But the inspectors weren't sure what to do next. One poll watcher, Sylvester Lewis, said that he objected to the women voting. This was not uncommon: The poll watchers were on hand to watch for irregularities, such as someone's name improperly listed on the voter rolls or a change of address. In such cases, voters were asked to validate their ballots by taking an oath assuring that they were legally permitted to vote. When asked to swear in her vote, Anthony willingly placed her hand on the Bible and swore that she was, in fact, able to vote. She then held her ballots out to the inspector.

"What do you say, Marsh?" one of the inspectors asked.

"I say put it in!" the second inspector replied.

"So do I," said the third inspector.

Anthony slipped her papers into the ballot box. She had voted. The other women followed her lead.

Later that day, Anthony shared the good news in a letter to Elizabeth Cady Stanton: "Well I have been & gone & done it!! Positively *voted* the Republican ticket—straight—this AM at 7 o'clock. . . . I hope you voted too."

ARREST

On November 14, almost two weeks after the election, US commissioner William C. Storrs issued a warrant for Anthony's arrest. She was charged with violating section 19 of the Enforcement Act of 1870, which made it illegal for someone to willfully cast an illegal ballot. Four more days passed before a US deputy marshal knocked on the door of Anthony's redbrick house on Madison Street. Her sister answered.

Anthony had been expecting the visit. She had previously been asked to call on Commissioner Storrs at this office. "I sent word to him that I had no social acquaintance with him," Anthony later said, "and didn't wish to call on him."

When her sister called her to the door, Anthony invited the marshal, Elisha J. Keeney, into the parlor. He made a comment about the pleasant weather they had been having, but Anthony made no effort to put him at ease. Finally, he said that Commissioner Storrs wanted to see her.

"What for?" she asked.

"To arrest you," the marshal said.

"Is that the way you arrest men?" she asked.

"No," he said.

The fifty-two-year-old woman then demanded that he arrest her properly. She held out her wrists to be handcuffed, but the marshal refused.

When she realized she was going to have to go downtown to the courthouse, Anthony excused herself and went upstairs to change clothes, leaving the flummoxed marshal waiting in the parlor.

When she was ready, Anthony and the marshal walked down to the horse-drawn trolley and headed to the Madison County courthouse. The conductor asked her for the five-cent fare, and Anthony said in a loud voice, "I am traveling at the expense of the government. Ask him for my fare."

At the courthouse, Judge Henry Selden and a second attorney, John Van Voorhis, met with her. Her attorneys refused to enter a plea, a preliminary hearing was set for two weeks later, and she returned home.

At the follow-up hearing on November 29, Van Voorhis asked Anthony, "Did you have any doubt yourself of your right to vote?"

"Not a particle," she said. Anthony had been accused of breaking a law that prohibited *willful and knowing* illegal voting; she argued that she didn't break the law because she believed her ballot was legal.

Commissioner Storrs was unconvinced. He set bail at $500 for Anthony and each of the other women who had been charged. The other women paid their bail, but Anthony refused. Storrs ordered her to be held by the marshal until the grand jury met in January.

Anthony was thrilled. She wanted to go to jail so that her attorney could use legal tactics to force the case before the US Supreme Court. If she was incarcerated, her lawyer could file a writ of

Henry Rogers Selden (1805–1885) agreed to serve as Susan B. Anthony's lawyer before she voted in the 1872 election. Earlier in his career, he had served as a judge on the New York State Court of Appeals and as the state's lieutenant governor from 1857 to 1858. He was an avid abolitionist, who helped Frederick Douglass escape from federal marshals in 1859. Selden supported female suffrage and never charged Anthony for the time he spent working on her case.

habeas corpus, which gives prisoners the right to challenge their imprisonment. If the writ was denied—as they expected it would be—then Anthony could appeal her case directly to the Supreme Court. And if the Supreme Court agreed with her, then it would uphold her interpretation of the law. In other words, if Anthony won at the Supreme Court, women across the United States would win the right to vote without waiting for Congress or the states to give them that right.

But when Anthony walked out of the courtroom, she was approached by Van Voorhis, who told her, "You've lost your chance to get your case before the Supreme Court."

She was livid. She confronted Selden and demanded an explanation.

Selden explained that he had paid her bail out of his own bank account. "I could not see a lady I respected put in jail," he said.

Without jail, there could be no writ of habeas corpus. Without that, there was no way to take the case to the Supreme Court. Anthony returned home dejected.

As expected, on January 24, 1873, a grand jury indicted Anthony for "knowingly, wrongfully, and unlawfully" voting. The trial was scheduled for May.

MAKING HER CASE

Anthony didn't plan to sit still and wait for a jury to convict her. Instead, she decided to take her case to the people. She prepared a lecture titled "Is It a Crime for a Citizen of the United States to Vote?" and delivered it at each of the twenty-nine post office districts in Monroe County, since her jury would be made up of men from the county. Night after night, she pulled her gray-streaked hair back into a tight bun at her neck and dressed in her gray silk dress with a white lace color. She looked earnestly into the crowd as she spoke:

> *Friends and Fellow-citizens: I stand before you to-night, under indictment for the alleged crime of having voted at the last Presidential election, without having a lawful right to vote. It shall be my work this evening to prove to you that in thus voting, I not only committed no crime, but, instead, simply exercised my citizen's right, guaranteed to me and all United States citizens by the National Constitution, beyond the power of any State to deny.*

Anthony also presented another speech, titled "Are Women Persons?" In that speech she said:

> *It was we, the people; not we, the white male citizens; nor yet we, the male citizens; but we, the whole people, who formed the Union. And we formed it, not to give the blessings of liberty, but to secure them; not to the half of ourselves and the half of our posterity, but to the whole people—women as well as men. And it is a downright mockery to talk to women of their enjoyment of the blessings of liberty while they are denied the use of the only means of securing them provided by this democratic-republican government—the ballot.*

In her speeches, Anthony cited the Declaration of Independence, the US Constitution, and the New York Constitution; she quoted American patriots. Audiences listened to her words, spellbound. After lecturing for an hour, Anthony got to the point: She asked the potential jurors not to return a verdict of "guilty" if chosen to determine her fate.

After months of lecturing, she wrote in a letter, "I have just closed a canvass of this county—from which my jurors are to be drawn—and I rather guess the U.S. District Attorney—who is very bitter—will hardly find twelve men so ignorant on the citizen's rights—as to agree on a verdict of Guilty."

But instead of trying to persuade the jury with a stronger argument, the prosecutor, the US district attorney, Richard Crowley, went to the judge and urged him to move the trial to a different county, where prospective jurors would not have heard Anthony's arguments.

The judge agreed to move the trial to Canandaigua, New York, in neighboring Ontario County. The trial date was pushed back to June 17.

Undaunted, Anthony organized another lecture tour and addressed crowds in Ontario County for twenty-one days in a row. This time she asked for help from suffragist Matilda Joslyn Gage. Gage prepared a speech titled "The United States on Trial, Not Susan B. Anthony," which she presented to sixteen groups.

On the night before her trial, Anthony presented her speech for the last time. She addressed a crowd in Canandaigua, near the courtroom where she would appear the next day. Exhausted, she knew she had done all that she could to convince the community that she should be found not guilty of the charges brought against her. The decision was out of her hands.

On the afternoon of June 17, 1873, Susan B. Anthony climbed

the front steps of the Ontario County Courthouse. She was wear-ing a new blue silk hat, draped with half a yard of spotted lace for a veil. When she entered the second-floor courtroom, she found it crowded with spectators.

Judge Ward Hunt sat at the bench. In a later account, Anthony described him as "a small-brained, pale-faced, prim-looking man, enveloped in a faultless suit of black broadcloth, and a snowy white neck-tie."

The US district attorney made the opening statement for the prosecution. "Whatever Miss Anthony's intentions may have been—whether they were good or otherwise," he said, "she did not have a right to vote upon that question, and if she did vote without having a lawful right to vote, then there is no question but what she is guilty of violating a law of the United States in that behalf enacted by the Congress of the United States."

Next, one of the inspectors for the Eighth Ward testified that Susan B. Anthony had cast a ballot.

The defense focused on the fact that Anthony believed she was entitled to vote. He called her as a witness in her defense.

But the district attorney interrupted. "She is not competent as a witness on her own behalf," he said.

The judge agreed. Anthony could not testify because she was a woman.

During his three-hour argument in Anthony's defense, Selden pointed out that she was being prosecuted because of her sex. "If the same act had been done by her brother under the same circum-stances, the act would have been not only innocent, but honorable and laudable," Selden argued. "The crime therefore consists not in the act done, but in the simple fact that the person doing it was a woman and not a man."

When both sides had finished presenting their evidence, Judge

Hunt pulled a piece of paper out of his pocket. He unfolded it and read an opinion that he had written—before the trial began. Clearly, Judge Hunt had had no intention of giving Anthony a fair and unbiased trial.

"The Fourteenth Amendment gives no right to a woman to vote, and the voting by Miss Anthony was in violation of the law," he said. He rejected the argument that she had voted in good faith. "Assuming that Miss Anthony believed she had a right to vote, that fact constitutes no defense if in truth she had not the right."

Everyone in the courtroom was shocked when the judge then told the all-male, all-white jury to find Anthony guilty. "Upon this evidence I suppose there is no question for the jury and that the jury should be directed to find a verdict of guilty," he said.

Selden turned to the judge. "That is a direction no Court has power to make in a criminal case," he said.

Judge Hunt ignored him.

Selden called for the jury to be polled.

Judge Hunt refused.

Selden requested a new trial.

The judge refused again. While unusual, Judge Hunt's directed verdict was not illegal at the time. Not until more than twenty years later, in 1895, did the Supreme Court rule that a judge of the federal courts could not direct a guilty verdict.

Before the sentencing, Judge Hunt asked Anthony if she had anything to say about why she should not be required to serve her sentence.

Anthony stood and stunned the spectators by chastising the judge in his own courtroom. "Yes, your honor, I have many things to say; for in your ordered verdict of guilty you have trampled under foot every vital principle of our government. My natural rights, my civil rights, my political rights, my judicial rights, are all alike ignored. Robbed of the fundamental privilege of citizenship,

I am degraded from the status of a citizen to that of a subject; and not only myself individually, but all of my sex are, by your honor's verdict, doomed to political subjection under this, so-called, form of government."

Judge Hunt interrupted the speech. "The Court cannot listen to a rehearsal of arguments the prisoner's counsel has already consumed three hours in presenting."

Undeterred, Anthony kept talking. "May it please your honor, I am not arguing the question, but simply stating the reasons why sentence can not, in justice, be pronounced against me. Your denial of my citizen's right to vote, is the denial of my right of consent as one of the governed, the denial of my right of representation as one of the taxed, the denial of my right to a trial by a jury of my peers as an offender against the law, therefore, the denial of my sacred rights to life, liberty, property, and—"

Frustrated, the judge interrupted again. "The Court cannot allow the prisoner to go on," he said.

"But your honor will not deny me this one and only poor privilege of protest against this high-handed outrage upon my citizen's rights," Anthony responded. "May it please the Court to remember that since the day of my arrest last November, this is the first time that either my self or any person of my disfranchised class has been allowed a word of defense before judge or jury."

"The prisoner must sit down," Judge Hunt said, his voice firm. "The Court can not allow it."

Anthony ignored the judge's warning. "All of my prosecutors, from the 8th Ward corner grocery politician, who entered the complaint, to the United States Marshal, Commissioner, District Attorney, District Judge, your honor on the bench, not one is my peer, but each and all are my political sovereigns; and had your honor submitted my case to the jury, as was clearly your duty, even then I should have had just cause of protest, for not one of those men was my peer; but native or foreign, white or black, rich or poor, educated or ignorant, awake or asleep, sober or drunk, each and every man of them was my political superior; hence, in no sense, my peer."

She drew a breath and kept on until the judge interrupted her again.

"The Court must insist," Judge Hunt said, trying to regain control of his courtroom. "The prisoner has been tried according to the established forms of law."

"Yes, your honor, but by forms of law all made by men, interpreted by men, administered by men, in favor of men, and against women; and hence, your honor's ordered verdict of guilty, against a United States citizen for the exercise of 'that citizen's right to vote,' simply because that citizen was a woman and not a man." Anthony continued for several minutes more, barely pausing to take a breath.

"The Court orders the prisoner to sit down," Justice Hunt said with increased frustration. "It will not allow another word."

Anthony would not be silenced, pressing on. "When I was brought before your honor for trial," she said, "I hoped for a broad and liberal interpretation of the Constitution."

"The Court must insist," Judge Hunt said more firmly.

Abruptly, almost unexpectedly, Anthony sat down, silent.

Judge Hunt seemed surprised that she had finally stopped talking. As soon as he gathered his wits, he realized that he had to ask her to stand again for sentencing. "The prisoner will stand up," he said.

Anthony stood.

"The sentence of the Court," the judge said, "is that you pay a fine of one hundred dollars and the costs of the prosecution."

Anthony immediately responded. "May it please your honor,"

she said, "I shall never pay a dollar of your unjust penalty. All the stock in trade I possess is a $10,000 debt, incurred by publishing my paper—*The Revolution*—four years ago, the sole object of which was to educate all women to do precisely as I have done, rebel against your manmade, unjust, unconstitutional forms of law, that tax, fine, imprison and hang women, while they deny them the right of representation in the Government; and I shall work on with might and main to pay every dollar of that honest debt, but not a penny shall go to this unjust claim. And I shall earnestly and persistently continue to urge all women to the practical recognition of the old revolutionary maxim that 'Resistance to tyranny is obedience to God.'"

Anthony should have been jailed until she paid the fine. The judge knew that's what she wanted; if she were imprisoned she could file an appeal to the US Supreme Court. Without being held, she had no standing for an appeal, because federal law did not allow appeals of criminal convictions. (The law has since been changed.)

Judge Hunt got the final word. He told Anthony, "Madam, the Court will not order you committed until the fine is paid."

By not jailing her, the judge left her no way to appeal. The case was closed.

When she got home that night, Anthony wrote in her journal, "The greatest judicial outrage history ever recorded! We were convicted before we had a hearing and the trial was a mere farce."

Although she lost the lawsuit, many people saw Anthony as the winner. One of the jurors told a newspaper reporter, "Could I have spoken, I should have answered 'not guilty,' and the men in the jury box would have sustained me."

"If it is a mere question of who got the best of it," another newspaper said, "Miss Anthony is still ahead. She has voted and the American constitution has survived the shock. Fining her one

THE DAILY GRAPHIC

AN ILLUSTRATED EVENING NEWSPAPER
39 & 41 PARK PLACE

VOL. I—NO. 81.   NEW YORK, THURSDAY, JUNE 5, 1873.   FIVE CENTS.

GRAPHIC STATUES, NO. 19.—"THE WOMAN WHO DARED."

This cartoon by Thomas West, which appeared in the June 5, 1873, issue of the
DAILY GRAPHIC, *shows a reversal of traditional sex roles: Susan B. Anthony
is wearing a man's top hat and spurs; the background includes a female police
officer, a man holding a baby, and a second man carrying a basket of food. Women
protesting for equality parade in the background.*

hundred dollars does not rule out the fact that . . . women voted,
and went home, and the world jogged on as before."

    Even newspapers that opposed female suffrage condemned the
way Judge Hunt handled the case.

    To prove her point that she considered the trial a miscarriage of
justice, Anthony had three thousand copies of the court transcript
printed and distributed across the country to politicians, libraries, and suffrage groups. And when she stood before audiences to
speak about the case, she took delight in opening her remarks by

saying, "I stand before you as a convicted criminal," although she never paid the fine or saw the inside of a jail cell.

Years later, Henry Selden reflected on the meaning of the case. "There never was a trial in the country with one half the importance of Miss Anthony's," he wrote. "If Anthony had won her case on the merit it would have revolutionized the suffrage of the country. . . . There was a prearranged determination to convict her. A jury trial was dangerous and so the Constitution was deliberately and openly violated."

While Susan B. Anthony's case never made it to the US Supreme Court, another case involving female suffrage and the Fourteenth Amendment did. Suffragists Francis and Virginia Minor also believed that the Fourteenth and Fifteenth Amendments granted women the right to vote, and they came up with a plan to put the issue to the test. In 1872, Virginia Minor tried to register to vote in St. Louis, Missouri, and when Reese Happersett, a registrar there, refused to allow it, the Minors sued him. They lost in the lower courts, so they appealed to the Supreme Court, arguing that the federal protections of a citizen's right to vote superseded any state law that says otherwise. In 1874, the US Supreme Court handed down a unanimous opinion upholding the lower court. The *Minor v. Happersett* decision said that the Constitution did not give citizens the right to vote. It said that citizenship meant "membership in a nation and nothing more."

One thing was clear: Neither Congress nor the federal courts were ready to grant women the right to vote. Until attitudes changed, suffragists were going to have to work for the passage of suffrage legislation one state at a time.

8 "WE ASK JUSTICE, WE ASK EQUALITY"

✳

Forward, Step by Step

IN 1876, WHEN THE NATION CELEBRATED ITS HUNDREDTH birthday, Susan B. Anthony and other suffragists considered encouraging women to march in their local Fourth of July parades draped in black and carrying banners reading TAXATION WITHOUT REPRESENTATION IS TYRANNY.

Ultimately, they settled on a more traditional protest at the Centennial Exposition in Philadelphia. The suffragists noted that the men who had organized the festivities did not include any women in the program. Did that mean, they asked, that women had done nothing worth recognizing during the past century?

Anthony's National Woman Suffrage Association responded to the insult by passing a resolution that said, in part, "One-half of the citizens of this nation, after a century of boasted liberty, are still political slaves."

The more conservative American Woman Suffrage Association was eventually given a small space inside the exhibition, but the National Woman Suffrage Association had to rent office space on Chestnut Street, nearby. They chose a spot close to the exposition's

A drawing by Frederic B. Schell depicting a crowd of people in the main building on opening day of the Centennial Exposition in Philadelphia

fairgrounds so that people attending the events would walk past the headquarters and could be asked to sign petitions about women's rights.

The core leadership—Susan B. Anthony, Elizabeth Cady Stanton, and Matilda Joslyn Gage, who was serving as president of the organization—wanted to prepare a formal statement, so they wrote a new declaration of women's rights.

The Declaration of Rights of the Women of the United States echoed the Declaration of Sentiments, written almost thirty years before, but it did not include the same demands. It did, of course, call for women to have the right to vote. The document stated: "We protest against this government of the United States as an oligarchy of sex, and not a true republic; and we protest against calling this a centennial celebration of the independence of the people of the United States."

Once it was complete, the women needed to figure out how to get the new declaration included in the Fourth of July festivities. Stanton wrote to the president of the Centennial Commission, General Joseph Roswell Hawley of Connecticut, and asked for fifty tickets to the ceremony.

Hawley turned her down, explaining that there were no extra tickets.

Stanton asked to present the declaration to the president of the United States "as an historical part of the proceedings."

Hawley refused. His excuse was that the schedule had been set and the programs had already been printed.

Stanton argued that his response proved her point, demonstrating that men had "run this government for one hundred years without consulting the women of the United States."

Hawley wasn't used to being challenged, especially by a woman. "We propose to celebrate what we have done the last hundred years," he said, "not what we have failed to do."

Frustrated, the women tried to get tickets to the Fourth of July event on their own. Anthony got a press pass for herself through her brother's Kansas newspaper. Hawley finally gave the suffragists four more seats.

At the Fourth of July celebration, the five suffragists squeezed into their seats in the press section as close to the front stage as possible. It was an oppressively hot and muggy day, and it was sweltering inside the crowded space of Independence Hall. The five women were sweaty from nerves and heat.

On a preestablished cue, the women stood, and Anthony led them down the aisle toward the stage. Her face was stern and determined, and she marched with purpose, her long dress swishing behind her.

The acting vice president of the United States, Thomas W.

Ferry, stood at the podium. He wasn't sure what Anthony and the other women intended as they stopped in front of him. They held out a three-foot long rolled-up parchment copy of the Declaration of Rights, tied with red, white, and blue ribbons.

"Mr. Vice President," Anthony said, "we present this Declaration of Rights of the women citizens of the United States."

The vice president thanked them and bent down to accept the document. The presentation of the declaration was now an official part of the proceedings.

Anthony nodded and marched back up the aisle, followed by the others, handing out additional copies of the Declaration of Rights to members of the audience.

On the stage, Hawley banged his gavel to bring the crowd back to order.

Once out of Independence Hall, Anthony spotted a bandstand that had been set up for a musical concert that evening. She climbed onto the stage and began reading the Declaration of Rights aloud to the gathering crowd. Matilda Joslyn Gage held an umbrella over Anthony to shade her from the unrelenting sun as she spoke.

"Woman has shown equal devotion with man to the cause of freedom and has stood firmly by his side in its defense . . . ," she loudly read. "And now, at the close of a hundred years, as the hour-hand of the great clock that marks the centuries points to 1876, we declare our faith in the principle of self-government. . . . We ask our rulers, at this hour, no special favors, no special privileges. . . . We ask justice, we ask equality, we ask that all civil and political rights that belong to the citizens of the United States be guaranteed to us and to our daughters forever."

The crowd cheered and clapped.

But the men in power ignored the declaration. The women had spoken, but they could not force the men to act.

WRITING *HISTORY OF WOMAN SUFFRAGE*

After seeing women omitted from history in the centennial cel-
ebrations, the suffragists decided to write their own account of
the women's suffrage movement. They believed that if they didn't
record their own history, it soon might be forgotten.

Several weeks after the centennial gathering in Philadelphia,
Susan B. Anthony visited Elizabeth Cady Stanton at her new home
in Tenafly, New Jersey. They had asked women involved in the
movement all over the country to send materials that might be
of interest, then they began to wade through enormous piles of
speeches, letters, portraits, written accounts, and newspaper articles. In addition, Anthony had an extensive collection of articles
and memorabilia that she had collected over the years and stored
in scrapbooks, trunks, and boxes.

Their goal was ambitious: to write *History of Woman Suffrage*,
a comprehensive chronicle of the women's movement. They didn't
see the need to wait until they had reached their goal to start writing the history.

"Men have been faithful in noting every heroic act of their half
of the race," Anthony said, "and now it should be the duty as well
as the pleasure, of women to make for future generations a record
of the heroic deeds of the other half."

Stanton did most of the writing and editing, and Anthony
organized the material and lined up a publisher. She arranged to
have the books distributed to schools and libraries nationwide.
Anthony both loved and loathed the project. In her diary, she
referred to it as "a perfect prison." She later told a friend, "I love to
make history but hate to write it."

Matilda Joslyn Gage also helped with the project, but it still
took more than ten years to produce three volumes, each about
one thousand pages long. When it was finished, *History of Woman*

Suffrage consisted of six enormous volumes. (Stanton did not help with the last three.)

This was not Anthony's only writing project. In 1897, she asked Ida Husted Harper to work with her on an authorized biography. The first two volumes of Harper's work, *The Life and Work of Susan B. Anthony*, came out in 1899; the third volume was published in 1908, two years after Anthony's death.

Unfortunately, Harper committed an outrageous and unconventional act when she completed her work for the first volume. In order to ensure that she would be the first and most authoritative Anthony biographer, Harper burned most of Anthony's letters and documents. Anthony was distraught, but the papers were gone forever.

THE ANTHONY AMENDMENT

In the late 1870s, Stanton and Anthony continued to work on behalf of a constitutional amendment that would grant women the right to vote. On January 10, 1878, Senator Arlen A. Sargent of California proposed a sixteenth amendment to the Constitution. (Three other amendments would be passed ahead of it, so that it ultimately became the Nineteenth Amendment.)

The brief but powerful text read, "The right of citizens of the United States to vote shall not be denied or abridged by the United States or by any State on account of sex." It became known as the Susan B. Anthony Amendment.

After the bill was introduced, Stanton had the opportunity to testify before the Senate Committee on Privileges and Elections. She was eager to do it, but she found the process disheartening. During her presentation, the men insulted her with their inattention. The senators read newspapers, jumped up and down opening

Elizabeth Cady Stanton addressing the Senate Committee on Privileges and Elections, from the January 16, 1878, issue of the NEW YORK DAILY GRAPHIC

and closing doors and windows, gazed at the ceiling, sharpened pencils, clipped their fingernails, stretched, and yawned. No one seemed interested in listening to what she had to say. "It was with difficulty that I restrained the impulse more than once to hurl my manuscript at his head," Stanton later wrote about the committee chairman.

Not surprisingly, the Committee on Privileges and Elections never voted to send the Susan B. Anthony Amendment to the full Senate for consideration that year. It was reintroduced dutifully every year, but the full Senate did not vote on it until 1887, when it was defeated 16 to 34, with twenty-five senators not even bothering to vote.

Despite congressional apathy and obstruction, the suffragists remained steadfast. Year after year, the National Woman Suffrage Association held its annual convention in Washington, DC, so that its members could lobby legislators.

Anthony became the face of the women's vote on Capitol Hill. "The members of Congress always knew when Miss Anthony had arrived in Washington," a fellow suffragist recalled. "Other women accepted their word that they were going to do something and waited patiently at home. Miss Anthony followed up and saw that [Congress members] did it. If she could not find them at the Capitol, she went to their homes. If they promised to introduce a certain measure on a certain day, she was in the gallery, looking them squarely in the face."

Anthony's bright-red shawl—the only flash of color in her otherwise dark and drab wardrobe—became iconic. When she once appeared before a group of reporters wearing a white shawl, some of the journalists joked that they would not write about suffrage unless she brought back the red wrap.

"All right, boys," she said. "I'll send to the hotel for it."

Someone brought it over. Anthony wrapped up in the fiery shawl, and the friendly crowd began to applaud.

SPREADING THE WORD IN THE WEST

When not lobbying in the Capitol in the 1870s, Elizabeth Cady Stanton and Susan B. Anthony were usually on the lecture circuit. They crisscrossed the country for eight or nine months of the year, speaking about suffrage, as well as other feminist topics.

With her soft white curls and graceful good manners, Stanton appeared harmless, but when she was at the podium she challenged her audiences with revolutionary ideas about divorce, religion, and women's role in society.

"Surely Mrs. Stanton has secured much immunity by a comfortable look of motherliness and a sly benignancy in her smiling eyes," wrote one newspaper reporter, "even though her arguments have been bayonet thrusts and her words gun shots."

No topic was off-limits for Stanton. Before her evening lectures, she often held afternoon meetings for all-female audiences about "the new science of marriage and maternity," meaning birth control. This was important, because women had limited access to information about sex, pregnancy, and childbearing.

Stanton could think on her feet, and she refused to be intimidated by those who dared to heckle her as she spoke.

During a lecture in Nebraska, an outspoken man interrupted her speech. "Don't you think that the best thing a woman can do is perform well her part in the role of wife and mother?" he asked. "My wife has presented me with eight beautiful children; is not this a better lifework than that of exercising the right of suffrage?" He thought he had trapped her.

Stanton took a moment to silently look him over, letting her eyes wander up and down his body. "Frankly, sir," she said, "I know of few men worth repeating eight times."

The man backed off, embarrassed by her boldness, and Stanton continued with her remarks.

Although she did not typically lecture with Stanton, Anthony also made the rounds on the lecture circuit. She once calculated that she had traveled thirteen thousand miles and conducted 171 lectures over the previous twelve months, earning $4,318 in gross receipts. No other reformer had logged as many miles on behalf of suffrage—or any other cause.

After more than a decade on the road, however, Stanton grew tired of touring. She returned to her home in New Jersey in 1881, when she was sixty-six years old. "I do not believe," she wrote in her diary, "there ever was a woman who esteemed it such a privilege to stay at home."

Susan B. Anthony and Elizabeth Cady Stanton carefully waded through thousands of documents when writing their part of the six-volume, 5,700-page History of Woman Suffrage.

When she got home, Stanton started work on the second volume of *History of Woman Suffrage*, which covered the period of the division of the women's suffrage movement in 1869.

While long and detailed, the book wasn't comprehensive. It made no mention of Lucy Stone, from whom Anthony had been estranged since their falling-out over Stone's marriage, or the rivalry between the Anthony's National and Stone's American Woman Suffrage Association. Stone said she didn't care about being left out of the book; she didn't want Stanton writing her history anyway.

Others suffragists thought that the books could only be authoritative if they included both sides of the movement. In fact, Harriot Stanton Blatch complained to her mother that the history was incomplete. Stanton told her she could write it herself if she wanted. So Blatch did just that.

She tried to be impartial in her writing, even though she saw the movement through her mother's eyes.

In late spring, when the page proofs for the second volume had been finished, Stanton and her daughter went to Europe for an extended stay. Stanton decided to pull away from the suffrage movement for a time. She felt that her radical ideas were out of step with an issue that seemed to have grown stagnant.

THE TEMPERANCE PARTNERSHIP

While Elizabeth Cady Stanton was overseas, Susan B. Anthony continued to be singularly devoted to the cause of female suffrage. To strengthen the movement, Anthony considered building alliances with almost any other organization willing to embrace women's right to vote. She developed relationships with the women's division of the Knights of Labor, the Universal Peach Union, and the Daughters of the American Revolution, to name a few.

One of the most important partners was the Woman's Christian Temperance Union (WCTU), an influential reform group of the late nineteenth century. Organizers in the temperance movement opposed the excessive consumption of alcohol, and most members objected to drinking any alcohol at all.

Women—including both Anthony and Stanton—had been involved with the temperance movement since the 1840s. Many reformers took up this cause before they took on other social issues, such as abolition and suffrage. The WCTU was the largest and best-known temperance organization. It was fairly modest in size until 1873, when a temperance revival swept across Ohio and western New York. During that time, small groups of women sang and prayed and forced almost three thousand saloon owners to close their doors. Most of these businesses reopened, however, which led temperance workers to realize that they would have to change the laws. It was a logical next step for them to realize that they could support suffrage as a means of realizing their temperance goals. When they lobbied their state legislatures, women found that without the vote they were ignored.

In 1879, Frances Willard was elected president of the WCTU. She energized the organization and helped to increase the membership from twenty-seven thousand to an astonishing two hundred thousand dues-paying members by 1890. Under her leadership the WCTU became a major political force.

Rather than narrowly focusing on alcohol, Willard and the WCTU adopted what she called the "Do Everything Policy," which called for the organization to be involved in dozens of reforms they said would protect the home. Their campaigns included prohibition (outlawing alcohol), prison reform, prosecution of pornographers, creation of kindergartens, and promotion of Sunday as a day of rest, among others. The group was divided into thirty-eight departments, each focused on a different social reform.

Suffrage became one of Willard's key concerns. In 1882, she said that as she prayed, God told her "to speak for woman's ballot as a weapon of protection to her home . . . from the tyranny of drink." She knew that gaining the vote would give women an important tool to bring about the entire social agenda she envisioned, since her membership and support for her cause were largely female.

Stanton and other suffragists were suspicious of the temperance alliance. Stanton warned Anthony not to be "dazzled by the promise of a sudden acquisition of numbers to our platforms with the wide-spread influence of the Church behind them." Stanton wanted to increase the number of suffragists, but she worried that most temperance workers had no real interest in women's rights.

Still, Anthony admired all that Willard had achieved, and she eagerly accepted help from the group.

But by aligning herself with the temperance movement, Anthony gained some new enemies—in the powerful liquor lobby, which now linked the women's vote with a threat to their industry. From that point forward, liquor lobbyists worked to defeat female suffrage.

Over time, a growing number of suffragists objected to the Woman's Christian Temperance Union's judgmental approach to reform. The problem came to a head in California in 1896 when voters there were considering a suffrage amendment to the state constitution. Suffragists worried that the WCTU was alienating male voters and costing them votes.

By that point, though, it was too late. The two movements had been merged in the minds of many voters. The suffrage amendment failed in California.

After that, Anthony tried to distance herself from the WCTU, and she remained devoted to the cause of suffrage. She didn't want the movement to be distracted by any issues that could interfere with or sidetrack the mission.

That included personal issues that could be controversial. In 1884, two years after his first wife died, abolitionist and civil rights leader Frederick Douglass married a white woman, Helen Pitts. When Elizabeth Cady Stanton found out about the marriage, she wrote Douglass a letter of congratulations. She also sent Anthony a letter, which she wanted her to sign, inviting Douglass to speak at the upcoming National Woman Suffrage Association meeting.

However, Anthony worried that the race issue would interfere with the suffrage agenda. She refused to sign the letter and

Frederick Douglass and his wife, Helen Pitts (sitting), with Helen's sister, Eva (standing). Helen Pitts said, "Love came to me, and I was not afraid to marry the man I loved because of his color."

encouraged Stanton not to "complicate or compromise" their efforts to win suffrage.

"I do hope you won't put your foot into the question of inter-marriage of the races," Anthony wrote to Stanton. "It has no place on our platform. . . . Our intention at this convention is to make every one who hears or reads believe in the grand principle of equality of rights and chances for women, and if they see on our program the name of Douglass every thought will be turned toward the subject of amalgamation and away from that of woman and her disfranchisement. . . . Do not throw around that marriage the halo of a pure and lofty duty to break down race lines. Your sympathy has run away with your judgment."

Stanton didn't challenge Anthony. Douglass was not invited to speak at the convention.

REUNITED

By the late 1880s, thousands of women had become suffragists, and women could vote in some school board and local elections across the country. But progress on the issue of women's suffrage on a national scale was moving at a painfully slow pace.

The National Woman Suffrage Association had been working toward an amendment to the US Constitution. They had gotten nowhere.

The American Woman Suffrage Association had worked on state-by-state campaigns to secure women's right to vote. They weren't getting anywhere, either.

After twenty years of working separately, the younger members of both groups began to see the wisdom of joining ranks and working on suffrage together. But a generation's worth of hard feelings and resentments separated the leadership. So for two years, Lucy

Stone's daughter, Alice Stone Blackwell, and one of Anthony's most trusted apprentices, Rachel Foster Avery, worked behind the scenes to reconcile the groups. The logic of combining forces was obvious to them: The groups would be stronger together.

Still, wrote Blackwell, "the elders were not keen for it on either side."

In addition to serious issues of strategy, Stanton and Anthony debated with Stone about which name should come first in a merger—should it be "American National" or "National American"?—and whether the annual meetings would be held in Washington, DC, or somewhere else. At last, in February 1890, the two organizations joined to form the National American Woman Suffrage Association (NAWSA).

There was squabbling over leadership roles, too. Lucy Stone refused to run for president of the new group. Eventually, Stanton and Anthony were both nominated for the position, but Anthony urged members to support Stanton.

"When the division was made twenty-two years ago, it was because our platform was too broad, because Mrs. Stanton was too radical," Anthony said. "A more conservative association was wanted. And now if we divide and Mrs. Stanton shall be deposed from the presidency you virtually degrade her."

Alice Stone Blackwell (1857–1950) was a suffragist, feminist, and journalist; she was an editor for the WOMAN'S JOURNAL. *She graduated Phi Beta Kappa from Boston University, and her otherwise all-male class elected her class president.*

Elizabeth Cady Stanton with her daughter Harriot Stanton Blatch and her granddaughter Nora in 1890

When the votes were tallied, Stanton was elected president, Anthony was elected vice president, and Stone became chair of the executive committee.

Stanton accepted the position but returned to England immediately after the convention. She didn't have the stamina she once did. She was quite overweight—of self-described "robust proportion"—and her eyesight was fading so much that she had a paid companion to help her get around during the day and to assist with reading and writing. Anthony described Stanton's physical decline in a letter to a friend, writing that it was a pity "that such mental powers must be hampered with such a *clumsy* body."

As expected, Anthony took charge and strengthened the new organization, bringing in a number of wealthy women to support the mission. Some considered NAWSA too comfortable with old approaches that weren't working well enough or fast enough. Despite the suffragists' steadfast effort, only a handful of states had even considered the suffrage issue on a state ballot.

As the twentieth century approached, Stanton and Anthony realized that they would not live long enough to see nationwide suffrage. Stanton wrote in her diary, "We are sowing winter wheat, which the coming spring will see sprout and which other hands than ours will reap and enjoy."

On January 18, 1892, Stanton—now seventy-six years old—resigned as president of NAWSA. She titled her farewell speech

"The Solitude of Self" and called it "the best thing I have ever written."

Stanton delivered the speech to the House and Senate Judiciary Committees and the convention. "The point I wish plainly to bring before you on this occasion, is the individuality of each human soul," Stanton said. "Who, I ask you, can take, dare take, on himself, the rights, the duties, the responsibilities of another human soul?"

To honor Stanton and her historic significance, the House Judiciary Committee had ten thousand copies of the speech printed and distributed across the country. Anthony wrote on one copy, "To Elizabeth Cady Stanton—This is pronounced the strongest and most unanswerable argument and appeal ever made by mortal pen or tongue for the full freedom and franchise of women."

However powerful Stanton's words, they were still not strong enough for Congress to follow up with concrete steps to grant women the right to vote.

THE WOMAN'S BIBLE

In 1895, more than three thousand people gathered at the Metropolitan Opera House in New York City for a grand celebration in honor of Stanton's eightieth birthday. Considering her failing health, many expected this to be the last major event of her career.

They were wrong. Two weeks after the party, Stanton published *The Woman's Bible*, a controversial book that challenged the way women were depicted in the Bible. She wrote, "Church and state, priest and legislators, all political parties and religious denominations have alike taught that woman was made after man, of man, and for man, an inferior being, subject to man."

Passage by passage, Stanton scrutinized and reinterpreted every part of the Bible that referred to women. She believed this

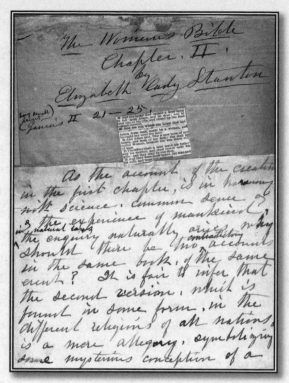

An early draft of Elizabeth Cady Stanton's
THE WOMAN'S BIBLE

critique was essential to getting equality between the sexes. "How can woman's position be changed from that of a subordinate to an equal," she wrote, "without opposition, without the broadest discussion of all the questions involved in her present degradation?"

Stanton spelled out the current understanding of women's status in the introduction, where she wrote that the Bible "teaches that woman brought sin and death into the world, that she precipitated the fall of the race. . . . Marriage for her was to be a condition of bondage, maternity a period of suffering and anguish, and in silence and subjection, she was to play the role of a dependent on man's bounty for all her material wants. . . . Here is the Bible position of woman all summed up."

But Stanton didn't agree with that position, of course. In the book, she asked readers to look a little deeper. She analyzed the text and offered a different interpretation. She began with a passage from the first chapter of Genesis: "So God created man in His own image, in the image of God created He him; male and female created He them."

"If language has any meaning," Stanton wrote, "we have in these texts a plain declaration of the existence of the feminine element in the Godhead, equal in power and glory with the masculine." She continued: "The masculine and feminine elements, exactly equal and balancing each other, are as essential to the maintenance of the equilibrium of the universe as positive and negative electricity, the centripetal and centrifugal forces, the laws of attraction which bind together all we know of this planet whereon we dwell and of the system in which we revolve." In other words, Stanton argued, the Bible says that woman is not subordinate to man, but equal in every way.

The Woman's Bible enraged just about everyone concerned with religion. Religious leaders denounced it as blasphemous. Churchgoers considered it irreverent. Bible scholars dismissed it as unimportant.

Stanton didn't mind a bit. "Women have just as good a right to interpret and twist the Bible to their own advantage as men have always twisted it and turned it to theirs," she told a reporter.

Anthony worried that Stanton's book would divide the coalition of women working for suffrage. Stanton had asked her to work on the project, but Anthony had refused.

"Stop hitting poor old St. Paul—and give your heaviest raps on the head of every Nabob—man or woman—who does injustice to a human being—for the crime of color or sex!!" Anthony wrote to Stanton. "I do wish you could center your big brain on the crimes we ourselves as a people are responsible for."

Anthony was right: Stanton's inflammatory text angered the membership of the National American Woman Suffrage

Association. At its annual convention in Washington, DC, a group of women offered a resolution officially dissociating the group from Stanton and *The Woman's Bible.*

"This association is non-sectarian, being composed of persons of all shadows of religious opinions, and has no official connection with the so-called *Woman's Bible* or any theological publication," the resolution read.

Anthony felt compelled to defend her friend with a passionate speech.

> *This resolution . . . will be a vote of censure upon a woman who is without a peer in intellectual and statesmanlike ability; one who has stood for half a century the acknowledged leader of progressive thought . . . in regard to all matters pertaining to the absolute freedom of woman. . . . When our platform becomes too narrow for people of all creeds and of no creeds, I myself shall not stand upon it. . . . I shall be pained beyond expression if the delegates . . . are so narrow and illiberal as to adopt this resolution. You [had] better not begin resolving against individual action or you will find no limit. This year it is Mrs. Stanton; next year it may be me or one of yourselves who will be the victim.*

Despite Anthony's speech, the delegates voted in favor of censure, 53 to 41.

Stanton was hurt and angry. "Much as I desire the suffrage," she wrote, "I would rather never vote than to see the policy of our government at the mercy of the religious bigotry of such women." Stanton wanted nothing more to do with the organization, and she wanted Anthony to give up her leadership role there as well.

For three weeks, Anthony wrestled with the issue, torn between loyalty to her closest friend and devotion to the organization she had worked for all her adult life.

Anthony decided not to resign. She wrote to Stanton, "Instead of my resigning and leaving those half-fledged chickens without any mother, I think it my duty, and the duty of yourself and all the liberals to be at the next convention and try to reverse this miserable narrow action."

In fact, the issue was never raised at the convention, and the censure was never reversed.

Although Stanton accepted Anthony's decision and didn't quit the group, she remained a bit peeved. She was growing weary of Anthony's single-mindedness about suffrage. "Miss Anthony has one idea and she has not patience with anyone who has two," Stanton wrote to a friend. "I cannot . . . sing suffrage anymore; I am deeply interested in all the questions of the day."

In January 1887, Elizabeth Cady Stanton was in England with her daughter when she learned that her husband of forty-six years had died. Years before, she had explained her marriage to a friend this way: "I fear . . . you may imagine my domestic relations not altogether happy." They are, she argued, "far more so than 99/100 of married people. . . . Mr. Stanton . . . is a very cheerful sunny genial man, hence we can laugh together. . . . He loves music so do I, he loves oratory so do I . . . but our theology is as wide apart as the north and south pole. . . . My views trouble him. I accept his philosophically. . . . if he could do the same we should be nearer and dearer I have no doubt."

VOICES OF OPPOSITION

Suffragists saw the vote as a way they could make the world a better place by using it to increase wages, eliminate child labor, and reduce government corruption. But some women continued to oppose their own suffrage, arguing that having the vote would threaten women's role in society and in the home.

The antis had first organized in 1869 when national pro-suffrage groups were first gaining power. Madeleine Vinton Dahlgren, wife of a Civil War admiral, led the Anti–Sixteenth Amendment Society and spearheaded a petition drive. The group collected signatures of five thousand women who did *not* want the right to vote. The petition or "protest" stated that "a higher sphere, apart from public life" required the "full measure of duties and responsibilities" of women, and it said that women were unwilling to "bear other and heavier burdens." It also claimed that suffrage would be harmful to children, because it would increase the likelihood of "discord" in marriages, increasing the "already alarming" rate of divorce in the country. "Marriage is a sacred unity. . . . Each family is represented through its head," Dahlgren said.

For more than thirty years, the antis argued that only an "insignificant minority" of women wanted the vote, and that women were "unfitted for the ballot" because they were "influenced by pity, passion and prejudice rather than by judgment." In addition, they said that society depended on women maintaining the domestic sphere—the home—which provided a refuge from the stresses of the outside world.

The vast majority of these "anti" women were educated, married, wealthy white women, who enjoyed the privileges of their status without considering the practical problems facing poor and powerless working-class women. They called women with an interest in politics or life beyond the home "manly" or "unsexed,"

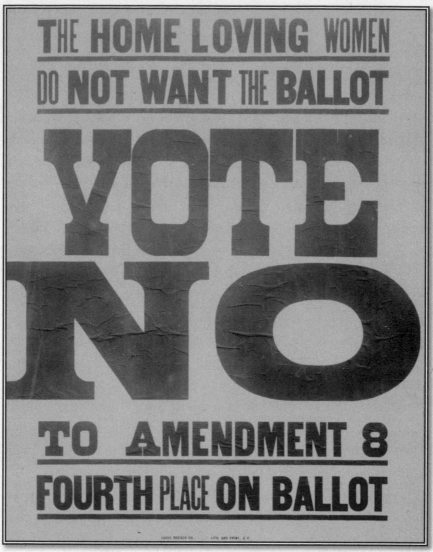

Anti-suffragists made posters encouraging the defeat of female suffrage.

and they argued that women enjoyed certain advantages over men, such as a legal requirement that husbands support their wives and children.

Instead of fighting with Dahlgren, the suffragists tried to change her mind. The women of the National Woman Suffrage

Association invited her and other members of the Anti–Sixteenth Amendment Society to their national convention in 1872. Dahlgren politely refused, explaining that by issuing the invitation the suffragists had "entirely ignored the principle which [the Anti–Sixteenth Amendment Society] sought to defend: 'the preservation of female modesty.'"

In 1878, the Senate Committee on Privileges and Elections invited both the suffragists and the anti-suffragists to present their views on a national suffrage amendment before Congress. Dahlgren did not appear—to do so would be to violate her own argument that women should not participate in public forums—but she offered a written statement titled "Protest against Woman Suffrage." In her remarks, Dahlgren argued that women had distinct duties in the home and that suffrage would threaten their special status. She also argued that fathers and husbands—male heads of households—represented the best interests of women. (Unmarried adult women or widowed women were out of luck, apparently.)

By the close of the nineteenth century, however, the biggest enemy of suffrage was not the antis but indifference. The energy had largely drained from the movement, and most women didn't talk much about suffrage, pro or con. In order to find out where women actually stood on the issue, in November 1895, Massachusetts conducted a nonbinding referendum.

This approach didn't please either side. The suffragists complained that the referendum wasn't binding, and the antis complained that they were expected to vote in order to show that they didn't want the vote.

The antis encouraged women *not* to vote in the referendum. That way, if voter turnout was low, the antis could claim that it was because women didn't want the ballot. Of about 612,000 women who were eligible to vote in the referendum, only about 7 percent registered and only about 4 percent voted. But of those who did vote, 96 percent supported suffrage. In other words, almost all of the women who voted supported suffrage. Still, the antis claimed that all of those who failed to vote opposed female suffrage.

Men could weigh in on the issue, too, and they were less supportive: Almost 70 percent of the men who voted opposed female suffrage. Overall, this measure ended up undermining the suffragists, because the low voter turnout suggested that women were apathetic about voting.

Several months before the referendum, Massachusetts Association Opposed to the Further Extension of Suffrage to Women (MAOFESW) was organized, an awkwardly named anti-suffrage group that recruited more than fifteen hundred women during its first year.

The group published a pamphlet titled *Why? Why Should Any Woman Be an Anti-Suffragist?* It said, "These women, who constitute the active members of the Anti-Suffrage majority, have realized that strength lies in organization and, therefore, they have formed themselves into societies to engage in active preventive measures." They believed that the stakes were nothing less than the "destruction of the home."

The suffragists had an uncharitable view of the antis. In *History of Woman Suffrage*, Ida Husted Harper described the MAOFESW this way:

> *Massachusetts was the home of the oldest and most influential*
> *anti-suffrage organization of women in the United States. . . .*
> *Few of its members did any active work but they were*
> *connected through the men of their families with the richest,*
> *most powerful and best organized groups of men in the*
> *State, who worked openly or behind the scenes against woman*

suffrage. They had an influence out of all proportion to their numbers. . . . While always posing as a woman's protest, the real strength of the movement was in the men.

In 1897, two years after the Massachusetts referendum, the antis formed the New York State Association Opposed to Woman Suffrage. And by the turn of the century, there were anti-suffrage groups in New York, Illinois, California, Massachusetts, South Dakota, Washington, and Oregon. While some of these groups boasted large memberships, the suffragists questioned the

Men line up in New York City to read the argument against giving women the right to vote. The National Association Opposed to Woman Suffrage was organized in 1911. Most of the members were wealthy, influential women and members of the clergy.

numbers reported by the antis. The suffragists noted that their "members" paid no membership dues and that people who may have signed a petition years before were still being counted as members. This led to the "exaggerated strength" of the anti-suffragist movement.

Whether the ranks of antis were exaggerated or not, it was clear that the time had not yet come for suffrage. As the nineteenth century came to a close, after fifty years of tireless effort, only four states—Wyoming (1869), Colorado (1893), Utah (1896), and Idaho (1896)—had full female suffrage. All had passed the legislation without significant involvement of the national suffrage leaders.

The suffrage movement was entering a phase that many historians refer to as "the doldrums." During the period from 1896 to 1910, not a single state adopted new suffrage legislation. The leadership of the movement was growing older and slowing down.

9

"FAILURE IS IMPOSSIBLE!"

The Next Generation

At the annual convention in February 1900, Susan B. Anthony resigned as president of the National American Woman Suffrage Association. She was eighty years old.

"I am not retiring now because I feel unable, mentally or physically, to do the necessary work," she told the delegates at the meeting. "I want to see you all at work, while I am alive, so I can scold you if you do not do it well."

During this period of her life, Anthony took a moment to look backward—and forward. The new century seemed to mark a shift in the women's movement. She told Elizabeth Cady Stanton, "The hardships of the last half-century are forgotten."

Stanton agreed. Many women, she said, "seem to know nothing of the . . . progressive steps made by their own sex in the last fifty years."

Women had made significant progress. At the time, a wife could own property in three-quarters of the states, and she could keep her own paycheck in two-thirds of the states. Most public universities had opened admission to women or were considering the possibility. There was a long way to go, and progress was slow—especially in the more conservative South—but the world was changing.

CHANGES IN LEADERSHIP

Who would follow Susan B. Anthony as president of the National American Woman Suffrage Association? Most members assumed the new leader would be Anna Howard Shaw, a Methodist minister who had a reputation as an excellent speaker and was in Anthony's inner circle. In addition to being a preacher, Shaw had gone to medical school at age thirty-five. After working with poor women in Boston as a doctor and a preacher, she decided that women's problems couldn't be solved by religion or medicine. "One's efforts must begin at the very foundation of the social structure," she said. She made suffrage her life's work.

Anthony had also worked with Carrie Chapman Catt, a superb organizer and fund-raiser who had helped to earn the vote for women in Colorado. While Anthony admired Shaw, she knew that Catt had the organizational skills that were needed for the job, and she chose Catt as the next president.

"In Mrs. Catt, you have my ideal leader," Anthony told the convention. "I present to you my successor."

"Your president, if you please," Catt said when she was introduced to the crowd. "But Miss Anthony's successor never! There is but one Miss Anthony, and she could not have a successor."

Anthony had no time for rest in her retirement. One of her first challenges involved a pledge she had made to raise money for the University of Rochester. Two years before, she and Elizabeth

Carrie Chapman Catt (1859–1947) grew up in Iowa and wanted to become a doctor. She became a law clerk, a teacher, and the superintendent of schools in Mason City, Iowa, before devoting her career to suffrage.

Cady Stanton had convinced the school to admit women, with the understanding that they would raise $50,000 to pay for the necessary new facilities. Anthony turned the fund-raising task over to a group of local women who raised $42,000, but then they stopped collecting money, as if they had reached their goal.

On the day before the final deadline, the local organizers told Anthony that they had failed.

Anthony immediately reached out to every donor she could think of. She told one woman who had promised to give a substantial donation once their school went coed, "Give it now . . . or the girls may never be admitted."

After twenty-four hours of tireless work, Anthony went to the university trustees and presented $8,000 in pledges to make up the shortfall. When one $2,000 pledge was rejected, Anthony offered her life insurance to cover the difference.

"They let the girls in," she wrote in her diary that night.

Two days later Anthony suffered a stroke that left her unable to speak. Over the course of several months, she regained her speech, but she never regained her previous vitality.

THE LAST GOOD-BYE

While they remained close friends, Susan B. Anthony and Elizabeth Cady Stanton didn't spend much time together anymore. Severe cataracts had left Stanton virtually blind, and heart failure made her weak and breathless. Her mind remained sharp, but she needed an assistant to read to her and to help her with her writing.

In May 1902, Anthony spent a week with Stanton in her home. "We have grown a little apart since not so closely associated as of old," Anthony admitted to a friend. "She thinks the church is now the enemy to fight—and feels worried that I stay back with the children—as she says—instead of going ahead with her."

Anthony held Stanton and wept when it was time for her to leave at the end of their visit. Both women were acutely aware that this could be their last good-bye.

"Shall I see you again?" Anthony asked.

"Oh, yes," Stanton answered. "If not here, then in the hereafter, if there is one—and if there isn't we shall never know it."

To make leaving easier, Anthony promised to come back for Stanton's eighty-seventh birthday in November. Then she went home to Rochester and wrote Stanton a letter. It said, in part:

> *We little dreamed when we began this contest, optimistic with the hope and buoyancy of youth, that half a century later we would be compelled to leave the finish of the battle to another generation of women. But our hearts are filled with joy to know that they enter upon this task equipped with a college education, with business experience, with the fully admitted right to speak in public—all of which were denied to women fifty years ago. . . . These strong, courageous, capable young women will*

take our place and complete our work. There is an army of
them where we were but a handful. . . . We, dear friend, shall
move on to the next sphere of existence . . . one where women
will not be placed in an inferior position but will be welcomed on
a plane of perfect intellectual and spiritual equality.
* Ever lovingly yours,*
* Susan B. Anthony*

One morning in late October, Stanton asked her daughter
Harriot to fix her hair and help her get dressed.

"I placed a table for her to rest her hands on," Harriot later
remembered. "She drew herself up very erect . . . and there she
stood seven or eight minutes, steadily looking out proudly before
her. I think she was mentally making an address."

Stanton did not speak her final thoughts aloud. Harriot encouraged her mother to rest.

The following day, Anthony received a telegram: MOTHER
PASSED AWAY AT THREE O'CLOCK.
HARRIOT.

Anthony spent the next several hours alone in her study.
When newspaper reporters
knocked on the door of her
Rochester home and asked for
a statement, she said, "I cannot express myself at all as I

Although they had differences, the
friendship between Susan B. Anthony
and Elizabeth Cady Stanton lasted
more than fifty years.

feel. . . . If I had died first she would have found beautiful phrases to describe our friendship, but I cannot put it into words."

Anthony came up with a more complete answer for a later interviewer. She told him that the best part of their lives together was "the days when the struggle was the hardest and the fight the thickest; when the whole world was against us and we had to stand the closer to each other; when I would go to her home and help with the children and the housekeeping through the day and then we would sit up far into the night preparing our ammunition and getting ready to move on the enemy."

A friend recalled, "To see poor Miss Anthony questioned over and over about her early times with her dead friend and climbing up to the attic to find a picture for the reporter with her hand shaking so that she could hardly lift the cards, was a piteous thing."

The following day, Anthony was on the train to New York City to attend the private funeral held in Stanton's apartment. "It is an awful hush," Anthony wrote to a friend. "It seems impossible—that the voice is hushed that I longed to hear for fifty years—longed to hear her opinion of things—before I knew exactly where I stood— It is all at sea—but the laws of nature are still going on. . . . What a world it is—it goes right on and on—no matter who lives or who dies!!"

Stanton had made her funeral arrangements in advance. "I should like to be in my ordinary dress," she had said of her plans. "No crepe or black . . . and some common-sense women to conduct the services."

Also in accordance with Stanton's wishes, next to her casket stood the mahogany table where she had sat as she drafted the Declaration of Sentiments in 1848, and on the casket rested a framed black-and-white photograph of Susan B. Anthony, her closest friend, her partner in activism, and her sister in suffrage work.

THE END OF AN ERA

Susan B. Anthony had outlived not only her longtime friend but all of her siblings as well, except her younger sister, Mary. But since her stroke, Anthony's doctors had advised her to ease up on her hectic schedule.

She ignored them. In the final years of her life, Anthony traveled to eighteen states and Europe; she finished editing the fourth volume of *History of Woman Suffrage*; and she attended six more suffrage meetings and four congressional hearings.

Anthony was always amazed at the reception she received when traveling. "Once I was the most hated and reviled of women," she said. "Now it seems as if everybody loves me."

Applause and affection weren't the same as the support of legislators, however. In 1902, she appeared for the last time before the Senate Select Committee on Woman Suffrage. She had appeared before that group and spoken on behalf of female suffrage for decades.

"We have waited," Anthony said. "How long will this injustice, this outrage, continue?" And she warned them, "I shall not be able to come much longer."

On February 15, 1906, Anthony traveled to Washington, DC, for her eighty-sixth birthday celebration. The hosts read letters and birthday wishes from people across the country, including President Theodore Roosevelt, who offered his "hearty good wishes for the continuation of her useful and honorable life."

Roosevelt's tribute did not impress Anthony. She rose from her chair, went to center stage, and said, "I wish the men would do something besides extend congratulations. I have asked President Roosevelt to push the matter of a constitutional amendment allowing suffrage to women by a recommendation to Congress. I would rather have him say a word to Congress for the cause than to praise me endlessly." The crowd cheered.

At the end of the evening, Anthony walked to the podium. The audience stood and applauded for more than ten minutes. When the cheering stopped, Anthony spoke.

She thanked her hosts and all those who had offered kind words. Then she ended her remarks with this statement: "There have been also others just as true and devoted to the cause—I wish I could name every one—but with such women consecrating their lives, failure is impossible!"

Two days later, Anthony arrived home in Rochester. She rested downstairs for a day before she felt strong enough to climb the stairs to her bedroom. She had double pneumonia—fluid in both of her lungs—and she could barely breathe.

Shaw hurried to her side.

"Just think," Anthony said. "I have been striving for over sixty years for a little bit of justice no bigger than that, and yet I must die without obtaining it. . . . It seems so cruel."

Shaw comforted her dear friend, but she knew that Anthony's words were true.

Anthony drifted in and out of consciousness.

"She suddenly began to utter the names of the women who had worked with her as if in a final roll call," Shaw later recalled. "Many of them had preceded her into the next world; others were still splendidly active in the work she was laying down. But young and old, living or dead, they all seemed to file past her dying eyes that day in an endless, shadowy review, and as they went by she spoke to each of them."

"They are still passing before me," Shaw remembered her saying. "Face after face, hundreds and hundreds of them. . . . I know how hard they have worked. I know the sacrifices they have made."

On Tuesday, March 13, 1906, Susan B. Anthony died.

Like Elizabeth Cady Stanton, Anthony had left instructions for her funeral. She did not want the shades drawn or black

*Anna Howard Shaw (1847–1919),
who followed Susan B. Anthony as
president of the National American
Woman Suffrage Association, was
also a physician and an ordained
Methodist minister.*

funeral crepe to be hung. Instead, she asked that a wreath of violets be hung on the front door of her house.

The table that had once belonged to Stanton—the one where the Declaration of Sentiments had been prepared—now sat in Anthony's front parlor. It featured a flower arrangement sent by the National American Woman Suffrage Association.

For her burial, Anthony wore a black silk dress with a white lace collar, accented by a flag pin given to her by the women of Wyoming. The pin glimmered with four diamonds, one for each of the states where women could vote. Before her casket was closed, the pin was removed and given to Anna Howard Shaw.

At the funeral, an honor guard of female students from the University of Rochester stood next to Anthony's body. During the service, ten thousand mourners filed passed her flag-draped coffin.

"The world is profoundly stirred by the loss of our great General," Shaw said in her eulogy, "and in consequence the lukewarm are becoming zealous, the prejudiced are disarming, and the suffragists are renewing their vows of fidelity to the cause for which Miss Anthony lived and died. Her talismanic words, the last she ever uttered before a public audience, 'Failure is impossible,' shall be inscribed on our banner and engraved on our hearts."

10 "VOTES FOR WOMEN"

The Second Wave of Suffragists

THE DEATHS OF ELIZABETH CADY STANTON AND SUSAN B. Anthony marked the end of the first wave of the American women's suffrage movement. The next generation of suffragists respected the accomplishments of their foremothers, but many of them were impatient with the slow progress of the movement. Some suffragists—especially younger women—were open to using new, more radical approaches to reach their goals.

By 1906, the year Anthony died, women in England were using civil disobedience in the battle for their voting rights. These women held demonstrations, interrupted government speakers, and shattered storefront and office windows to bring attention to their cause.

The longer their demands were ignored, the more militant their tactics became. They set fires in mailboxes, cut telephone wires, and vandalized train cars. Critics called these women "suffragettes," a word intended to be disparaging, but the women embraced the term as one of power and rebellion.

Police arrested and jailed many of the British suffragettes, often treating them harshly. However, instead of backing down, the women continued their protests in prison by starting hunger strikes. The prison officials then responded with aggressive force-feedings to keep the women alive. In England, more than a thousand suffragettes spent time in jail, and dozens were force-fed.

Harriot Stanton Blatch, the youngest daughter of Elizabeth Cady Stanton, lived in England for twenty years and worked with British suffragettes. When she moved home to the United States in 1902, Blatch noted that, by comparison, "There did not seem to be a grain of political knowledge in the [US] movement." Blatch said, "The suffrage movement . . . bored its adherents and repelled its opponents."

Blatch stirred up new interest in the American suffrage movement. She recruited working women, set up lecture tours for British suffragettes, and brought in a number of wealthy supporters to the cause. In January 1907, she formed the Equality League of Self-Supporting Women. Less than two years later, the organization had more than nineteen thousand members.

Blatch came up with a number of publicity strategies. She sponsored a trolley campaign in New York State and an automobile tour across Illinois. She organized the first suffrage parade in New York City, with women carrying yellow banners and wearing yellow sashes boldly declaring VOTES FOR WOMEN. She led several dozen marchers on a two-week hike from New York City to Albany,

Harriot Eaton Stanton Blatch (1856–1940) was a writer and suffragist who helped to reinvigorate the American women's suffrage movement.

the state capital. During their pilgrimage, they talked to everyone they met about women's rights. These aren't radical acts by today's standards, but they were bold measures in their day.

These new publicity campaigns brought renewed attention to the movement. Suddenly, suffrage was a young person's fight, not a battle once fought by her mother and her mother's friends. "As for the suffrage movement," a young college graduate noted, "it is actually fashionable now."

The newly reenergized suffrage movement finally started having some success after a long period of stagnation. In 1910, Washington became the first state to pass suffrage legislation in fourteen years. Success in other states followed, with California, Kansas, Arizona, and Oregon passing laws in the next few years. Times were changing.

INTRODUCING ALICE PAUL

Elizabeth Cady Stanton had predicted that the next generation of suffragists would not display "the infinite patience we have for a half a century." Younger suffragists considered the National American Woman Suffrage Association (NAWSA) too slow and too passive in its approach. They wanted suffrage and they wanted it now.

One of these new-wave suffragists was Alice Paul.

Paul grew up in a wealthy Quaker family in a New Jersey suburb outside Philadelphia. As a child she learned about social justice and even attended suffrage meetings with her mother. During her senior year at Swarthmore College, she took a course in political science, which sparked her interest in political activism.

After graduation, Paul worked in a settlement house—a facility that provided social services to an inner-city community—in New York City and studied social work at the New York School

ALICE PAUL (1885–1977) *decided that radical reform was necessary to bring about change after hearing militant suffragettes speak at the University of Birmingham in England.*

of Philanthropy (now part of Columbia University). She went on to earn a master's degree in sociology from the University of Pennsylvania, followed by a fellowship to study at the Woodbrooke Quaker Study Centre in Birmingham, England.

While in England, Paul wanted to experience what it was like to be a member of the working class. "I dressed as a working girl—they gave me the clothes at the Settlement," she wrote in a letter to her mother. She then tried to get work at a jam factory, but she couldn't, so she went to a rubber factory instead. "There were about 40 girls waiting in the yard. The foreman came out & looked at us as though we were so many cows."

Paul got the job and worked twelve-hour days threading cords into automobile tires for less than five dollars a week. She worked from 6 a.m. to 6 p.m., with a half-hour break for breakfast and an hour at noon for lunch. "I got my own food & supported myself on my wages," she wrote proudly.

While at Woodbrooke Quaker Study Centre, she heard a speech by Christabel Pankhurst, the British suffragette, and she was invited to participate in suffrage protests, but she didn't jump into radical politics easily. While she wasn't opposed to joining the protest, she said, "I thought all my family and everybody I knew would object."

Finally, in 1908, at age twenty-three, Paul joined the British suffragettes. It did not take long for her to be arrested.

After her first encounter with police, Paul wrote to her mother: "Dear Mamma," she began. "On Tuesday I went on a deputation of the Suffragettes to the House of Commons & 108 of us were arrested. I never did anything militant till now, for I could not risk having to give up my work, in case of being sent to prison." She assured her mother that she would return home to finish her doctoral degree after the trial. "And if I am sent to prison," she wrote, "I will come as soon as I am released."

Paul was arrested at least seven times in Great Britain and jailed at least three times.

In June 1909, Alice Paul met Lucy Burns at a London police station after they had both been arrested for participating in a protest. Paul noticed that Burns was wearing an American flag pin on her suit, so she introduced herself as a fellow American. Burns told Paul she was an Irish Catholic from Brooklyn. The two women hit it off immediately.

When Paul returned to the United States in 1910 to finish her PhD thesis, "Towards Equality: A Study of the Legal Position of Women in Pennsylvania," at the University of Pennsylvania, she was invited to speak before the Philadelphia branch of NAWSA.

The national leadership noticed Paul's eloquence and devotion to suffrage, and after her lecture she was asked to serve on their board. Harriot Stanton Blatch invited Paul to come to New York City to speak at Cooper Union.

After one of Paul's speeches, a Quaker woman questioned her about her militancy. Paul responded, without apology, "I attach no particular sanctity to a twenty-five-cent window pane." She said that she had broken forty-eight windows during her time in England "because it is a means to an end."

She also criticized modern Quakers as too passive. "It seems indeed a far cry from the aggressive vigor with which the early Friends challenged the evils of their time," she said. She did, however, make it clear that she did not support the use of violence if it could be avoided.

When Lucy Burns returned to the United States in 1912, she reconnected with Alice Paul. The two suffragists complemented one another, much like Anthony and Stanton. "They seemed in those early days to have one spirit and one brain," a mutual friend said. Both women agreed with the motto of the British suffrage movement: "Deeds, Not Words."

While Paul and Burns did become involved with NAWSA, they didn't support its emphasis on state campaigns. Like Stanton and Anthony before them, they favored bolder campaigns with a focus on a federal amendment.

In 1912, Paul applied to lead the association's congressional committee, the group that lobbied legislators on Capitol Hill. In recent years, the committee had been virtually inactive, but Paul envisioned a more dynamic future.

Anna Howard Shaw thought Paul was too young and too militant for the job, but she decided to give her a chance after progressive reformer and suffragist Jane Addams spoke up on Paul's behalf. Paul agreed to accept a ten-dollar annual budget and not to

In addition to being a suffragist, Jane Addams (1860–1935) was a social worker and an advocate for world peace. She created the first American settlement house, a home in Chicago where poor and middle-class women lived together.

ask for more money. If she needed more money, she was expected to raise the funds herself.

Inspired by Harriot Stanton Blatch, Paul wanted to use pageants and parades to rekindle interest in a federal amendment for women's suffrage, as well as to influence members of Congress. She believed that people would support the movement if they knew more about it.

"OUR RIGHT TO THE AVENUE"

As part of her campaign, Alice Paul wanted to organize a parade in the nation's capital. She imagined a colorful extravaganza with bands and floats and thousands of marchers from all over the country, an event so bold and beautiful that it would demand notice from federal legislators. Paul's parade would announce to the world that a new generation of suffragists had arrived, one that was ready to make some real changes.

She wanted the grand procession to take place on March 3, 1913, the day before the inaugural parade for the twenty-eighth president of the United States, Woodrow Wilson.

Paul had moved to Washington, DC, in December 1912, after assuming leadership of NAWSA's congressional committee, but the organization's leadership remained wary of her, and they wanted to keep the radicalism of the British suffragettes out of their organization. They told Paul that she could hold a parade but that she would have to raise the money on her own.

Paul didn't complain; she got busy. First, she had to find office space. She chose a basement room located under a real estate firm on F Street in a well-traveled part of Washington, DC. The rent was sixty dollars a month—six times the annual budget for her entire committee—but she knew the location would bring in additional volunteers, who would learn about suffrage by walking past the office. She signed the lease even though she didn't have the money in the bank.

Paul didn't want problems with the authorities, so early in the planning process she met with the District of Columbia's police superintendent, Richard Sylvester, to obtain a parade permit.

"It's totally unsuitable for women to be marching down Pennsylvania Avenue," Sylvester said. He warned that the parade route Paul had requested passed near a number of bars and saloons and that some of the men may get rowdy and disruptive. He told

First headquarters of the congressional committee of the National American Woman Suffrage Association in Washington, DC, in 1913

her that he didn't have enough police officers to cover two parades, back-to-back, and that the president's event took precedence. He suggested other dates and routes: How about doing it a week later, or going down Sixteenth Street, which was wider and could handle a bigger crowd?

Paul insisted on using the same route as the president's inaugural parade, down Pennsylvania Avenue from the Capitol to the White House. She wanted to march where the men marched. She had chosen the date for her parade to get attention from the spectators and the press already in town for the inauguration. And she knew that the trains were offering discounted fares that weekend, so transportation would be less expensive for marchers who didn't have much money.

Paul could be both stubborn and tough. She lacked physical presence—she weighed less than one hundred pounds—but she was determined, and she refused to take no for an answer.

So Alice Paul launched a public relations campaign. She pleaded for "our right to the Avenue," and she convinced the local board of trade, chamber of commerce, merchants' association, and other community groups to back her. She asked women who had marched in suffrage parades in New York City to speak to the police superintendent and told him that things would go smoothly "if the police protection was half as good as it was in New York." With public support behind her, Sylvester eventually gave in.

Now that she had her way, Paul stayed up at night worrying that her parade would be a flop, especially compared to the New York City event, which had become an annual tradition. So instead of talking about putting on a "parade," she began to talk about a suffrage "procession." She told one supporter, "We are endeavoring to make the procession a particularly beautiful one, so that it will be noteworthy on account of its beauty even if we are not able to make it so on account of its numbers."

GETTING TO WORK

Alice Paul couldn't do it alone. She proselytized about suffrage to anyone who would listen and recruited volunteers to help with the work.

Paul may have been small and delicate physically, but she had an intensity and passion for her work that those around her found inspiring. People found it hard to say no to her. "She's no bigger than a wisp of hay, but she has the most deep and beautiful violet-blue eyes, and when they look at you and ask you to do something, you could no more refuse," one volunteer said.

"When you ask her a question, there ensues, on her part, a moment of stillness so profound you can almost hear it," another suffragist said. "I think I have never seen anybody who can keep so still as Alice Paul. . . . . Superficially she seems cold, austere, a little remote. But that is only because the fire of her spirit burns at such a heat that it is still and white. She has the quiet of a spinning top."

Paul wasn't one for small talk or gossip, and she didn't flatter or pass out compliments easily. Once, when a volunteer quit her post, Paul asked why the woman had left, and someone explained that she had been offended that Paul had not thanked her for her work.

"But she did not do it for me," Paul said. "She did it for suffrage."

Still, she didn't make the same mistake again. From that point on, she made an effort to express appreciation.

Paul worked tirelessly on the campaign. She kept a room in a Quaker boardinghouse near the office, but she kept her room quite cold so that she wouldn't be tempted to sit up at night and give in to her favorite guilty pleasure, reading mysteries and detective novels. She went out of her way to avoid walking past bookstores that might tempt her to stop and browse. There would be time for that later, she told herself, after women had won the right to vote.

GETTING READY

The details of preparing for the suffrage parade were daunting, even the simplest ones. Paul had ordered purple, white, and green flags, but some women objected, because those were the colors of the British suffragettes. The choice of colors "will surely be offensive to a large number of our members who are hotly opposed to the militants," a NAWSA leader wrote to her. Anna Howard Shaw, for example, said she would never march "under the suffragette flag" of the British protesters.

It seemed a petty concern but an easy issue to address. To keep the peace, Paul changed the green to gold and ordered two thousand replacement pennants. They were purple, for justice, white, for purity, and gold, for courage.

Paul wanted the women to dress in solid colors and to be arranged to create a rainbow. Social workers, businesswomen, and librarians were to wear blue; artists,

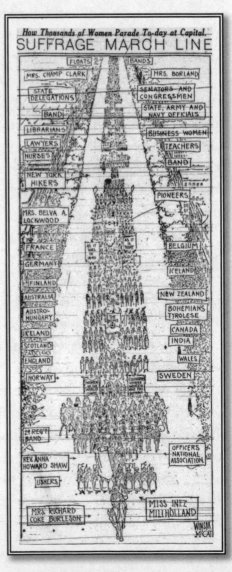

This illustration from the NEW YORK EVENING JOURNAL *shows the intended organization of the marchers in the 1913 suffrage parade.*

*Cover of the official program of the National American Woman
Suffrage Association procession in Washington, DC, on March 3, 1913*

actresses, and musicians were to wear rose; and so forth; so that
the marchers would form a kaleidoscope of color and professions.

When she heard rumors that a group of college boys planned
to release dozens of mice along the parade route, hoping to create
chaos, Paul said, "The idea that any of the women would desert
and run for shelter is absurd. All would walk bravely on, merely for
the principle of the thing, if for nothing else."

The police superintendent wasn't so sure. He responded to the
threat by arranging for several hundred Boy Scouts to stand guard
along the route.

Two weeks before the event, Paul realized that there would
be many more marchers than the two thousand she had initially
expected, but when she asked the Washington, DC, commissioners for additional protection, she was told nothing more could be
done.

But the police superintendent came through. Sylvester depu-
tized police officers for the occasion. In fact, he assured Paul that

there would be 575 police officers on patrol during the parade, significantly *more* than the 367 that would be working on the day of the presidential inauguration.

Still, Paul worried about security. So the night before the parade, one of the suffragists, Elizabeth Selden Rogers, took her to see her brother-in-law Henry Lewis Stimson, the secretary of war. Paul explained the situation and begged for more officers.

Stimson promised to send the US Cavalry, if necessary. And true to his word, he arranged to have the Fifteenth Cavalry from Fort Myer, Virginia, moved to the western perimeter of Washington, DC, to be ready to assist if trouble developed.

Thirteen suffragists or pilgrims walked 250 miles, from New York to Washington, DC, to join the March 3 suffrage procession. They were followed by a wagon carrying twenty thousand suffrage leaflets, which they shared with interested people along the way, taking every chance to discuss the issue of voting rights for women. Even anti-suffragists acknowledged that they respected the women's devotion to their cause.

11

"HOW LONG MUST WOMEN WAIT FOR LIBERTY?"

Parades and Protests

THE MORNING OF MARCH 3, 1913, DAWNED TO IDEAL conditions—cloudless skies, a light breeze, and temperatures expected to reach the mid-fifties. The mile-and-a-half-long parade was scheduled to begin at 3 p.m. and end at 5 p.m.

The crowds began to gather first thing in the morning. By noon, the streets near Capitol Hill were already filling with participants and spectators. By early afternoon, the crowds were growing dangerously large. The streets had become so congested that the city issued an emergency decree to suspend the trolley service until after the parade because there was no room for the passengers to disembark downtown.

The numbers surpassed everyone's expectations. Estimates vary, but at least five thousand and as many as eight thousand women arrived that morning, ready to take part in the march. Between one hundred thousand and three hundred thousand spectators lined the streets to watch.

While the crowds gathered, the marchers tried to get organized

Crowds overwhelmed the streetcars on the morning of the suffrage procession, March 3, 1913.

into their various groups. Unit leaders held up flags to help steer people in the right direction as the women formed ranks in various divisions. The marchers knew where they were expected to stand, with one notable exception: the African American marchers.

THE AFRICAN AMERICAN SUFFRAGISTS

In early January, an African American woman had asked if she could participate in the parade, and Alice Paul assured her that she was welcome. But when word spread that black women were going to join the procession, some Southern women complained. They threatened that a majority of the white marchers "will refuse to participate if negroes in any number formed a part of the parade."

Paul didn't want the race issue to compromise her event. She said that she was "predisposed to side with, and not against, the negro in any question of racial difference," but she wasn't willing to risk the success of the parade to take a stand for the African American marchers. For weeks, she had tried to ignore the complaints; her plan was "to say nothing whatever about the question" and try to keep it out of the press.

The issue couldn't be so easily sidestepped, though. So in an attempt at compromise, Paul suggested that the African American suffragists march as a bloc at the back of the parade.

This response offended just about everyone. "The suffrage movement stands for enfranchising for [sic] every single woman in the United States," argued Mary Ware Dennett, the secretary of the National American Woman Suffrage Association. Other white women didn't think the African American women belonged in the parade at all.

Several weeks before the parade, an African American sorority from Howard University asked to march with the college women. Paul arranged for them to walk with the New York City Woman Suffrage Party. Mary Church Terrell, an Oberlin College graduate who was active in the civil rights movement, accepted Paul's compromise.

Some women still objected; they said "a southern minority was terrorizing the northern majority."

A few days before the parade, Paul received a telegram: WE HAVE APPLICATION FROM A COLORED WOMAN TO MARCH—WILL NEGRO WOMEN BE ADMITTED TO THE SUFFRAGE PARADE—ANSWER—QUICK.

The African American woman in question was Ida Wells-Barnett, who planned to come from Chicago to Washington, DC, to march side by side with her suffrage sisters from Illinois. Wells-Barnett was a founding member of the National Association for the Advancement of Colored People, as well as a writer, the leader of a national campaign against lynching, and the founder of the

IDA BELL WELLS-BARNETT (1862–1931) *was a journalist, suffragist, and civil rights leader. She was one of the founders of the National Association for the Advancement of Colored People.*

Alpha Suffrage Club, the first organization to work specifically for African American women's suffrage.

Paul told the leadership to allow Wells-Barnett to join the parade, thinking she could figure out a solution when the time came.

On the morning of the parade, the issue of where the African American women would march remained up in the air. Wells-Barnett arrived in Washington, DC, with sixty-two other Illinois suffragists, all white. When the group gathered in a rehearsal area to review the order of the parade, the leader of the Illinois delegation announced that Alice Paul had advised them "to keep [their] delegation entirely white." She explained that the African American women were to march with the all-black contingent at the back of the parade.

"We should like to have Mrs. Barnett march with us," one of the Illinois delegates said. "If the national association has decided it is unwise to include the colored women, I think we should abide by its decision."

Another Illinois delegate, Virginia Brooks, disagreed. "We

have come down here to march for equal rights," she said. "I think that we should allow Mrs. Barnett to walk in our delegation. If the women of other states lack moral courage, we should show them that we are not afraid of public opinion. We should stand by our principles. If we do not the parade will be a farce."

Everyone turned to Wells-Barnett to hear what she had to say. Tears rolled down her cheeks, and her voice trembled as she said, "If the Illinois women do not take a stand now in this great democratic parade then the colored women are lost."

The Illinois suffragists knew she was right. They decided to challenge Alice Paul and to urge her to allow them to march together. "It is time for Illinois to recognize the colored women as a political equal," said the president of the Illinois Equal Suffrage Association.

Illinois may have been ready to take on the issue of segregation, but the rest of the parade leadership was not. The leadership told the Illinois delegation to follow Paul's request and have Wells-Barnett march with the other African American women.

"I shall not march at all unless I can march under the Illinois banner," Wells-Barnett said. "When I was asked to come down here I was asked to march with the other women of our state, and I intend to do so or not take part in the parade at all."

"If I were a colored woman, I should be willing to march with the other women of my race," one Illinois suffragist said.

"There is a difference . . . which you probably do not see," Wells-Barnett replied. "I shall not march with the colored women . . . I am not taking this stand because I personally wish for recognition. I am doing it for the future benefit of my whole race." She turned and walked away.

The others assumed that Wells-Barnett had resigned herself to joining the other African Americans at the back of the line.

Two Illinois delegates—both white—offered to march with

Lining up for the opening of the suffrage procession in Washington, DC

Wells-Barnett in the African American section. But when it came time to gather in formation, one of those women said she was sick and she would not march at all. The other planned to stand with Wells-Barnett, even though several of her fellow delegates accused her of trying to steal publicity. "Let anyone say anything they please. I cannot prevent that, but I can prevent having one of our delegation left to march alone, almost as if she were a disgrace."

The women formed their ranks, but no one could find Wells-Barnett.

According to a *Chicago Tribune* report, when the Illinois group lined up to begin the march, "Suddenly from the crowd on the

OPPOSITE PAGE

*The 1913 parade was an elaborate spectacle. It included women marching under the banner of the National Woman Suffrage Association (*TOP*), as well as horse-drawn floats (*CENTER*). The parade ended with a tableau, or silent play, staged on the steps of the U.S. Treasury Building (*BOTTOM*).*

sidewalk Miss Barnett walked calmly out to the delegation and assumed her place." The marchers made room for her, and she fell into line with them.

OUT OF ORDER

At 3:25 p.m.—almost a half hour after the announced beginning time—a starting gun sounded and the parade officially began. Inez Milholland Boissevain, a young attorney with long wavy dark hair, led the procession. Dressed in a white gown and a pale-blue cloak, she rode her white horse, Grey Dawn. Many described her as a modern-day Joan of Arc.

Behind Boissevain, two horses pulled a cart carrying a model of the Liberty Bell and the "Great Demand" banner, which read

Inez Milholland Boissevain (1886–1916) riding one of four horses that were at the head of the March 3, 1913, suffrage procession. She supported suffrage as a means of improving the working conditions of children and African Americans.

WE DEMAND AN AMENDMENT TO THE CONSTITUTION OF THE UNITED STATES ENFRANCHISING THE WOMEN OF THIS COUNTRY.

Next came women on floats, on horseback, and on foot. There were twenty-six horse-drawn floats, six golden chariots, ten marching bands, and six mounted brigades. The first group represented women from countries where suffrage was legal— Australia (1902), the Cook Islands (1893), Finland (1906), the Isle of Man (1881), and Norway (1913). They were followed by thousands of women marching in groups representing college students, doctors, nurses, lawyers, business leaders, artists, educators, librarians, actresses, and musicians. There were women representing the Red Cross, PTAs, political parties, religious groups, and social clubs, as well as women marching behind banners from every state. Many of the marchers wore badges or sashes that read VOTES FOR WOMEN.

Earlier that morning, the police had strung half-inch steel cables along the sidewalks to restrain the crowd. Police escorts formed a wedge at the front of the procession as the marchers began down Pennsylvania Avenue, followed by sixteen mounted officers. But as soon as the police passed, the spectators pushed through the lines.

The crowds pressed in toward the marchers. At the start of the parade, the women walked four across, but as the spectators spilled into the streets, the women narrowed their ranks to three across, then two, and finally they marched single file. Then, before the marchers had gone more than a few blocks, the line stopped and they were surrounded by a "horrible howling mob."

Most of the spectators were men, and many were drunk. According to the *Washington Post*, the women "practically fought their way foot by foot up Pennsylvania Avenue. . . . No inauguration has ever produced such scenes, which in many instances amounted to little less than riots."

Crowds spilling onto Pennsylvania Avenue during the suffrage procession in Washington, DC

"Why don't you go home and cook dinner?" asked some of the men.

"Who is minding the babies?" asked others.

Men snatched and trampled the suffragists' banners and climbed onto their floats. They yelled obscenities, pinched and groped the women, and used canes to knock off the women's hats. They spit at the women and threw lighted cigarettes and matches in their direction.

The police were on hand, but they didn't help. "They seemed to be doing absolutely nothing, simply standing there on their horses," said one marcher. The police "just stood by and laughed," said another. When a marcher asked the police for help, the officer folded his arms and said, "I can do nothing with this crowd, and I ain't agoing to try." Another police officer watched a drunk man spit chewing tobacco in an older woman's face; when someone complained to him, he said, "There would be nothing like this if you would stay at home."

Assistance *did* come from the four hundred Boy Scouts

positioned along Pennsylvania Avenue. Witnesses reported that they were "active and determined," and that "you could see the little fellows were red in the face from perspiring."

Alice Paul and Lucy Burns pushed to the front of the parade. Paul had planned to march with the college women, so she was wearing her black academic gown. She and Burns tried to push back the crowds to make way, but it didn't do much good.

Eventually, the police called for help. A regiment of National Guard troops, on hand for the inaugural parade, arrived on the scene and pushed back the crowd at one intersection. As promised, US Cavalry troops also rode into town to restore order. The horsemen forced their way into the crowd and made room so that the marchers could inch forward.

Woodrow Wilson arrived by train at Union Station on the day of the suffrage procession. He had expected to be welcomed by cheering supporters, but no one was there to meet him. "Where are the people?" he asked. "On the Avenue watching the suffragists parade," an aide responded. This would not be the last time that Wilson would be upstaged by a group of suffragists. From his first day in office as president, he would be reminded of the movement.

But it seemed that each time the marchers made progress, they stalled, again and again. They eventually completed the route, but they were several hours behind schedule.

AFTERWARD

The day after the parade, Harriot Stanton Blatch sent Woodrow Wilson a telegram and released copies of it to the press:

> As you ride today in comfort and safety to the Capitol to be inaugurated as President of the people of the United States, we beg that you will not be unmindful that yesterday the Government which is supposed to exist for the good of all, left women while passing in peaceful procession in their demand for political freedom at the mercy of a howling mob on the very streets which are being at this moment efficiently officered for the protection of men.

Alice Paul immediately began collecting notarized depositions from the marchers to document the failures of the police department. She had learned that the Senate was going to conduct hearings about the parade, and she wanted to gather testimony before the suffragists returned to their hometowns.

Newspaper coverage about the parade exceeded Paul's greatest expectations. The event probably got more attention as a fiasco than it would have if things had gone smoothly. "This mistreatment by the police was probably the best thing that could ever have happened to us," Paul later wrote to a friend. "It aroused a great deal of public indignation and sympathy."

The *Washington Post* reported that one hundred spectators

were injured and taken to the hospital emergency room, including two dozen people who suffered wounds or fractures, fourteen people who fainted, and eight people who were drunk. None of the marchers were injured.

A report in the *Woman's Journal* said, "Women were spat upon . . . slapped in the face, tripped up, pelted with burning cigar stubs, and insulted by jeers and obscene language too vile to print or repeat."

Nonetheless, throughout the ordeal, the suffragists had stayed calm and handled themselves with dignity. "Never was I so ashamed of our national capital before," said Anna Howard Shaw. "The women in the parade showed wonderful dignity and self-respect by keeping cool in the midst of insult and lewd remarks."

The Senate held two weeks of hearings into the police conduct during the procession. More than 150 witnesses testified. One marcher said that "[the police] would have taken better care of a drove of pigs." Another said, "There seemed to be a tacit agreement to make our efforts a failure."

Paul told the Senate that she had warned the police about the large crowds. "We exhausted every possible means of getting protection on that day," she said, "and we made it known to every official the immense number of women that were coming, and that they must be prepared."

The police superintendent said his conscience was clear. "I did my duty," he said.

The Senate investigators didn't agree; the committee censured the police superintendent. He was not fired, but he was soon forced to resign when additional complaints were brought against him on other matters.

No one blamed Alice Paul for the shortcomings of the parade. In fact, Anna Howard Shaw praised her for the "splendid work" that she had done organizing the parade. "While it may seem

WOMAN'S JOURNAL
AND SUFFRAGE NEWS

VOL. XLIV. NO. 10   SATURDAY, MARCH 8, 1913   FIVE CENTS

PARADE STRUGGLES TO VICTORY DESPITE DISGRACEFUL SCENES

Nation Aroused by Open Insults to Women—Cause Wins Popular Sympathy—Congress Orders Investigation—Striking Object Lesson

Washington has been disgraced. Equal suffrage has scored a great victory. Thousands of indifferent women have been aroused. Influential men are incensed and the United States Senate demands an investigation of the treatment given the suffragists at the National Capital on Monday.

Ten thousand women from all over the country had planned a magnificent parade and pageant to take place in Washington on March 3. Artists, pageant leaders, designers, women of influence and renown were ready to give a wonderful and beautiful piece of suffrage work to the public that would throng the National Capital for the inauguration festivities. The suffragists were ready; the whole procession started down Pennsylvania avenue, when the police protection that had been promised, failed them, and a disgraceful scene followed. The crowd surged into the space which had been marked off for the paraders, and the leaders of the suffrage movement were compelled to push their way through a mob of the worst element in Washington and vicinity. Women were spit upon, slapped in the face, tripped up, pelted with burning cigar stubs, and insulted by jeers and obscene language too vile to print or repeat.

The cause of all the trouble is apparent when the facts are known. The police authorities in Washington opposed every attempt to have a suffrage parade at all. Having been forbidden a place in the inaugural procession, the suffragists asked to have a procession of their own on March 3. They were finally told that they could have a procession but that it could not be on Pennsylvania avenue, but must be on a side street. At last they got permission to have the suffrage parade on the avenue, and asked that traffic be excluded from the street during the parade. For a long time this was denied, and only on Saturday were they successful.

Everything was at last arranged; it was a glorious day; ten thousand women were ready to do their part to make the parade beautiful to behold, to make it a credit to womanhood and to demonstrate the strength of the movement for their enfranchisement.

The police were determined, however, and they had their way. Their attempt to afford the marchers protection and keep the space of the avenue free for the suffrage procession was the flimsiest sham. Police officers stood by with folded arms and grinned while the picked women of the land were insulted and roughly abused by an ignorant and uncouth mob.

Miss Alice Paul and other suffragists were compelled to drive their automobiles down the avenue to separate the crowds so the suffragists with the banners and floats could pass. The police officials say their force was inadequate to handle the crowds, but it is noted that there was no disorder on the avenue during the inaugural procession. It is stated that federal troops were offered to the chief of police for the suffrage procession, but that he refused their aid. At any rate, assistance was finally called from Fort Myer, and mounted soldiers drove back the crowd so that a straggling line of marchers could pass through.

Not only were the suffragists bitterly disappointed in having the effect

(Continued on Page 78)

AMENDMENT WINS IN NEW JERSEY

Easy Victory in Assembly 45 to 5—Equal Suffrage Enthusiasm Runs High

The New Jersey Legislature passed the woman suffrage amendment in the Assembly last week by a vote of 46 to 5. The Senate had already voted favorably 14 to 5.

A large delegation of suffragists crowded the galleries, and when the overwhelming vote was announced there was a scene of great enthusiasm. Women stood in their seats and waved handkerchiefs and "votes for women" flags and cheered themselves hoarse.

Dr. Jekyll Becomes Mr. Hyde

Opposition was confined exclusively to the old sentimental arguments.

(Continued on Page 79)

MICHIGAN AGAIN CAMPAIGN STATE

Senate Passes Suffrage Amendment 26 to 5 and Battle Is Now On

Michigan is again a campaign State after a short lapse of four months. The amendment will go to the voters on April 7. The State-wide feeling that the women were defrauded of victory last fall will help the suffragists.

The final action of the Legislature was taken last week, when the Senate, by a vote of 26 to 5, passed the suffrage amendment, with a slight amendment to make the requirements for foreign-born women the same as those for male immigrants.

Governor Watches Debate

The debate in the Senate lasted an hour and a quarter, and was characterized by the persistent efforts of Senator Weadock and a few others to tack on crippling amendments. Several suggestions, including the disabling of women for holding office or serving on juries, were voted down in quick succession.

Gov. Ferris was among the visitors who crowded the chamber and gallery. Mrs. Clara B. Arthur, Mrs. Thomas R. Henderson and Mrs. William Brotherton, of Detroit; Mrs. Jennie Law Hardy, of Tecumseh, and other State leaders were present, supported by a large delegation of Lansing suffragists.

The final stand of the opposition was made by Senator Murtha in the hope of putting off the submission till November, 1914, and this also failed. Of the five who opposed the measure on the final roll-call, three were from Detroit.

A complete campaign of organization and education has been mapped out by the State Association. The

(Continued on Page 78.)

General Rosalie Jones in Pilgrim Costume; Miss Inez Milholland on White Steed Leading the Parade; One of the Scores of Imposing Floats; One View of the Procession

---

The front page of the WOMAN'S JOURNAL *announced* PARADE STRUGGLES TO VICTORY DESPITE DISGRACEFUL SCENES.

to you that the work of all these months was lost in the fact that the parade as a spectacular display was destroyed," Shaw wrote in a letter to Paul later, "nevertheless I think it has done more for suffrage and will do more for suffrage in the end than the parade itself would have done."

BUILDING ON SUCCESS

In addition to planning and coordinating the parade, Alice Paul and her committee had to spend time raising money to pay for it. They sold buttons, flags, banners, and sashes, and they solicited funds by writing letters and making phone calls. In the final accounting, the parade expenses totaled $13,750—an amount equal to more than $330,000 in today's dollars—and the bills were paid in full.

Paul didn't rest after the parade. Two weeks after the event, she and a group of suffragists met with President Wilson to ask if he would support suffrage. He said that he had not considered the issue and had no opinion at that point. As weeks passed, Paul returned twice more with the same question, and each time he said he hadn't made up his mind.

Paul refused to wait patiently. She had learned about the power of the press and planned to use it to her advantage. One month after the parade, she gathered a group of 531 women—two women from every state, plus one from each congressional district—and they walked the parade route in reverse. Dressed in white, the marchers delivered petitions to each member of Congress. The event was less elaborate than the parade, but it, too, generated press coverage.

In mid-April 1913, Paul set up a political organization known as the Congressional Union for Woman Suffrage to work exclusively on passing a federal suffrage amendment, in conjunction with the congressional committee of the National American Woman Suffrage Association. The group collected petitions, recruited additional supporters and volunteers, raised funds, and started a weekly newspaper, the *Suffragist*, which kept readers up to date on the status of the federal suffrage amendment.

The Congressional Union also started "suffrage schools" to educate women about the issue and, according to Paul, they conducted "an uninterrupted series of indoor and outdoor meetings, numbering frequently from five to ten a day." They wanted women to understand the importance of suffrage, convinced that they would then support the campaign. It wasn't long before Paul's staff had to expand its office from a basement room to ten rooms on two floors.

Meanwhile, the leadership of NAWSA—including both Anna Howard Shaw and Carrie Chapman Catt—had begun to worry that the congressional committee was growing too powerful, too fast. They also had concerns that Paul's new group was overshadowing the parent organization, and that the two groups were competing for volunteers and for funds.

At the NAWSA convention in December 1913, leaders praised the congressional committee's efforts. They also expressed apprehension that the committee operated so independently. Some within the leadership didn't trust Paul. They had concerns that she might turn to the more violent and controversial methods of the British suffragettes. Basically, they weren't sure what she was going to do next.

Officers decided that the powerful Congressional Union could remain part of the congressional committee and NAWSA only if Paul agreed to allow the national board to control the group's finances and approve its decisions. Paul had developed her organization without support from the national board, and she wasn't eager to hand over the bank account and her decision-making power.

She refused. She continued to work with the congressional committee, but she separated the Congressional Union from NAWSA and established it on its own.

PAUL'S POLITICAL STRATEGY

During her time in England, Alice Paul had learned the British suffragists' political approach to their cause, which involved holding the party in power responsible for not passing the suffrage amendment. This blame-the-party-in-power approach made sense in Great Britain, where the prime minister is an elected member of Parliament who serves only as long as his or her party holds a majority of the parliamentary seats.

The same logic didn't apply in the United States, where the president is independently elected and often does not represent the party that has a majority in the Congress. The president cannot force the passage of constitutional amendments, which must be passed by two-thirds of both houses of Congress and ratified by three-quarters of the state legislatures.

Alice Paul steadfastly held to her party-in-power campaign, even though most other suffragists objected. With six full suffrage states and two million female voters, there already existed a ready-made voting bloc with the potential to influence state and national elections.

Despite those logical pitfalls with the party-in-power approach, Paul stuck with it. She believed that by campaigning against the president and his party—in this case, President Woodrow Wilson and the Democratic Party—the suffragists could convince politicians to take a more active role in working for a federal amendment.

The leadership of the National American Woman Suffrage Association strongly objected to this political strategy, but Paul remained unyielding. She and her political supporters went to the states where women had won the right to vote, and they campaigned against Democrats—*all* Democrats, even those who supported suffrage.

Paul insisted that her approach would work in the long run. She argued that the strategy would send a strong message and that it would motivate more politicians to take a stand on the suffrage issue. She didn't want politicians to voice lukewarm support for suffrage; she wanted them to work for change until it was accomplished.

ON HER OWN

President Woodrow Wilson kept trying to dodge the suffrage question. In 1914, he still hadn't come out as clearly for or against the issue. That wasn't good enough for Alice Paul. While some suffragists chose to support Wilson and hoped he would support suffrage in return, Paul planned to send a message by working *against* his reelection.

The National American Woman Suffrage Association didn't support her approach. The leadership saw Wilson as sympathetic to suffrage, even if he wasn't ready to move on the issue quite yet. This left the suffragists divided over political strategy. As a result, in 1914 the women's suffrage movement once again split into two political groups—the larger and more conservative NAWSA, run by Carrie Chapman Catt and Anna Howard Shaw (which supported a state-by-state approach to suffrage and stood with Wilson), and the smaller and more radical Congressional Union led by Alice Paul (which favored a federal amendment and held Wilson accountable for his lack of support).

Paul wasted no time putting her plan into action. She hired railroad cars, decorated them with banners, and set out on a whistle-stop campaign dedicated to campaigning *against* twenty Democrats who had supported suffrage, saying that she held these officials accountable for the failure of the amendment.

Her tactics seemed to help: That year the Senate held the first vote on women's suffrage since 1887. The measure failed, but the vote was a small victory in its own right. At last, Congress was at least considering the suffrage question.

That also meant that legislators could be held accountable for their positions. More than a third of the senators abstained from voting. Of those who did vote, only thirty-five voted in favor, well below the required two-thirds majority of sixty-four votes.

Several months later, in January 1915, the House of Representatives considered the Susan B. Anthony Amendment. In the House, the measure fell nearly one hundred votes short of the total needed—with 174 in favor and 204 opposed.

The suffragists had a long way to go. But at least the issue was getting more attention.

THE WINNING PLAN

In 1915, Carrie Chapman Catt took over the leadership of the National American Woman Suffrage Association. The next year, using a different political approach than the Congressional Union,

NAWSA launched what Catt called "the Winning Plan." She didn't tell the membership the details of the plan, but she did promise it would be a "red-hot, never-ceasing campaign."

Essentially, Catt's plan involved simultaneously going after both state and federal measures, working for progress wherever it could be found. Her plan involved addressing the needs of each state. In states that already had female suffrage, the emphasis would be on support for a federal amendment. In states considering suffrage, the emphasis would be on winning voting rights, either full suffrage (freedom to vote in all elections) or partial suffrage (the right to vote in local elections, school boards, or presidential primaries). Catt believed that her plan would result in full female suffrage in less than six years.

In 1916, President Woodrow Wilson was running for reelection. He wanted support from the suffragists and welcomed delegations from NAWSA at the White House.

In June, Wilson wrote to Catt and told her that he would encourage the Democratic Party to include a suffrage endorsement in its platform.

Finally, in October 1916, Wilson came out and declared his official support for female suffrage.

The month before, President Wilson had accepted an invitation to speak at NAWSA's annual convention. "I have not come to ask you to be patient, because you have been," he said. He assured the women that they would soon be triumphant. But when Anna Howard Shaw expressed the hope that victory would come in a Wilson administration, he didn't promise anything.

Alice Paul wasn't willing to beg for Wilson's weak support during his reelection campaign. In June 1916, she founded the National Woman's Party, yet another group dedicated to only one issue, female suffrage. (The Congressional Union then fell under the auspices of the National Woman's Party, and the leadership of both groups was the same until the Congressional Union disbanded the following year, leaving the National Woman's Party as Paul's political base.)

"MR. PRESIDENT, HOW LONG MUST WOMEN WAIT FOR LIBERTY?"

After her appearance on horseback leading the 1913 parade, Inez Milholland Boissevain continued to work for women's suffrage. Then, in October 1916, while onstage in Los Angeles at a suffrage event, Boissevain collapsed. The final words she spoke before she dropped were "Mr. President, how long must women wait for liberty?"

A doctor diagnosed severe anemia and infected tonsils. Without the medicines available today to treat infection, her condition rapidly declined. She died on November 25.

Her words became a rallying call for the suffrage movement. President Wilson would hear them many times in the coming years.

Alice Paul recognized the power of the simple phrase, and she often used it in her lobbying campaigns. She became a skilled lobbyist, organizing a system to track members of Congress, using cards to note each legislator's position on suffrage, as well as personal information, such as birthplace, family, opinion of wife and daughters, religion, military service, personal achievements, and anything else that might be of use. She had influential residents of home states send birthday cakes with a suffrage banner and flag to members of the Judiciary Committee; in purple writing on the cake, the message read "May the coming year bring you joy, and the Susan B. Anthony amendment."

In late November, Paul planned a new form of protest. She and the Congressional Union obtained ten tickets to the president's first speech to Congress since his reelection. One of the women in the group wore an oversize brown coat. She looked pregnant, but she was actually smuggling a large banner under her coat. They arrived at the event early and went upstairs to the balcony overlooking the House floor.

During the speech, at a preestablished cue, the women in the front row of the balcony grabbed the satin banner and lowered it over the gallery rail. In bold black lettering, it read, Mr. President, What Will You Do for Woman Suffrage?

During his remarks, Wilson looked up and appeared to read the banner, but he continued with his speech without acknowledging it.

An usher, however, had clearly seen the banner and hurried over to remove it.

The women stayed seated and listened to the rest of Wilson's remarks.

The following day, the newspaper headlines read Suffragists Bother Wilson.

And it would not be the last President Wilson heard from the suffragists.

12 "POWER BELONGS TO GOOD"

The Silent Sentinels

ON THE MORNING OF JANUARY 10, 1917, ALICE PAUL AND eleven other women walked out of the headquarters of the National Woman's Party and started marching in the direction of the White House. Each of the women carried an oversize cloth banner suspended from an eight-foot pole. As they started out, some of the women found the banners unwieldy, but they tightened their grips on the wooden rods and kept moving forward.

The women were bundled in hats, gloves, and ankle-length wool coats topped with striped satin sashes. The marchers stood tall and walked with purpose. They looked just as Paul had intended—unified, respectable, and solidly middle-class.

People walking past wondered what they were up to. Some paused to read the words written on the banners.

The first banner cited Inez Milholland Boissevain's famous words: HOW LONG MUST WOMEN WAIT FOR LIBERTY?

The second banner said MR. PRESIDENT, WHAT WILL YOU DO FOR WOMAN SUFFRAGE?

The other women carried plain cloth panels showing the colors of the American women's suffrage movement: purple, white, and gold.

When they reached the White House, the women divided into two groups of six and headed toward the east and west entrances. As Paul had instructed, the marchers stood next to the gates and held the banners high. Her instructions may have echoed through their minds: "Stand on either side of the two gates with your backs to the wall. If the police interfere with you . . . step from place to place on the sidewalk. . . . Don't come back here until your time is up."

The women didn't smile. They stood statue-like from 9 a.m. to 1 p.m., when another group of women took their places for the second shift, 1 p.m. to 5 p.m.

The women didn't chat with one another or with people walking on the street. Paul understood that their silence would make those who saw them feel uncomfortable. She knew from her Quaker upbringing the power of silence—and discomfort. The women earned the name "the Silent Sentinels."

When passersby asked what they were doing, one member spoke and answered simply and directly that they were marching in support of women's right to vote.

President Woodrow Wilson wasn't in the White House when the protesters first arrived. The day had been unusually mild for January, with temperatures in the mid-fifties, so he had slipped away for an early round of golf. But at 10:40 a.m., he returned.

As his car approached the gates, Wilson stared at the picketers. Although such protests are common today, in 1917 no one had ever picketed the White House before, so he wasn't sure what to do.

As his car pulled through the gate, the president acknowledged the women by tipping his hat in their direction, but he did not smile. The car drove right on by.

The Silent Sentinels gathered in front of the White House. "We always tried to make our lines as beautiful as we could," Paul recalled years later.

BACK AGAIN

The weather in Washington, DC, can be erratic, especially in winter. After a balmy first day of protesting, a bitterly cold wind blew in. On the second day of picketing, the temperature barely reached above freezing.

From the comfort of the White House, President Wilson watched the women standing outside in the cold. He asked the head usher to invite them into the White House for warm coffee or tea.

A few minutes later, the usher returned. "Excuse me, Mr. President," he said, "but they indignantly refused."

Rather than seek refuge from the cold inside the White House, the women paced back and forth on wooden planks to get their feet off the icy-cold sidewalks. They also stood on heated bricks and trapped the warmth under their skirts.

These protests were a change of strategy for Alice Paul and

the suffragists. Since the 1913 procession, they had tried lobbying, meeting with President Wilson, and holding additional parades, but nothing seemed to generate political support for women's suffrage.

Paul had wanted to try another dramatic but nonviolent form of protest. "We can't organize bigger processions . . . We have got to take a new departure. We have got to keep the question before [the president] all the time," argued Harriot Stanton Blatch to the National Woman's Party board when explaining her new idea: the picketing campaign.

Paul immediately loved the idea. She was acutely aware of the symbolism of the Silent Sentinels. Instead of entering the White House—a place of power—Paul wanted the suffragists to stand *outside*, showing that they had been unjustly shut out of the political process.

"Principle is sure to win—injustice and evil have no power back of them for power belongs to good," Paul wrote in a letter to her sister, explaining the campaign. Their message would be clear: The banners would spell it out for Wilson—and everyone else—to see. Paul insisted that the picketing would "visualize the movement to the man and woman on the street."

Not everyone agreed with the approach. Some suffragists favored more militancy, arguing that silence was a sign of weakness, not strength. "I know some people think that it is cowardice and all that sort of thing to take the present attitude," Anna Howard Shaw wrote, "but it requires a good deal more courage to work steadily and steadfastly for forty or fifty years to gain an end, than it does to do a [sic] impulsive rash thing and lose it."

With rare exceptions, the protesters picketed six days a week—every day but Sunday—through rain and snow and summer heat. To show the diversity of their supporters, Paul came up with themes for picketing days, such as Maryland Day, when all the picketers came from Maryland, and other days when the picketers

Suffragists from New York at their posts in the rain

came from a specified college or profession. The National Woman's Party press releases about the themes generated ongoing newspaper coverage about the protests.

During the campaign, almost two thousand women, representing more than half of the states, took turns protesting. They were as young as nineteen and as old as eighty. Many were college-educated and the descendants of Quakers, abolitionists, and other social reformers. Some returned to the picket line regularly. Others joined in only once or twice while on vacation; a few picketed while on their honeymoons. For a time, the picketers were a tourist attraction, and people would ask to hold a banner and pose for a photograph.

Some people on the street supported the protesters by smiling, offering words of encouragement, or bringing them thermoses filled with hot coffee. One Civil War veteran brought the protesters a two-dollar bill. "I am living at the Old Soldier's Home," he said, "and I ain't got much money, but here's something for your campaign."

The suffragists received letters of complaint, as well as the occasional expression of gratitude, sometimes with a donation enclosed. Once, when sifting through the mail, Alice Paul noticed a letter with familiar handwriting on the envelope. She opened it and read: "I wish to make a protest against the methods you are adopting in annoying the President," the letter writer said. "Surely the Cong. Union will not gain converts by such undignified actions. I hope thee will call it off." The letter was from her mother.

Paul would have preferred her mother's support, but she had been raised to think for herself and to work for social justice. She would not back down.

AN INAUGURAL PROTEST

On the day of Woodrow Wilson's second inauguration, March 4, 1917, one thousand protesting women encircled the White House in the biting wind, sleet, and pouring rain. Many of them were in Washington, DC, to attend a convention of the National Woman's Party, but they wanted to show their support for suffrage by marching with the picketers. Despite the harsh weather, the protesters walked around the block in front of the White House four times, a distance of about four miles.

In the days that followed, newspaper reporters covered the suffrage debate. "Before Alice Paul and the pickets came, days would pass when the word suffrage didn't appear in the dispatches," a journalist wrote in the *New York Sun*. "Since their activities, no word occurs more frequently than this."

Some newspapers that initially criticized the picketers came to respect their tenacity and sincerity. After the inaugural protest, the chief Washington correspondent for a news agency wrote this report:

Suffragists continued their protests in the rain during President Woodrow Wilson's second inauguration, on March 4, 1917. This was the first action of Alice Paul's new National Woman's Party, the organization that grew out of the Congressional Union.

During the eighteen years I have been a newspaper correspondent in Washington I have seen no more impressive sight than the spectacle of the pickets surrounding the White House on the afternoon on March fourth. The weather gave this affair its character. Had there been fifteen hundred women carrying banners on a fair day the sight would have been a pretty one. But to see a thousand women—young women, middle-aged women, and old women—and there were women in the line who had passed their three score years and ten— marching in a rain that almost froze as it fell; to see them standing and marching and holding their heavy banners, momentarily growing heavier—holding them against a wind that was half a gale—hour after hour, until their gloves were wet and their clothes soaked through . . . was a sight to impress even the jaded sense of one who has seen much.

CHOOSING WORDS WISELY

The words chosen for the banners were the backbone of the National Woman's Party protest. They needed to convey the right message to the president and the passersby, and to people seeing the photographs in the newspapers. The Silent Sentinels engaged in nonviolent protest: Instead of fighting with weapons, Alice Paul and the National Woman's Party fought with words and images.

A few days after the first banners were introduced, Paul changed them to keep the message fresh:

THE RIGHT OF SELF-GOVERNMENT FOR HALF OF ITS
   PEOPLE IS OF FAR MORE VITAL CONSEQUENCE TO THE
   NATION THAN ANY OR ALL OTHER QUESTIONS.

DEMOCRACY SHOULD BEGIN AT HOME.

RESISTANCE TO TYRANNY IS OBEDIENCE TO GOD.

On Susan B. Anthony's birthday the women carried a banner that read, IN OUR HANDS IS THE POWER TO BRING TO A TRIUMPHANT CONCLUSION THE WORK FOR THE NATIONAL SUFFRAGE AMENDMENT WHICH MISS ANTHONY BEGAN.

On President Abraham Lincoln's birthday, they held up a banner that said, LINCOLN STOOD FOR WOMAN SUFFRAGE SIXTY YEARS AGO—MR. PRESIDENT, YOU BLOCK THE NATIONAL SUFFRAGE AMENDMENT TODAY. WHY ARE YOU BEHIND LINCOLN?

As the picketing expanded, however, some suffragists became more outspoken in their disapproval of the campaign. The leadership of the National American Woman Suffrage Association opposed what they considered to be Alice Paul's daily harassment of the president. "No one can feel worse than I do over the foolishness of their picketing the White House," said Anna Howard

Anna Howard Shaw (left) and Carrie Chapman Catt (right) both served as president of the National American Woman Suffrage Association. In 1900, Catt succeeded Susan B. Anthony as president, but she resigned in 1904, when her husband was ill. Shaw served as president from 1904 to 1915. Catt resumed the presidency in 1915 and served until 1947.

Shaw, former president of NAWSA. The group's current president, Carrie Chapman Catt, agreed, calling the protesters "unwise and unprofitable to the cause."

Conservative suffragists considered picketing rude and unwomanly. An article in the *New American Woman*, a conservative

Suffragists tailored their signs to world events, like the text on this banner: DENMARK ON THE VERGE OF WAR GAVE WOMEN THE VOTE. WHY NOT GIVE IT TO AMERICAN WOMEN NOW.

Women leaving the headquarters of the National Woman's Party ready to march to the White House

suffrage journal, said, "Good ladies, why all this rudeness? Of what avail is all this bombast? Of what combination of gray matter is that which leads gently bred women to violate all conventional rules of polite assemblages? Women of no class nor of any party can ever be excused for thus disporting themselves."

President Wilson was growing tired of the protests, and he asked the press to limit coverage of the protesting suffragists. Editors from the *Washington Times* and *Washington Star* decided that they would "refrain from giving the suffragette ladies any publicity." They would publish short notices of the news, but nothing "to feed their vanity."

The *Washington Post*, however, refused to participate in the press blackout. The public had an ongoing interest in the picketers, they reasoned, and the editors believed that readers had the right to know what was going on.

A VOTE FOR WAR

On April 2, 1917, members of the Sixty-Fifth Congress were sworn in to a special session. Among the legislators who took the oath of

office was Jeannette Rankin of Montana, the first female member
of Congress. On the same day, President Woodrow Wilson asked
Congress to declare war on Germany in the conflict that became
known first as the Great War and then as World War I. The call
to war was no surprise.

Many people were interested in seeing where Rankin stood on
the issue. She was a committed pacifist, but she was receiving pressure from constituents who wanted her to support the president's
call to arms. A few days before the vote, Carrie Chapman Catt and
several other women from the National American Woman Suffrage
Association visited Rankin and urged her to vote for war. They
were fearful that if she voted her conscience she would make women
appear weak, which could compromise the suffrage campaign.

Alice Paul disagreed. The night before the vote, Paul visited
Rankin and encouraged her to vote against the war. "We thought
it would be a tragedy for the first woman ever in Congress to vote
for war," Paul said. She went on to explain her belief that "women
were the peace-loving half of the world and that by giving power
to women we would diminish the possibilities of war."

Rankin didn't tell either side how she was going to vote. She
wasn't sure herself.

At 3 p.m., the roll call vote began on the question of entering
the war. When Rankin's name was called, she did not answer. She
understood both sides of the argument, and she could not force
herself to voice an opinion.

The clerk moved on, but he returned and called her name
again a few minutes later. "Rankin."

She had to vote. This is what she had been elected to do. "I
want to stand by my country, but I cannot vote for war," Rankin
said. Her voice grew quieter: "I vote no."

In the chaos of the chamber, only those sitting closest to her
could hear her. The crowd yelled, "Vote! Vote! Vote!"

JEANNETTE RANKIN (1880–1973) *was the first woman elected to the US Congress. Voters in Montana gave women the right to vote in 1914. After winning in 1916, she said, "I may be the first woman member of Congress, but I won't be the last."*

Jeannette Rankin's portrait, by Sharon Sprung. During her first term in Congress, the Montana legislature changed the boundaries of its voting districts, and Rankin found herself in a politically unfavorable area. Instead of running for reelection to the House, she ran for Senate and lost. She was reelected to the House more than twenty years later, in 1940.

"No!" Rankin called out. She could not vote for what she did not believe. She covered her face with her hands and wept.

The final vote on the measure was 373 in favor, 50 against. The *Helena Independent* called Rankin "a dagger in the hands of the German propagandists, a dupe of the Kaiser . . . a crying school-girl," even though a majority of her constituents opposed the war. Catt considered Rankin's vote an act of cowardice; Paul praised it as an act of courage.

WARTIME PROTEST

Now that the country was at war, suffragists had to decide once again whether to suspend their efforts, as they had been forced to do during the Civil War. The National American Woman Suffrage Association decided to stand with President Woodrow Wilson and back the war effort, hoping that their cooperation would earn Wilson's support of suffrage after the war.

Alice Paul and the other members of the National Woman's Party knew how the suffragists had been treated after the Civil War; they decided to continue picketing. "Our decision to reestablish picketing is prompted by the highest patriotic motives," Paul said, arguing that the most patriotic thing women could do was to fight for inclusion in the democratic process. "In war time a mild conventional appeal for justice will not be heard."

Paul, a pacifist who did not support the war, was cautious not to criticize pro-war suffragists or the war itself. She stuck to the argument that in a democracy, women must have the right to vote, noting that female suffrage "serves the highest interest of the country."

Her mailbox filled with letters from suffrage sympathizers

who objected to picketing during the war. Some said that picketing had become "little less than criminal" and called it the most outrageous of the "foolish, childish methods you have used trying to harass our overburdened president." One woman from Pennsylvania resigned from the National Woman's Party, saying, "I am an American before I am a suffragist."

Carrie Chapman Catt asked Paul to stop the campaign. Catt called the picketing "an unwarranted discourtesy to the President and a futile annoyance" to Congress. She also said it was "hurting our cause," because one congressman had said that he wouldn't vote for suffrage as long as the women picketed.

Catt also issued a public statement to the president pledging NAWSA's support of the war effort and accepting Wilson's invitation to serve on the Woman's Committee of the Council of National Defense.

A CHANGE IN MESSAGE

Alice Paul and the National Woman's Party used the United States' entry into the war to argue that President Woodrow Wilson's support of democracy around the world contradicted his refusal to support full democracy at home. This was the beginning of Paul's most blatant militancy.

"The world must be made safe for democracy," Wilson said in his declaration of war to Congress. "We shall fight for the things which we have always held nearest to our hearts—for democracy, for the right of those who submit to authority to have a voice in their own governments."

Paul and the National Woman's Party picketers put Wilson's words on a banner to remind the American people that the

Curious passersby look at the banners held by the Silent Sentinels.

president had taken the country to war to protect democracy around the world, while American women could not vote.

"It was really a big turning point," Paul said about using Wilson's words against him. "That's when the militancy really began."

THE RUSSIAN BANNER

When the National Woman's Party learned that representatives of the Russian government were going to visit the White House on June 20, 1917, they decided to turn up the heat again.

Around noon that day, Lucy Burns and another suffragist, Dora Lewis, walked over to the White House. They waited until right before the Russian envoy was scheduled to arrive to unfurl their banner. At 12:23 p.m., they revealed it:

To the Russian Envoys: We the Women of America Tell You That America Is Not a Democracy. Twenty Million American Women Are Denied the Right to Vote. President Wilson Is the Chief Opponent of Their National Enfranchisement. Help Us Make This Nation Really Free. Tell Our Government It Must Liberate Its People Before It Can Claim Free Russia as an Ally.

At 12:30 p.m., the diplomats' car drove past the protesters. The Russians may or may not have been able to read the wordy message, written in English, from their moving car. Other people on the street did read the banner, though. "Traitors!" they shouted. "Treason!"

The Silent Sentinels did not respond.

"Why don't you take that banner to Berlin?" one spectator asked.

"You are helping Germany," another bystander said.

A man in a plaid suit and a checked cap called to his friends, "Come on, boys, let's tear that thing down." The man pulled a penknife out of his pocket and slashed the cloth banner off the poles.

Alice Paul had known that the words would inflame the public and get a response. She issued a press release in which she blamed the government for its own embarrassment. "The responsibility . . . ," the press release said, "is with the government and not with the women of America, if the lack of democracy at home weakens government in its fight for democracy three thousand miles away."

The next day, the protesters returned with a duplicate banner. By noon, several thousand people had crowded around the White

House entrance. Then the wife of an army officer spit at the protesters and tore down the banner. She trampled it into the ground.

Paul had crossed a line.

Wilson was ready to push back.

UNDER ARREST

The day after the Russian banner first appeared, the new District of Columbia police superintendent, Raymond W. Pullman, visited Alice Paul. He told her to stop the protests.

"We have picketed for six months without interference," she said. "Has the law been changed?"

"You must stop it," the police superintendent repeated.

"Why? Has picketing suddenly become illegal?" Paul asked. "Certainly it is as legal in June as in January."

"If you do persist in going—and we hope you won't—we have no alternative except to arrest you," the police superintendent said. "These are our instructions."

"Well, I think that we feel that we ought to continue," Paul said, "and I feel that we will continue."

The following day, June 22, 1917, the picketers took their places in front of the White House, just as they had been doing since January. But this time, two picketers—Lucy Burns and Katharine Morey—were arrested and charged with obstructing traffic. The women did not resist arrest.

On June 23, the police superintendent warned Paul again. She politely ignored him. The police arrested four more picketers.

On June 25, the women picketed, and the police arrested twelve more protesters.

Day after day, women walked to the White House carrying

banners, knowing that they would be arrested. The police refused to offer any protection to the protesters, who now were picketing in violation of a government order.

On June 26, Alice Paul and Lucy Burns were carrying a banner that read DEMOCRACY SHOULD BEGIN AT HOME when a group of boys started heckling them. The women ignored the taunts, but the boys eventually snatched the banner away from them and tore it apart. The women did not speak out or defend themselves. Near the National Woman's Party headquarters, a second mob accosted several suffragists carrying banners. Again, the women did not offer resistance.

The police arrested nine suffragists. No one in the mob was arrested or charged with a crime.

By the end of June, twenty-seven women had been arrested for "causing a crowd to gather and thus obstructing traffic." Some were not prosecuted, typically because they were first-time offenders who were issued warnings, but six of the women—including three teachers and a nurse—went to trial.

In court, the suffragists argued that they had refused to stop picketing because their action was legal under the Constitution. They quoted the First Amendment guarantee of "the right of the people peacefully to assemble, and to petition the Government for a redress of grievances." They also cited the Clayton Antitrust Act, passed in 1914, which ensured the rights of citizens and union members to strike, boycott, and picket.

The court agreed with the suffragists' legal arguments. But instead of letting them go, the judge changed the charges and convicted them of "obstructing the highways."

The court fined each of the protesters twenty-five dollars.

The protesters refused to pay. "Not a dollar of your fine shall we pay. To pay a fine would be an admission of guilt," one of the women said. "We are innocent."

The women, who were held for three days, became the first suffragists to go to jail for protesting in support of women's right to vote.

THE FOURTH OF JULY PROTEST

The arrests didn't slow down the campaign. If anything, they encouraged Alice Paul and her allies to stage more provocative protests that attracted larger crowds and led to more arrests. Paul believed that the persecution of nonviolent protesters would help the cause of suffrage.

On July 4, a group of five women left the National Woman's Party headquarters carrying a banner referencing the Declaration of Independence: JUST GOVERNMENTS DERIVE THEIR POWER FROM THE CONSENT OF THE GOVERNED. As the five picketers crossed Pennsylvania Avenue, twenty-nine police officers swept in to arrest them. One of the women arrested, Helena Hill Weed, was wearing a Daughters of the American Revolution pin decorated with bars that represented her fourteen ancestors who had given their lives in the fight. Another group of six protesters, including Lucy Burns, was arrested at the west gate for obstructing traffic.

Paul recognized the symbolic value of women being arrested on the Fourth of July for exercising the rights to seek freedom. The following day, newspapers carried the story, many on the front pages.

When they went to court, the suffragists hung their dirty tattered banners on the wall of the courtroom. All eleven picketers accepted jail sentences rather than paying a fine.

Ten days later, on Bastille Day (France's independence day), sixteen suffragists protested, and all sixteen were arrested for carrying banners that read, LIBERTY, EQUALITY, FRATERNITY, JULY 14, 1789 and MR. PRESIDENT, HOW LONG MUST AMERICAN WOMEN WAIT FOR LIBERTY? One of the women arrested was a descendant of a signer of the Declaration of Independence. Another was a grandmother. This time, the women were sentenced to sixty days in jail. Because some of the women who were arrested were well-connected, the sentence was especially shocking and caused outrage.

Officials worried that the women would become martyrs. So after three days, the government backed down and President Wilson pardoned the protesters. Some of the president's advisors even recommended that he approve suffrage as a war measure so that the protests would stop.

The suffragists didn't want to appear to be cooperating with Wilson. The picketers didn't want to be pardoned by the government for something they didn't believe was a crime. They made new banners that said, WE ASK NOT PARDON FOR OURSELVES, BUT JUSTICE FOR ALL AMERICAN WOMEN.

Helena Hill Weed (1875–1958), a graduate of Vassar College, was a geologist, as well as the daughter of a member of Congress and vice president of the Daughters of the American Revolution. She was also a member of the Congressional Union and the National Woman's Party. She was sentenced to three days in jail for carrying a banner that said JUST GOVERNMENTS DERIVE THEIR POWER FROM THE CONSENT OF THE GOVERNED.

Lucy Burns in a cell at the Occoquan Workhouse. Burns led the picketing demonstrations and served more time in jail than any other suffragist in the United States. She also served four prison terms in England.

In the *Suffragist*, Paul suggested that women might not be arrested for picketing anymore. She was wrong.

The women resumed picketing on July 23. Throughout the summer, protesters circulated from the picket lines to the courtrooms to the jail cells and back to the picket lines.

"KAISER WILSON"

President Wilson responded by changing strategy and no longer arresting the protesters. He ignored them and hoped they would go away.

In late July and early August, fewer spectators gathered to watch the picketers, and the press coverage dropped off. Alice Paul needed to do something bold to recapture the headlines.

On August 10, 1917, she ignited the movement again with a banner she knew would create a stir. The suffragists carried a banner that read, KAISER WILSON, HAVE YOU FORGOTTEN YOUR SYMPATHY WITH THE POOR GERMANS BECAUSE THEY WERE NOT SELF-GOVERNED? 20,000,000 AMERICAN WOMEN ARE NOT SELF-GOVERNED. TAKE THE BEAM OUT OF YOUR OWN EYE.

Suffragist Virginia Arnold

This banner and two similar ones were particularly provocative because the country was at war with Germany. At that time, the anti-German feeling in the United States was so strong that frankfurters were renamed "hot dogs," sauerkraut was called "liberty cabbage," and orchestras refused to play music by the composer Ludwig van Beethoven because he was German. Calling the president of the United States a "kaiser" was an outrage.

The suffragists marched with the Kaiser Wilson banners for six days, and each day the crowds grew more excited and violent. The first day, three sailors dragged Lucy Burns out of the line and into the street, where they shredded her banner. The suffragists then hung the salvaged banner from the second-story balcony of the National Woman's Party headquarters several blocks away.

Several days later, the sailors, still enraged, went to the National Woman's Party headquarters and tore down the Kaiser Wilson banner and an American flag. Later that afternoon, someone fired a bullet through a second-story window. No one was injured, and, despite the assaults, the women returned to picket day after day. Over the course of several days, more than two hundred banners were destroyed.

MORE ARRESTS

On August 17, almost two months after the first round of arrests, the police superintendent again warned Alice Paul that there would be another round of arrests if the protests continued.

The suffragists returned to their posts, and fourteen women, including Lucy Burns, were arrested for carrying banners that said, MR. PRESIDENT, HOW LONG MUST WOMEN BE DENIED A VOICE IN THE GOVERNMENT THAT IS CONSCRIPTING THEIR SONS?

This time they were sentenced to thirty days in the Occoquan Workhouse in rural Virginia.

The protests continued, and so did the arrests.

September 13: Six women were arrested and sentenced to thirty days in the workhouse.

September 22: Four women were arrested and sentenced to thirty days in the workhouse.

October 6: Eleven women were arrested and had their sentences suspended.

October 15: Four women were arrested; two received suspended sentences, and two repeat offenders were sentenced to six months in the workhouse.

October 20: Alice Paul and three other protesters were arrested. Paul had been carrying a banner quoting Wilson: THE TIME HAS COME TO CONQUER OR SUBMIT. FOR US THERE IS BUT ONE CHOICE. WE HAVE MADE IT.

Of the four women, two were sentenced to thirty days in the workhouse. But Paul, who was referred to as the ringleader, and the other woman who had been repeatedly arrested were sentenced to a surprising seven months in jail. It seemed that if the government couldn't control Paul through intimidation, it would try to control her through incarceration.

The day after the police announced that future picketers would be sentenced to up to six months in prison, Alice Paul led the picket line with a banner reading THE TIME HAS COME TO CONQUER OR SUBMIT. FOR US THERE IS BUT ONE CHOICE. WE HAVE MADE IT.

After sentencing, Paul wrote a letter home: "Dear Mother: I have been sentenced today to seven months imprisonment. Please do not worry. It will merely be a delightful rest. With love, Alice."

13

"THIS ORDEAL WAS THE MOST TERRIBLE TORTURE"

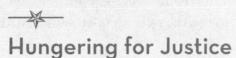

Hungering for Justice

ON OCTOBER 20, 1917, ALICE PAUL WAS ESCORTED FROM a courtroom to the District Jail to begin serving a seven-month sentence for obstructing traffic. She knew what she was getting into, because she had been imprisoned for picketing when she lived in London several years before.

Paul realized that some women weren't cut out for a stay in prison. She always made sure that women understood what to expect when they volunteered for the picket line. Women who picketed might be arrested, and those who were arrested could expect to be mistreated. The women served their time at the Occoquan Workhouse in northern Virginia or the District Jail in Washington, DC. The conditions in both facilities were deplorable.

While in jail, the suffragists slept on blankets that were washed only once a year.

They drank from cups dipped directly into an open pail of dirty water.

They shared a single piece of soap with other prisoners, including those with open sores and diseases such as tuberculosis and syphilis.

They wore scratchy prison uniforms, including one-size-fits-all shoes with interchangeable right and left feet.

They had to use the toilet in open stalls in front of male prison guards.

They were often denied access to toothbrushes, combs, and toilet paper.

The food was disgusting. A typical meal consisted of raw salt pork, bread, and soup, and sometimes molasses. Once, the suffragists were served ginger cakes with a dead fly and a piece of newspaper cooked inside. A cook at the workhouse signed an affidavit testifying that "the beans, hominy, rice, corn meal . . . and cereal have all had worms in them. Sometimes the worms float on top of the soup. Often they are found in the corn bread." At one point, the women held a contest among tables to see how many

Suffragist Pauline Adams of Norfolk, Virginia, in the prison garb she wore during a sixty-day sentence. By the fall of 1917, more than 500 suffragists had been arrested and 168 had spent time in jail, most for "obstructing sidewalk traffic."

worms they could find in their food. When one table counted fifteen, the women lost interest in the game—and their meals.

One of the jailed suffragists complained that the workhouse "was full of rats. I minded them more than anything else. I can still hear them squealing and fighting, and the sound they made as they fell from the table to the floor and scurried away."

Because of the harsh conditions, some husbands refused to allow their wives to go to jail, and paid the fines instead. Many others supported their wives' decisions. One woman's husband recovering from a stroke still told his wife he could get along without her while she went to jail.

THE POWER OF NONVIOLENCE

Alice Paul believed that the suffering of the protesters would not be in vain. She had faith that this assertive but peaceful protest would help women win the federal suffrage amendment in the shortest time possible. Nonviolence would overpower violence; justice would win.

Paul knew that the treatment the women received in jail would create a public relations crisis for President Wilson, even in wartime. Letters to Wilson supporting the suffragists already far outnumbered those supporting the president's position. Many of those who took the time to write accused the government of violating the suffragists' right to free speech.

Many newspapers also published articles and editorials supporting the protesters. Belle Case La Follette praised the National Woman's Party in *La Follette's Weekly*, a magazine started by her husband, Senator Robert La Follette. She wrote that the picketers had neither violated the law nor committed violence. Paul's nonviolent protest appeared to be turning the tide.

HUNGER STRIKE

From the moment she arrived at the District Jail, Alice Paul asked for political prisoner status. She and the other suffragists argued that they were being jailed because they had opposed the government and not because they had blocked traffic or stood too long on the sidewalks or city streets.

Her jailers ignored her request.

Paul responded by going on a hunger strike. She was tiny and thin, but she was mentally strong and determined. She wanted the world to know that she was willing to give her life for suffrage.

Some of the jailers and custodians were sympathetic, which allowed the women to pass notes from cell to cell. Word about the hunger strike spread to the other women behind bars, and soon thirty other inmates from the District Jail and the Occoquan Workhouse joined the effort.

To break their resolve, the warden at the Occoquan Workhouse tried to tempt the hunger strikers by serving them fried chicken and fresh salad.

In response, Lucy Burns wrote a note to the other suffragists: "I think this riotous feast which has just passed our doors is the last effort of the institution to dislodge all of us who can be dislodged. They think there is nothing in our souls above fried chicken."

The women still refused to eat.

The warden and officials in President Woodrow Wilson's administration didn't want to be held responsible for the illness or death of Paul or any of the other hunger strikers. So after several days, the warden ordered force-feedings.

During the procedure, three or four prison guards pinned the women down and forced their heads back. A doctor, James Alonzo Gannon, then shoved a hard feeding tube down their throats and poured in a concoction of two raw eggs mixed with a pint of

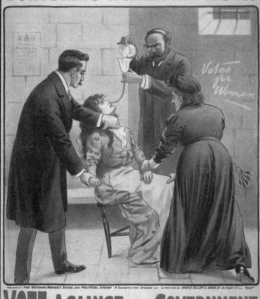

This poster from the National Women's Social and Political Union in England shows the force-feeding of a British suffragette. The practice was introduced in the fall of 1909 after the female prisoners went on a hunger strike.

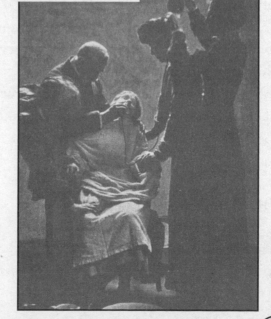

A suffragist being force-fed using a nasal tube. The official term for the practice was "gavage."

ice-cold milk. The feedings were repeated three times a day.

Some of the women wrote accounts of the force-feedings, which were smuggled out of the jail by visitors. These statements horrified the public. "Dr. Gannon . . . forced the tube through my lips and down my throat, I gasping and suffocating with the agony of it," Dora Lewis wrote. "I didn't know where to breathe from, and everything turned black when the liquid began pouring in."

Rose Winslow, another of the hunger strikers, smuggled a statement out of the jail with a prisoner who was being released. "Yesterday was a bad day for me in feeding," she wrote. "I was vomiting continuously during the process. . . . Don't let them tell you we take this well. Miss Paul vomits much. I do too. It's the nervous reaction, and I can't control it much. We think of the coming feeding all day. It is horrible."

Lucy Burns had experienced force-feeding in England, so she knew what to expect. With five people holding her down, she was able to fight off all attempts to force the tube into her mouth and down her throat. Instead, the doctor inserted the tube through her left nostril.

Burns described the feeding tube in clinical, almost impersonal terms: "It hurts nose and throat very much and makes nose bleed freely. Tube drawn out covered with blood. Operation leaves one very sick. Food dumped directly into stomach feels like a ball of lead. Left nostril, throat, and muscles of neck very sore all night."

THE PSYCHIATRIC WARD

The warden threatened that if Alice Paul did not end her hunger strike she would be transferred to Saint Elizabeth's Insane Asylum.

Paul refused to eat.

Prison officials moved her to solitary confinement and treated her like a psychiatric patient while they decided what to do with her next. She was not allowed to communicate with family, friends, or her lawyer.

"There were two windows in the room," Paul later recalled. "Dr. Gannon immediately ordered one window nailed from top to bottom. He then ordered the door leading into the hallway taken down and an iron-barred door put in its place. He departed with the command to a nurse to 'observe her.'"

Every three hours through the night, a nurse interrupted Paul by shining a flashlight in her face. "This ordeal was the most terrible torture," she said, "as it prevented my sleeping for more than a few minutes at a time."

When the superintendent of Saint Elizabeth's, Dr. William White, went to Paul's cell to evaluate her mental health, she was expecting the worst. But instead, he was kind. "Please talk," he said. "Tell me about suffrage; why you have opposed the president; the whole history of your campaign; why you picket; what you hope to accomplish by it."

"Indeed I'll talk," Paul said. She presented a thoughtful and coherent lecture about suffrage, unaware that the question was intended to test her sanity.

The doctor determined that Paul was not mentally ill, and he refused to allow her to be transferred to his facility. This was a very lucky break for Alice Paul. In the early twentieth century, husbands and doctors had the right to have their wives and patients held in psychiatric wards for indefinite periods, sometimes confined by straitjackets and leg irons. Too often this was used to force women to submit, rather than to address their underlying mental health issues.

Paul was transferred back to the regular part of the jail to serve out her sentence.

THE NIGHT OF TERROR

Alice Paul's fellow suffragists were distraught about how she was being treated. Three weeks into her sentence, more than forty women, ranging in age from nineteen to seventy-three, protested Paul's treatment by marching through the streets of Washington, DC.

The police arrested the women, then let them go with a warning.

The following day, most of the women returned to the picket line. This time the police arrested thirty-five protesters, who were sentenced to between six days and six months, depending on whether they had been arrested previously.

The judge sentenced the suffragists to the District Jail, but the police took them to the Occoquan Workhouse, because the prison officials didn't want to let the women near Paul, who was held in the jail.

When they arrived at the workhouse, the women refused to give their names until they saw Raymond Whittaker, the superintendent.

The Occoquan Workhouse In Lorton, Virginia, was built in 1910 and closed in 2001. It was designed to house low-risk inmates in dormitory complexes rather than cell blocks. The brick buildings were constructed by prisoners themselves, using bricks made on site. In 2008 it was converted into a cultural arts center.

Suffragists marched in defense of Alice Paul while she was being held at the District Jail. Paul was willing—even eager—to share the well-publicized indignities suffered by the suffragists who had been imprisoned. She also wanted to prove to the women she led that she was willing to suffer for the cause.

"You'll sit here all night," the matron said.

"We will await his return," Dora Lewis said. The women sat down to wait.

Several hours later, a stocky man burst through the door. "He has stiff white hair, blazing little eyes, and a dull purple birthmark on the side of his face," recalled one of the suffragists.

"Mr. Whittaker," Lewis said, standing. "I am authorized by my companions to say that we wish to be treated as political prisoners."

"Shut up," Whittaker said. "Sit down."

Lewis tried to speak, but Whittaker interrupted. "Take her," he said to two of the guards.

The guards stood on either side of Lewis and pulled her out of the room—"like a dressmaker's dummy," one of the women later recalled.

Whittaker then ordered the guards to remove the other women. As one of the protesters was being dragged out of the room, her bag caught on the arm of a chair. The guard thought the woman was resisting, so he twisted her wrist and yanked her forward. "I felt that I was in the midst of a football scrimmage. . . . My feet were completely off the floor, my arms and shoulders were almost twisted out of joint and my back was bruised," the woman said. "One man's hand was at my throat." Fortunately, the handle of the purse tore and she was free.

In what became known as the "Night of Terror," the women were taken across a grassy yard to the men's prison, where they were placed in individual cells. "The dungeon I was in was very filthy," said one of the protesters. "Tobacco spit on the floor and all along the side of the filthy bunk; dirty horse blankets, open dirty toilet, no water, dark and damp. I was so cold my teeth chattered all night. Superintendent Whittaker ran up and down the corridor screaming to the guards to bring the handcuffs, straight jackets and gags."

One of the inmates, Mary Nolan, a frail seventy-three-year-old woman from Jacksonville, Florida, walked with a limp. She called to the guards, "I'll come with you; don't drag me." They pulled her down the steps and shoved her into a cell. She landed on the bed.

A second inmate, Alice Cosu, was thrown into the same room and smashed against a stone wall.

One of the guards yelled, "Damned Suffrager! My mother ain't no Suffrager! I will put you through hell!"

One by one, the other cells were filled.

Dora Lewis had been left by herself while the other women were taken to their cells.

"Are you going to give your name or not?" Whittaker asked her, raising a clenched fist.

"No," she said. The guards came and hauled her out of the room.

Mary Nolan and Alice Cosu watched as a guard opened the

door and another threw Dora Lewis's limp body onto a mattress on the floor. The women thought that Lewis was dead.

They called for help, but no one listened.

A moment later, Lewis revived and told them she was okay. She did not know why she had lost consciousness.

Whittaker came to the cell and threatened to gag the women if they weren't quiet.

That night, Lewis shivered with cold, but Cosu began vomiting and complaining of chest pain. The women worried that she was having a heart attack. It took two hours for anyone to come and take Cosu to the prison hospital.

As one of the leaders, Lucy Burns, called roll to check on the other women, Whittaker warned her to shut up, but Burns didn't listen. She wanted to make sure all of the women were okay.

A moment later, one of the guards appeared and handcuffed Burns's wrists together and fastened them to the cell door above her head. She had to stay in that position for several hours, until an elderly guard released her arms. In the morning, her wrists were bruised and swollen.

After the Night of Terror, several dozen other women joined with Alice Paul in her hunger strike to protest their unfair and intolerable treatment.

BACK IN COURT

President Woodrow Wilson sent a representative to the prison to find out what was happening. The man assumed the president wanted to hear good news, so that's what he reported. Wilson certainly must have known that the women were being treated harshly, but he could now deny that he knew they were being abused.

While the women waited in jail, the National Woman's Party

lawyers filed a writ of habeas corpus, which would require the government to bring the inmates to court and explain why some of the women were in the Occoquan Workhouse when they had been sentenced to the District Jail.

The women had their day in court on November 23, 1917. When the inmates entered the courtroom, reporters and family members were shocked at how thin and haggard they appeared. Some could barely walk; some were so weak that they had to lie down on the benches with their coats tucked under their heads for pillows. Some were still bruised and battered from the Night of Terror almost two weeks before.

The judge immediately released the women who were considered too frail to continue to serve their sentences. The others were moved to an abandoned jail.

When they returned to jail, many of the women continued with their hunger strike. To undermine their effort, one of the district commissioners ordered the warden to install two gas stoves

The abandoned jail near the District Jail, where the picketers were confined during a long hunger strike

near the women's cells and to hire six women to cook ham and bacon twenty-four hours a day.

"I kept those cooks busy day and night frying ham," Commissioner Louis Brownlow recalled. "I was convinced that the fragrance of frying ham was the greatest stimulus to appetite known to man. It was terribly hard on the women."

The women did not eat.

President Wilson had a nightmare on his hands. Newspapers covered the story of the suffragists day after day. The *New York Times* published regular updates on Alice Paul's condition, as well as the full text of a statement from her that had been smuggled out of the prison. In it, Paul described how two of three windows in her cell had been nailed shut. She said that Dr. Gannon seemed "determined to deprive [her] of air" because she had complained about the stale air when asking to be recognized as a political prisoner. She also noted that she and the other suffragists had been deprived of letters, books, visitors, and decent food.

A November 7, 1917, *New York Times* article quoted Paul's physician as saying that she "was refusing food, and would not touch a morsel until she and her companions received the same treatment as seventeen murderers [in the same facility], who have the privilege of special food, air, exercise, and the newspapers."

The prisoners had become martyrs.

At that point, the Wilson administration changed its approach: It let the suffragists out of jail.

On November 27, most of the suffrage protesters, including Paul, were suddenly released from their cells. Paul had spent five weeks in jail; she had been on a hunger strike for twenty-two days.

She immediately issued a press release that detailed what had happened to the suffragists while they were in prison. She also argued that their sudden release proved that their sentences had

On December 9, 1917, the National Woman's Party hosted a dinner honoring the eighty-nine women who had served time in the District Jail or the Occoquan Workhouse. Each of them was awarded a small sterling silver pin that was a replica of a cell door with a heart-shaped lock. The "Jailed for Freedom" pin was designed by artist Nina Evans Allender.

been unjust. "We are put out of jail as we were put in it—at the whim of the government," she said.

CONGRESS CONSIDERS SUFFRAGE

On January 9, 1918, President Woodrow Wilson gave a speech to Congress offering his support for women's suffrage, describing it as a war measure. He met with a dozen important Democrats and urged them to support the Susan B. Anthony Amendment. He also released a statement saying that he "frankly and earnestly" supported the amendment "as an act of right and justice to the women of the country and of the world."

The next day—exactly one year after the first picketers took their posts outside the gates to the White House—the House of Representatives gathered to vote on the amendment that would give women the right to vote in national elections.

Everyone knew the vote was going to be close, so many legislators made extraordinary efforts to be on hand to cast their ballots. Representative Thetus Sims of Tennessee had broken his arm and shoulder by slipping on ice several days earlier, but he refused to seek medical care until he cast his vote in favor of the amendment. Representative James R. Mann of Illinois came from his hospital bed in Baltimore, where he had been for six months, so that he could vote yes. Representative Henry Barnhart of Indiana was carried in on a stretcher from a Washington, DC, hospital after an appendectomy; he stayed just long enough to vote. Representative Frederick C. Hicks of New York left his dying wife's bedside to that he could vote yes; she was said to have been an ardent suffragist, and it was a way he could pay his respects to her. After the vote, he went home to her funeral.

The amendment passed in the House by a vote of 274 to 136, exactly the needed two-thirds majority. The suffragists present cheered and waved handkerchiefs. The House floor was so chaotic that the roll call was repeated three times to be sure of its accuracy.

For the amendment to be sent to the states for ratification, however, both houses of Congress had to approve it by a two-thirds majority. Now it was up to the US Senate.

For more than eight months, the Senate refused to vote. Then on September 30, 1918, Wilson pressured the anti-suffrage Democrats to support the measure. "We have made partners of the women in this war," he said in an address to the Senate. "Shall

WOODROW WILSON (1856–1924) *was the twenty-eighth president of the United States. In a speech before Congress on September 30, 1918, Wilson said, "This war [World War I] could not have been fought . . . if it had not been for the services of the women. . . . We shall not only be distrusted but shall deserve to be distrusted if we do not enfranchise them."*

we admit them only to a partnership of suffering and sacrifice and toil, and not to a partnership of privilege and right?" During the war, five million men had left their jobs and joined the military, leaving women to fill those vacant jobs and raise their children as well.

Finally, on October 1, 1918, the Senate voted, 34 to 62, two votes short of the required two-thirds majority. The bill had been defeated.

WATCHFIRES FOR FREEDOM

After Congress failed to pass the amendment, Alice Paul turned up the heat on her campaign and changed her tactics yet again. The suffragists would still carry protest banners, but they would also burn copies of President Wilson's speeches in front of the White House, symbolically destroying his declarations of democracy. They called the fires "Watchfires for Freedom."

Even though Wilson had spoken out in favor of suffrage, the National Woman's Party continued to hold him, as the nation's leader, responsible for the failure of the measure. On December 16, 1918, three hundred women marched down to Lafayette Square in Washington, DC, dropped pages of Wilson's speeches into a cauldron there, and set them on fire. According to an account written in the *Suffragist*, they burned "all the words he has ever uttered or written on the subject of democracy."

On January 1, 1919, the suffragists began a new "watchfire" protest in front of the White House. "We had a sort of perpetual flame going in an urn . . . ," Alice Paul said, describing it. "It was really very dramatic, because when President Wilson went to Paris for the peace conference [to set the terms among countries at the end of World War I], he was always issuing some wonderful, idealistic

Suffragists guard a bonfire on the sidewalk in front of the White House. The wood used for the fires came from all over the country, symbolizing the unity of women nationwide. Spectators sometimes overturned the urns and trampled on the ashes, but the women relit the fires.

statement that was impossible to reconcile with what he was doing at home. And we had an enormous bell . . . and every time Wilson would make one of these speeches, we would toll this great bell, and then somebody would go outside with the President's speech and, with great dignity, burn it in our little caldron."

Arrests began again, as the suffragists expected. This time the women were charged with "congregating in the park," "holding a meeting without a permit," or "building a bonfire on a public highway between sunrise and sunset." The judge issued shorter sentences—ten to fifteen days—so that hunger strikes wouldn't be an issue.

A month later, Congress had another chance to take up the bill. So on the afternoon on February 9, 1919—the day before the Senate planned to consider the amendment—nearly forty suffragists marched to the White House. President Wilson was in Europe.

This time, the angry suffragists burned not only Wilson's words but also a straw-stuffed figure about two feet tall meant to represent the president. When they put the "little figure" into the urn, the crowd erupted. A suffragist from Tennessee said, "We burn not the effigy of the President of a free people, but the leader of an autocratic party organization whose tyrannical power holds millions of women in political slavery."

Almost forty of the one hundred participants were arrested and taken to court, where the judge began sentencing the women to the District Jail. But after hearing twenty-six of the cases, the judge grew weary and gave up on the process, freeing the women who had not yet been tried.

Paul's watchfire campaign didn't work. The Senate voted on the suffrage amendment on February 10, and it failed to pass again, but this time by only a single vote.

A QUIET RESOLUTION

After the February defeat, Alice Paul and the suffragists continued to protest, but not as consistently or flamboyantly. However, President Wilson knew that if the bill did not pass early in the next session, the suffrage protests would start up again.

On May 19, 1919, the Sixty-Sixth Congress was called into session. The president was again in France for a peace conference, but he took time out to cable a message to the new Congress encouraging support of the suffrage amendment, among other measures.

On May 21, 1919, the new House passed the suffrage amendment by a vote of 304 to 89, more than the required two-thirds.

On June 4, 1919, with little debate, the Senate passed the amendment by a vote of 56 to 25, two more votes than necessary.

The suffragists in the chamber broke into applause that lasted two minutes.

This time, the suffragists had predicted victory. Paul did not attend the final vote, because she had already gone on to Minnesota to start the state ratification campaign. When she heard the news, she wrote to her supporters. "Women who have taken part in the long struggle for freedom feel today the full relief of victory," she said. "Freedom has come not as a gift but as a triumph."

The final wording of the amendment was exactly the same as it was when it was defeated in 1878: "The right of citizens of the United States to vote shall not be denied or abridged by the United States or by any State on account of sex."

President Wilson telegrammed Carrie Chapman Catt to congratulate her; he did not contact Alice Paul. Catt had remained dedicated to traditional lobbying—privately meeting with legislators and the president to persuade them to support suffrage—whereas Paul's campaign had been designed to humiliate the president.

While an enormous hurdle had been cleared, the suffragists knew their work was not done: Before the amendment would become law, three-fourths of the states needed to ratify it.

14

"DON'T FORGET TO BE A GOOD BOY"

The Battle for Ratification

THE SUFFRAGISTS DIDN'T EXPECT THE RATIFICATION OF the Nineteenth Amendment to be easy. It wasn't supposed to be. The system had been designed to make changes to the Constitution possible but difficult, requiring both houses of Congress to pass any amendment with a two-thirds majority vote, after which three-fourths of the states must approve—or ratify—it. In 1919, there were forty-eight states in the union, meaning the approval of thirty-six states was required for ratification.

The suffragists were ready. The National American Woman Suffrage Association, led by Carrie Chapman Catt, had about two million women and men eager to work for the amendment, and Alice Paul's National Woman's Party had about fifty thousand more. These energetic volunteers knew their state legislators and the local issues, so they knew how to maximize their influence.

Of course, the antis—those who opposed women's suffrage— were gearing up for a fight, too. They were especially powerful in the South, where many people didn't support female suffrage.

Some considered the federal amendment a challenge to states' rights to make their own choices and laws, and others worried that expanding African American suffrage to include women could threaten white political control.

The antis used the same arguments they had used all along: Suffrage would destroy the home; it was "unwomanly"; mothers would neglect their children, and wives would divorce their husbands over political disagreements. "I honor women too highly to allow them to descend into the dirty pool of politics," one anti politician said. An anti-suffrage leaflet warned, A VOTE FOR FEDERAL SUFFRAGE IS A VOTE FOR ORGANIZED FEMALE NAGGING FOREVER.

GETTING STARTED

The suffragists started their state ratification campaigns by reaching out to governors and urging them to consider the amendment. Their timing couldn't have been worse. Most state legislatures were out of session, and some met biannually and would not gather until the following year, unless the governor called a special legislative session.

The suffragists didn't want to lose momentum. They wanted women to be able to vote in the 1920 presidential election. They also knew that the country would probably become more conservative in the years following the end of the war.

The antis knew that, too. They believed that if they stalled until after the November elections, the suffrage "fad" would probably lose steam.

So the suffragists turned ratification into a race. Wisconsin won by voting for the amendment on June 10, 1919, less than a week after Congress had passed it. Illinois was second, and Michigan

Each time a state ratified the 19th Amendment, Alice Paul sewed a star on the purple, white, and gold "ratification banner" she kept at the National Woman's Party headquarters.

third. Eleven more states ratified the amendment quickly. And then things slowed down.

By the spring of 1920, thirty-five states had ratified the 19th Amendment, and eight states—Georgia, Alabama, South Carolina, Virginia, Maryland, Mississippi, Louisiana, and Delaware—had voted against ratification.

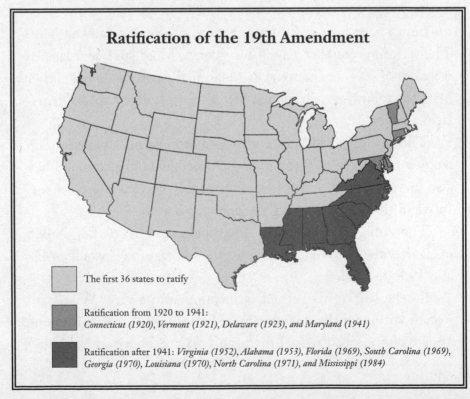

Ratification of the 19th Amendment

The first 36 states to ratify

Ratification from 1920 to 1941: *Connecticut (1920), Vermont (1921), Delaware (1923), and Maryland (1941)*

Ratification after 1941: *Virginia (1952), Alabama (1953), Florida (1969), South Carolina (1969), Georgia (1970), Louisiana (1970), North Carolina (1971), and Mississippi (1984)*

Just one more state was needed for ratification, but the suffragists were running out of possibilities. Only seven states had not yet voted on the issue, and most of these were in the Deep South, where the suffragists knew they didn't stand a chance of winning. Eventually, Tennessee emerged as the most likely battleground.

Tennessee's governor, Albert H. Roberts, was up for reelection, and he knew that supporting suffrage would cost him votes in a tight election. On the other hand, he was a Democrat, and he was getting pressure from the party to support ratification. After receiving a telegram from President Woodrow Wilson urging him to support the amendment, he agreed to call a special legislative session, but he planned to wait until August, after the state's Democratic party primary.

"WE NOW HAVE 35½ STATES"

At noon on Monday, August 9, 1920, the Tennessee legislature opened a special session. Both the state house and the state senate had to ratify. Governor Roberts spoke in favor of the amendment. "Tennessee occupies a pivotal position and the eyes of all America are upon us," he said. "Millions of women are looking to this Legislature to give them a voice and share in shaping the destiny of the Republic."

The leadership of the state senate agreed with the governor. Its committee on constitutional amendments recommended adoption. "National woman's suffrage is at hand," a committee report stated. "It may be delayed but it cannot be defeated, and we covet for Tennessee the signal honor of being the thirty-sixth and last State necessary to consummate this great reform." On August 13, after a number of long speeches, the Senate approved ratification of the Nineteenth Amendment by a vote of 25 to 4.

"We now have 35½ states," Catt wrote to a friend. "We are up to our last half of a state."

The final battle was going to be the most difficult. Politicians who had opposed suffrage in North Carolina urged members of Tennessee's House of Representatives to fight suffrage "to the last ditch, and then some." A journalist described the special legislative session as "the bitterest, bare-fisted, name-calling, back-biting session in the state's history." Suffragists called the showdown in Tennessee "Armageddon."

For five days, members of the Tennessee House debated the question. The Speaker of the House opposed suffrage, but he had promised to be fair to the suffragists. He lied: He did everything possible to block ratification, and he tried to time the vote to ensure its defeat.

Because it was clear that the vote would be very close, parties on both sides worked to influence the vote. But when Carrie Chapman Catt went to Nashville to lobby the legislators, the antis treated her as an outside agitator.

Catt later said that she had never before experienced the unfair tactics she witnessed in Tennessee. "Never in the history of politics has there been such a nefarious lobby as labored to block the ratification in Nashville," she wrote. "They appropriated our telegrams, tapped our telephones, listened outside our windows and transoms. . . . Even if we win, we who have been here will never remember it with anything but a shudder."

In addition to spying, Catt accused the antis of "buying" votes. Joe Hanover, a pro-suffrage legislator from Memphis, said he was approached by another lawmaker who told him, "Sorry, Joe, but I'm going to have to leave you suffrage boys. The antis just paid me three hundred dollars."

"Well, you're a cheap vote," Hanover said. "I hear they're paying the others a thousand."

The pro-suffrage lobbyists used a more subtle approach. They were accused of flirting with lawmakers as they invited them to garden parties, parades, and pro-suffrage dinners to earn their support.

Neither side was confident that they had the votes to win.

The night before the decision, the suffragists met in Catt's hotel room to discuss strategy. "There is one more thing we can do—only one," she said. "We can pray."

THE FINAL VOTE

On August 18, 1920, members of the Tennessee House of Representatives gathered in their chamber to vote on the ratification of the Nineteenth Amendment.

It was too close to call. No one knew how the final tally would go. Win or lose, everyone knew the vote would make history. As a result, some legislators made herculean efforts to cast their ballots.

"The hour has come," Speaker of the House Seth Walker said. The roll call began.

When the votes were counted, there was a tie: 48 for ratification, 48 against. The legislators had to vote again.

One by one, the clerk called the names of the legislators a second time. The seventh congressman to vote was Harry Burn, twenty-four, the youngest member of the legislature. He represented a solidly anti-suffrage district in the mountains of Tennessee, and in the first round, his vote had been a nay.

What no one but Burn knew at the time was that he had a letter in his pocket from his mother, Febb Burn, a suffrage advocate. She was an educated woman who read four newspapers a day. "Hurrah and vote for Suffrage," she had said in her seven-page letter, "and don't keep them in doubt. . . . I've been watching to see how you stood but have not seen anything yet. . . . Don't forget to be a good boy, and help Mrs. 'Thomas Catt' with her 'Rats.' Is she the one that put rat in ratification. Ha! . . . With lots of love, Mama."

The Speaker of the House called Burn's name a second time.

"Aye," he answered.

The final tally: 49 for, 47 against. Tennessee had ratified the Nineteenth Amendment, which would now become part of the US Constitution. The suffragists screamed and waved their banners and tossed yellow flowers. Some wept.

Burn rushed out of the chamber to escape opponents who wanted to beat him up. He hurried upstairs and hid in the attic until the crowds left and he could slip home safely.

The antis called Burn a "traitor to manhood's honor." Anti-suffrage newspapers accused him of having been bribed. They claimed he had been paid $10,000 to change his vote.

Burn wanted to explain his change of heart, so the next day he inserted a personal statement into the *House Journal*. He said he voted in favor of ratification "first, because I believe in full suffrage as a right; second, I believe we had a moral and legal right to ratify; third, I knew that a mother's advice is always safest for a boy to follow, and my mother wanted me to vote for ratification; fourth, I appreciated the fact that an opportunity such as seldom comes to a mortal man to free seventeen million women from political slavery was mine; fifth, I desired that my party in both state and nation might say that it was a Republican from the mountains of East Tennessee . . . who made national woman suffrage possible on this date, not for personal glory but for the glory of his party."

When Burn next went back to his hometown to visit his constituents, he had a bodyguard, but it turned out that wasn't necessary. In fact, he was elected to a second term.

Years later, he said, "It was a logical attitude from my standpoint. My mother was a college woman, a student of national and

Febb Ensminger Burn, Harry Burn's mother, who wrote to her son encouraging him to support the Nineteenth Amendment

Harry Burn on a campaign poster in 1918. He served in the Tennessee House of Representatives from 1918 to 1922 and in the state senate from 1948 to 1952.

Your Vote and Influence Solicited

HARRY T. BURN

NIOTA, TENNESSEE

Republican Nominee for Representative
Election Tuesday, November 5th, 1918

to fix for school. She
wants you here to
go with her.
Write mother every
time you have a
chance, for I am always
looking for a letter
when you are away.
Dont forget to be a
good boy, and help
Mrs "Thomas Catt"
with her "Rats."
Is she the one that
put "Rat" in ratification
Ha' no more from
mama This time
With lots of love, mama.
(over)

Page six of the letter Febb Burn wrote to her son

Alice Paul sewed the thirty-sixth star on the suffrage banner and displayed it on the balcony of the National Woman's Party headquarters when Tennessee became the thirty-sixth state to ratify the amendment on August 18, 1920.

international affairs who took an interest in all public issues. She could not vote. Yet the tenant farmers on our farm, some of whom were illiterate, could vote. . . . I had to vote for ratification."

The opponents of suffrage in Tennessee challenged the vote. For several days, Tennessee officials tried to use technicalities to overthrow the decision. Antis harassed the legislators in an attempt to get them to change their votes. Two representatives complained that they "were called up every half hour day and night so that they had no sleep." Another was threatened with the loss of his teaching job. Still, all of the pro-suffrage legislators held strong.

Then a county judge issued a five-day restraining order forbidding the governor from certifying the result.

Governor Roberts ignored the order. On August 24, he signed the ratification certificate and sent it by registered mail to Washington, DC.

The signed document arrived at the residence of Secretary of State Bainbridge Colby at 3:45 a.m. on August 26. Colby reviewed

Alice Paul raises a glass in celebration of the ratification of the Nineteenth Amendment.

the documents and asked his assistant to meet him at his home as soon as possible.

At 8 a.m., he signed a proclamation adding the women's suffrage amendment to the US Constitution. He didn't use a special pen or make any kind of statements or declarations. The only witness present was his assistant as the Nineteenth Amendment officially became law.

A FINAL SNUB

At 8 a.m., Alice Paul received a call telling her to go to the State Department. She thought she was going to witness the official signing of the Nineteenth Amendment. She waited several hours at the State Department before learning that Secretary of State Bainbridge Colby had already signed the document. She and Carrie Chapman Catt had been arguing about how to handle the signing, so Colby had decided to avoid the issue by not allowing either side to attend.

Paul asked if he would re-create the signing for movie cameras to document the historic event, but Colby refused. He told her to go home and return with other suffragists for photographs later that afternoon.

But when Paul returned at the designated time, Carrie

Chapman Catt was leaving Colby's office with a photographer. It appeared that Colby had planned to meet with the women's groups separately. Paul waited in the hallway of the State Department to be seen by Colby, but the appointment was delayed by a visit from the Spanish ambassador.

Paul waited.

And waited. Others from the National Woman's Party gave up and went home, and after hours waiting in the corridor, Paul left, too.

The lack of courtesy was not lost on Paul and her associates. The slight had been a way of punishing her for her militancy and her refusal to adhere to the more moderate approach of the National American Woman Suffrage Association. She had not made friends within the Wilson administration.

Abby Scott Baker, an officer of the National Woman's Party, called the signing "quite tragic." "This was the final culmination of the women's fight," she said, "and women, irrespective of factions, should have been allowed to be present when the proclamation was signed."

President Wilson did not even send a message of congratulations to Alice Paul. He did, however, send word to Catt, who shared his words on behalf of suffrage at a celebratory party that night. He had said, "I deem it one of the greatest honors of my life that this great event [the ratification of this amendment] should have occurred during the period of my administration."

THE SINGLE LINK

Carrie Chapman Catt accepted the president's congratulations, but she recognized the cost of the accomplishment. She had tallied NAWSA's efforts over the years: Since the 1848 Seneca Falls

Convention, there had been 480 campaigns in state legislatures, 56 state referendums, 47 attempts to add suffrage to state constitutions, and 19 biannual campaigns to 19 different Congresses. "To get the word male out of the Constitution cost the women of the country . . . years of pauseless campaigning," she later wrote. "It was a continuous, seemingly endless chain of activity. Young suffragists who helped forge the last links of that chain were not born when it began. Old suffragists who forged the first links were dead when it ended."

In fact, there *was* a single link that unified the suffrage movement's past and present. One woman, Charlotte Woodward Pierce, signed the Declaration of Sentiments in 1848 and lived long enough to see the ratification of the Nineteenth Amendment in 1920. Pierce was about nineteen years old when she attended the first women's rights convention at Seneca Falls, and she was ninety-one when she became eligible to vote for the first time.

Unfortunately, Pierce never made it to the polls. She was sick and bedridden on Election Day, November 2, 1920. Shortly after that, she lost her eyesight and couldn't leave home. "I'm too old," she said. "I'm afraid I'll never vote." There is no record that she ever did.

Pierce had remained an active and steadfast suffragist all her life. She had worked with the American Woman Suffrage Association, and she knew Susan B. Anthony, calling her "a great and noble woman." Women's suffrage—which had seemed like a radical idea when it was first proposed seventy-two years earlier in central New York—had finally become the law of the land.

Charlotte Woodward was one of the youngest women to attend the 1848 Seneca Falls Convention.

AFTER WINNING THE VOTE

Once suffrage was won, the National American Woman Suffrage Association changed its name and its mission: In 1920, it reestablished itself as the League of Women Voters, a nonpartisan organization dedicated to educating women about political issues. This poster celebrates suffrage and the League of Women Voters.

Alice Paul was thirty-five years old when the Nineteenth Amendment was ratified. She promptly went back to school and earned three degrees in law from the Washington College of Law at American University. She supported the Equal Rights Amendment, proposed in 1923; Congress passed the bill in 1972, but it was never ratified by three-fourths of the states. It read "Equality of rights under the law shall not be denied or abridged by the United States or by any State on account of sex."

The Nineteenth Amendment enfranchised women, but some states quickly moved to deny nonwhite women—and men—the right to vote. Native Americans were not granted the right to vote until the Indian Citizenship Act was passed in 1924. Chinese Americans didn't get the right to vote until 1943. Japanese Americans and other Asian Americans weren't granted the right to vote until 1952. And the voting rights of African Americans in the South were restricted until President Lyndon Johnson signed the Voting Rights Act of 1965.

Hillary Rodham Clinton won the Democratic Party's nomination for president of the United States in 2016.

At the Democratic National Convention in 2016, 102-year-old Jerry Emmett of Prescott, Arizona, announced that the Arizona delegation was casting fifty-one of its eighty-five votes for Hillary Clinton for president. Born before women had the right to vote, she carried a sign that read, CENTENARIAN FOR HILLARY.

IN HER OWN WORDS

KEY PRIMARY SOURCES

This book refers to a number of other books and writings that have proven critical to the suffrage movement and to women's history. The following appendix provides descriptions of these texts, as well as links to the full manuscripts.

A VINDICATION OF THE RIGHTS OF WOMAN (1792)
Mary Wollstonecraft

A Vindication of the Rights of Woman is considered one of the earliest works of feminist philosophy. In the book, Mary Wollstonecraft advocates for educational and social equality for women, arguing that educated women would be better mothers to their children and wives to their husbands.

For the full text, visit: **http://www.gutenberg.org/ebooks/3420**

LETTERS ON THE EQUALITY OF THE SEXES, AND THE CONDITION OF WOMAN (1838)
Sarah Grimké

Sarah Grimké and her sister, Angelina, were abolitionists, suffragists, and women's rights advocates. They were among the first women to engage in public speaking, including addressing audiences of both men and women. Audiences were drawn to them because they had a unique perspective on the slavery issue: They had grown up on a plantation in Charleston, South Carolina, where they witnessed the horrors of slavery. As young adults, the sisters moved to Philadelphia, where they became Quakers and joined the abolitionist movement. Their 1836 writings, *An Appeal to the Christian Women of the South* and *An Epistle to the Clergy of the Southern States*, inspired an anti-slavery movement. Sarah's *Letters on the Equality of the Sexes*, published two years later, advocated female equality of opportunity.

For the full text, visit **https://books.google.com/books/about/Letters_ on_the_Equality_of_the_Sexes_and.html?id=6w0LbHT6Ei0C** or **https:// archive.org/stream/lettersonequalit00grimrich/lettersonequalit00grim- rich_djvu.txt**.

DECLARATION OF SENTIMENTS (1848)
Elizabeth Cady Stanton

The Declaration of Sentiments was the statement of purpose presented at the first women's rights convention, held in Seneca Falls, New York, on July 19, 1848. Elizabeth Cady Stanton wrote the text, assisted by Lucretia Coffin Mott, Martha Coffin Wright, Mary Ann McClintock, and Jane Hunt. The text is modeled on the Declaration of Independence.

Of the original signers, only one—Rhoda Palmer (1816–1919)—ever legally voted; she cast a ballot in 1918 after New York passed female suffrage. A second original signer, Charlotte Woodward Pierce, lived to see the passage of the Nineteenth Amendment, but she was ill and unable to cast her vote in the 1920 election, and she died in 1921.

For the full text and the list of resolutions, see *History of Woman Suffrage*, Vol. 1, by Elizabeth Cady Stanton (Rochester, NY: Fowler and Wells, 1889), 70–71; or visit **https://archive.org/details/historyofwomansu01stanuoft** or **http://www.nps.gov/wori/learn/historyculture/declaration-of- sentiments.htm**.

"AIN'T I A WOMAN?" (1851)
Sojourner Truth

As a slave in New York's Hudson Valley, Sojourner Truth was known as Isabella Baumfree. In 1843, sixteen years after she gained her freedom, she changed her name and began to preach about the abolition of slavery. On May 29, 1851, she delivered a stirring speech at a women's rights convention in Akron, Ohio. The first reports of the speech were published in the *New York Tribune* and the *Liberator* in early June, and a transcript of the speech was published in the *Anti-Slavery Bugle* later that month. The speech became more famous a decade later—in 1863—when Frances Dana Barker Gage published a different version, based on notes she took as president of the Akron convention. The Gage version, often referred to as the "Ain't I a Woman?" speech, is the version referred to most often by historians. Sojourner Truth was illiterate, so she offered no written account of her own.

For more information, see **http://www.sojournertruth.org/Library /Speeches**.

WEDDING VOWS OF LUCY STONE AND HENRY BLACKWELL (1855)

Instead of exchanging traditional wedding vows, abolitionists and social reformers Lucy Stone and Henry Blackwell read a "protest."

For the full text, see *History of Woman Suffrage*, Vol. 1, 260; or visit **http://www.gutenberg.org/ebooks/28020**.

"ARE WOMEN PERSONS?"
Susan B. Anthony's Address after Her Arrest for Illegal Voting (1873)

In 1872, Susan B. Anthony voted in the presidential election in Rochester, New York. She was arrested and charged with voting illegally. In the months she waited for her trial, she spoke out for women's rights.

For the full text of her speeches, see *A History of US Sourcebook and Index: Documents That Shaped the American Nation*, edited by Steven Mintz (New York: Oxford University Press, 2003), 172–173.

NINETEENTH AMENDMENT TO THE UNITED STATES CONSTITUTION (1920)

> *The right of citizens of the United States to vote shall not be denied or abridged by the United States or by any other State on account of sex.*
> *Congress shall have power to enforce this article by appropriate legislation.*

THE SUFFRAGE SISTERS
A TIMELINE

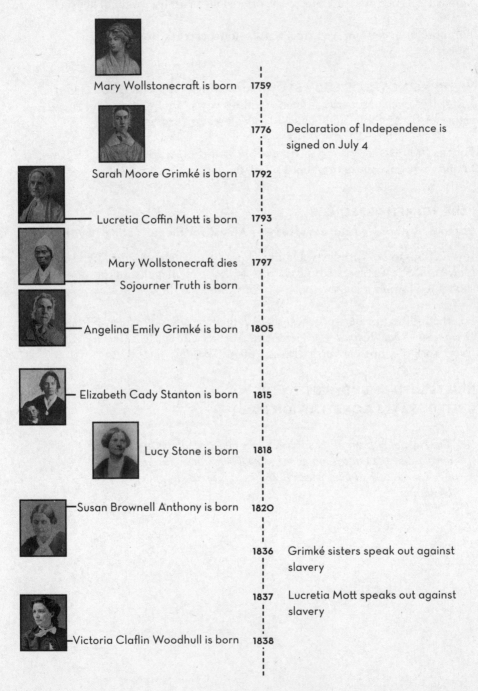

Mary Wollstonecraft is born **1759**

1776 Declaration of Independence is signed on July 4

Sarah Moore Grimké is born **1792**

Lucretia Coffin Mott is born **1793**

Mary Wollstonecraft dies **1797**

Sojourner Truth is born

Angelina Emily Grimké is born **1805**

Elizabeth Cady Stanton is born **1815**

Lucy Stone is born **1818**

Susan Brownell Anthony is born **1820**

1836 Grimké sisters speak out against slavery

1837 Lucretia Mott speaks out against slavery

Victoria Claflin Woodhull is born **1838**

1840	Elizabeth Cady Stanton meets Lucretia Mott at the World Anti-Slavery Convention in London
1848	First women's rights convention, Seneca Falls, New York
1851	Amelia Bloomer publishes articles about dress reform
	Sojourner Truth makes her "Ain't I a Woman?" speech in Ohio

Harriot Eaton Stanton Blatch is born — 1856

— Alice Stone Blackwell is born — 1857

— Carrie Chapman Catt is born — 1859

1861	American Civil War begins

— Ida Bell Wells-Barnett is born — 1862

1865	American Civil War ends
1868	Congress passes Fourteenth Amendment, which introduces the word "male" into the Constitution
1869	National Woman Suffrage Association and American Woman Suffrage Association are founded
	Wyoming is the first state or territory to grant women the right to vote

	1872	Victoria Woodhull is nominated for president of the United States
Sarah Moore Grimké dies	**1873**	Susan B. Anthony stands trial for illegally voting in the presidential election
	1878	Susan B. Anthony writes a women's suffrage constitutional amendment
Angelina Emily Grimké dies Lucy Burns is born	**1879**	Frances Willard becomes president of the Woman's Christian Temperance Union
Lucretia Coffin Mott dies	**1880**	
Sojourner Truth dies	**1883**	
Alice Paul is born	**1885**	
Inez Milholland Boissevain is born	**1886**	
	1890	Suffrage groups merge to create National American Woman Suffrage Association
Lucy Stone dies	**1893**	
	1895	Elizabeth Cady Stanton publishes *The Woman's Bible*
	1900	Carrie Chapman Catt and Anna Howard Shaw emerge as leaders of the suffrage movement
Elizabeth Cady Stanton dies	**1902**	

Susan Brownell Anthony dies	**1906**	
	1913	Alice Paul and Lucy Burns organize the Congressional Union
		Suffrage procession is held in Washington, DC
Inez Milholland Boissevain dies	**1916**	Jeannette Rankin of Montana becomes the first woman elected to the US House of Representatives
	1917	The United States enters World War I; Alice Paul begins to picket the White House
	1918	The Nineteenth Amendment passes the US House or Representatives but fails in the Senate
Anna Howard Shaw dies	**1919**	The Nineteenth Amendment passes the House and the Senate
	1920	The Nineteenth Amendment is ratified by the states
Victoria Claflin Woodhull dies	**1927**	
Ida Bell Wells-Barnett dies	**1931**	
Harriot Eaton Stanton Blatch dies	**1940**	
Carrie Chapman Catt dies	**1947**	
Alice Stone Blackwell dies	**1950**	
Lucy Burns dies	**1966**	
Alice Paul dies	**1977**	

BIBLIOGRAPHY

BOOKS

Adams, Katherine H., and Michael L. Keene. *Alice Paul and the American Suffrage Campaign*. Urbana: University of Illinois Press, 2008.

Armitage, Susan, and Elizabeth Jameson. *The Women's West*. Norman: University of Oklahoma Press, 1987.

Bacon, Margaret Hope. *Valiant Friend: The Life of Lucretia Mott*. Philadelphia: Friends General Conference, 1999.

Baker, Jean H. *Sisters: The Lives of America's Suffragists*. New York: Hill and Wang, 2005.

Bausum, Ann. *With Courage and Cloth: Winning the Fight for a Woman's Right to Vote*. Washington, DC: National Geographic, 2004.

Benjamin, Anne Myra. *Women Against Equality: The Anti-Suffrage Movement in the United States from 1895 to 1920*. Lulu Publishing Services, 2014.

Bordin, Ruth. *Frances Willard: A Biography*. Chapel Hill: University of North Carolina Press, 1986.

Brody, Miriam. *Victoria Woodhull: Free Spirit for Women's Rights*. New York: Oxford University Press, 2003.

Bryant, Jennifer Fisher. *Lucretia Mott: A Guiding Light*. Grand Rapids, MI: Eerdmans, 1996.

Burgan, Michael. *The 19th Amendment*. Minneapolis: Compass Point, 2006.

Cahill, Bernadette. *Alice Paul, the National Woman's Party and the Vote: The First Civil Rights Struggle of the 20th Century*. Jefferson, NC: McFarland, 2015.

Clift, Eleanor. *Founding Sisters and the Nineteenth Amendment*. Hoboken, NJ: John Wiley, 2003.

Colman, Penny. *Elizabeth Cady Stanton and Susan B. Anthony: A Friendship That Changed the World*. New York: Henry Holt, 2011.

DuBois, Ellen Carol. *Harriot Stanton Blatch and the Winning of Woman Suffrage.* New Haven, CT: Yale University Press, 1997.

DuBois, Ellen Carol, and Richard Cándida Smith. *Elizabeth Cady Stanton, Feminist as Thinker: A Reader in Documents and Essays.* New York: New York University Press, 2007.

Dudden, Faye E. *Fighting Chance: The Struggle Over Woman Suffrage and Black Suffrage in Reconstruction America.* New York: Oxford University Press, 2011.

Dumbeck, Kristina. *Leaders of Women's Suffrage.* San Diego: Lucent Books, 2000.

Flexner, Eleanor, and Ellen Fitzpatrick. *Century of Struggle: The Woman's Rights Movement in the United States.* Cambridge, MA: Belknap Press of Harvard University Press, 1996.

Foner, Philip S., and Yuval Taylor, eds. *Frederick Douglass: Selected Speeches and Writings.* Chicago: Chicago Review Press, 1999.

Fradin, Dennis Brindell, and Judith Bloom Fradin. *Ida B. Wells: Mother of the Civil Rights Movement.* New York: Clarion, 2000.

Giddings, Paula J. *Ida: A Sword Among Lions.* New York: Amistad, 2008.

Ginzberg, Lori D. *Elizabeth Cady Stanton: An American Life.* New York: Hill and Wang, 2009.

Goodier, Susan. *No Votes for Women: The New York State Anti-Suffrage Movement.* Chicago: University of Illinois Press, 2013.

Griffith, Elisabeth. *In Her Own Right: The Life of Elizabeth Cady Stanton.* New York: Oxford University Press, 1984.

Grimké, Sarah. *Letters on the Equality of the Sexes, and the Condition of Woman.* Boston: Isaac Knapp, 1838.

Havelin, Kate. *Victoria Woodhull: Fearless Feminist.* Minneapolis: Twenty-First Century Books, 2007.

Hollihan, Kerrie Logan. *Rightfully Ours: How Women Won the Vote.* Chicago: Chicago Review Press, 2012.

Hull, N. E. H. *The Woman Who Dared to Vote: The Trial of Susan B. Anthony.* Lawrence: University Press of Kansas, 2012.

Keller, Kristin Thoennes. *Carrie Chapman Catt: A Voice for Women.* Minneapolis: Compass Point, 2006.

Lumsden, Linda J. *Rampant Women: Suffragists and the Right of Assembly.* Knoxville: University of Tennessee Press, 1997.

Lunardini, Christine. *Alice Paul: Equality for Women.* Boulder: Westview Press, 2013.

McMillen, Sally G. *Lucy Stone: An Unapologetic Life.* New York: Oxford University Press, 2015.

———. *Seneca Falls and the Origins of the Women's Rights Movement.* New York: Oxford University Press, 2008.

Mintz, Steven, ed. *A History of US Sourcebook and Index: Documents That Shaped the American Nation.* New York: Oxford University Press, 2003.

Monroe, Judy. *The Nineteenth Amendment: Women's Right to Vote*. New York: Enslow, 1998.

Myers, Walter Dean. *Ida B. Wells: Let the Truth Be Told*. New York: Amistad, 2008.

Naden, Corinne J. *Jeannette Rankin*. New York: Cavendish Square, 2014.

Riley, Glenda. *The Female Frontier: A Comparative View of Women on the Prairie and the Plains*. Lawrence: University Press of Kansas, 1988.

Ruth, Janice E., and Evelyn Sinclair. *Women of the Suffrage Movement: Women Who Dare*. Petaluma, CA: Pomegranate Communications, 2006.

Sherr, Lynn. *Failure Is Impossible: Susan B. Anthony in Her Own Words*. New York: Times Books, 1995.

Stanton, Elizabeth Cady. *Eighty Years and More: Reminiscences 1815–1897*. New York: European Publishing, 1898; CreateSpace, 2015. (Also available online: **http://digital.library.upenn.edu/women/stanton/years/years.html.**)

———. *The Woman's Bible*. With foreword by Maureen Fitzgerald. Boston: Northeastern University Press, 1993.

Stanton, Elizabeth Cady, et al. *History of Woman Suffrage, Vol. 3, 1876–1885*. Rochester, NY: Charles Mann, 1886.

Sterling, Dorothy. *Lucretia Mott*. New York: Feminist Press, 1999.

Terrell, Mary Church. *A Colored Woman in a White World*. With foreword by Debra Newman Ham. Amherst, NY: Humanity Books, 2005.

Tetrault, Lisa. *The Myth of Seneca Falls: Memory and the Women's Suffrage Movement, 1848–1898*. Chapel Hill: University of North Carolina Press, 2014.

Underhill, Lois Beachy. *The Woman Who Ran for President: The Many Lives of Victoria Woodhull*. Bridgehampton, NY: Bridge Works, 1995.

Van Voris, Jacqueline. *Carrie Chapman Catt: A Public Life*. New York: Feminist Press, 1987.

Walton, Mary. *A Woman's Crusade: Alice Paul and the Battle for the Ballot*. New York: Palgrave Macmillan, 2010.

Ward, Geoffrey C., and Ken Burns. *Not for Ourselves Alone: The Story of Elizabeth Cady Stanton and Susan B. Anthony*. New York: Knopf, 1999.

Weatherford, Doris. *A History of the American Suffragist Movement*. New York: MTM, 2005.

Wells, Ida B. *Ida B. Wells: The Light of Truth, Writings of an Anti-Lynching Crusader*. Edited by Henry Louis Gates Jr. New York: Penguin Classics, 2014.

Wheeler, Marjorie Spruill, ed. *One Woman, One Vote: Rediscovering the Woman Suffrage Movement*. Troutdale, OR: NewSage Press, 1995.

Wollstonecraft, Mary. *A Vindication of the Rights of Woman*. London: Joseph Johnson, 1792; New York: Dover, 1996.

Zahniser, J. D., and Amelia Fry. *Alice Paul: Claiming Power*. New York: Oxford University Press, 2014.

The following historical documents can be read online at **http://books.google.com, www.gutenberg.org**, or **www.archive.org**.

A Vindication of the Rights of Woman by Mary Wollstonecraft (1792)
An Account of the Proceedings on the Trial of Susan B. Anthony, on the Charge of Illegal Voting, at the Presidential Election in Nov., 1872 (1874)
History of Woman Suffrage by Elizabeth Cady Stanton, Susan B. Anthony, Matilda Joslyn Gage, and others (1881)
"The Solitude of Self" by Elizabeth Cady Stanton (1892)
The Life and Work of Susan B. Anthony by Ida Husted Harper (1898)
The Woman's Bible by Elizabeth Cady Stanton (1895 and 1898)
Eighty Years and More by Elizabeth Cady Stanton (1898)
Elizabeth Cady Stanton as Revealed in Her Letters, Diary, and Reminiscences, edited by Theodore Stanton and Harriot Stanton Blatch (1922)

FILMS

Burns, Ken, and Paul Barnes. *Not for Ourselves Alone: The Story of Elizabeth Cady Stanton and Susan B. Anthony*. PBS, 1999.
Iron Jawed Angels. HBO, 2004.
"One Woman, One Vote." *American Experience*. Narrated by Susan Sarandon. PBS, 1995.

MANUSCRIPT COLLECTIONS

Cambridge, MA
    Schlesinger Library, Radcliffe Institute
    Alice Paul Papers
    Anna Howard Shaw Papers
Chicago, IL
    Regenstein Library, University of Chicago
    Ida B. Wells Papers
Evanston, IL
    Willard Memorial Library
    Frances Willard Diaries
    National Woman's Christian Temperance Union Papers
Indianapolis, IN
    Institute for American Thought
    Frederick Douglass Papers
New Brunswick, NJ
    Rutgers University
    Elizabeth Cady Stanton and Susan B. Anthony Papers Project
Swarthmore, PA
    Friends Historical Library, Swarthmore College
    Mott Manuscript Collection

Washington, DC
    Library of Congress
        Carrie Chapman Catt Papers
        Frederick Douglass Papers
        National American Woman Suffrage Association Records
        National Woman Suffrage Association Collection
        National Woman's Party Papers
        Susan B. Anthony Papers

WEBSITES
Alice Paul Institute
    www.alicepaul.org
Susan B. Anthony Center: History of Women's Suffrage
    www.rochester.edu/sba/suffrage-history
Elizabeth Cady Stanton and Susan B. Anthony Papers Project
    http://ecssba.rutgers.edu
Jeannette Rankin Peace Center
    www.jrpc.org
National Women's History Project
    http://nwhp.org
Victoria Woodhull: The Spirit to Run the White House
    www.victoria-woodhull.com

PLACES OF INTEREST
Women's Rights National Historical Park
Visitor's Center, Elizabeth Cady Stanton House,
    and Wesleyan Chapel
www.nps.gov/wori
136 Fall Street, Seneca Falls, NY 13148
(315) 568-0024

National Susan B. Anthony Museum & House
www.susanbanthonyhouse.org
17 Madison Street, Rochester, NY 14608
(585) 235-6124

Frances Willard House Museum & Archives
www.franceswillardhouse.org
1730 Chicago Avenue, Evanston IL 60201
(847) 328-7500

NOTES

PREFACE
"Aye"

"The hour has come," Marjorie Spruill Wheeler, ed., *One Woman, One Vote: Rediscovering the Woman Suffrage Movement* (Troutdale, OR: NewSage Press, 1995), 346.

CHAPTER 1:
"Oh, my daughter, I wish you were a boy!":
Before Seneca Falls

"A young man of great talent and promise . . ." Elizabeth Cady Stanton, *Eighty Years and More: Reminiscences 1815–1897* (CreateSpace, 2015), 20.
"Oh, my daughter, I wish you were a boy!" Ibid.
"I will try to be all my brother was," Ibid., 21.
"Then and there I resolved . . ." Ibid.
"All that day and far into the night . . ." Ibid.
"Why, girls, to be sure . . ." Ibid.
"For months afterward, at the twilight hour . . ." Ibid., 22.
"At last the frosts and storms . . ." Ibid.
"Tell my father how fast I get on," Ibid.
"I taxed every power . . ." Ibid.
"Now, my father will be satisfied . . ." Ibid., 23.
"There, I got it!" Ibid.
"You should have been a boy!" Ibid.
"A conservative's conservative," Geoffrey C. Ward and Ken Burns, *Not for Ourselves Alone: The Story of Elizabeth Cady Stanton and Susan B. Anthony* (New York: Knopf, 1999), 12.
"Though gentle and tender . . ." Stanton, *Eighty Years and More*, 3.
"Tall, queenly looking woman . . ." Ibid.

"I heard so many friends remark . . ." Ibid., 4.

"When you are grown up . . ." Ibid., 32.

"I could take them back and lock them up . . ." Ibid.

"Nothing pleased me better than a long argument . . ." Ibid., 48.

"I soon noticed that . . ." Ibid.

"How to keep house and make puddings," Ward and Burns, *Not for Ourselves Alone*, 15.

"The thought of a school . . ." Stanton, *Eighty Years and More*, 35.

"I had already studied . . ." Ibid.

"The large house . . ." Ibid., 36.

"A terrifier of human souls," Ibid., 41.

"Fear of the judgment . . ." Ibid., 43.

"I often at night roused my father . . ." Ibid.

"Religious superstition gave place to rational ideas . . ." Ward and Burns, *Not for Ourselves Alone*, 17.

"Here one was sure to meet . . ." Stanton, *Eighty Years and More*, 52.

"The rousing arguments . . ." Penny Colman, *Elizabeth Cady Stanton and Susan B. Anthony: A Friendship That Changed the World* (New York: Henry Holt, 2011), 18.

"An atmosphere of love . . ." Stanton, *Eighty Years and More*, 52–53.

"I have a most important secret to tell you . . ." Ibid., 62.

"Harriet, I have brought . . ." Ibid.

"She will start this evening . . ." Ibid.

"The details of her story . . ." Ibid., 63.

"We needed no further education . . ." Ibid.

"Intolerably offensive," Colman, *Elizabeth Cady Stanton*, 22.

"I ask no favors . . ." Grimké, *Letters on the Equality of the Sexes, and the Condition of Woman*, 10.

"Why, my dear brothers . . ." Eleanor Flexner and Ellen Fitzpatrick, *Century of Struggle: The Woman's Rights Movement in the United States* (Cambridge, MA: Belknap Press of Harvard University Press, 1996), 44.

"I had become interested . . ." Stanton, *Eighty Years and More*, 59.

"The most eloquent . . ." Ibid., 58.

"As I had a passion for oratory . . ." Ibid.

"The enthusiasm of the people . . ." Ibid., 59.

"What do you say . . ." Ibid.

"It was better to announce . . ." Ibid., 61.

"Mr. Stanton's present business cannot be regarded . . ." Ward and Burns, *Not for Ourselves Alone*, 19–20.

"A tall, fully developed man . . ." Stanton, *Eighty Years and More*, 27.

"He was soon a great favorite in the family . . ." Ibid.

"A season of doubt and conflict," Colman, *Elizabeth Cady Stanton*, 24.

"Heretofore my apprehensions . . ." Stanton, *Eighty Years and More*, 61.

"We did not wish the ocean to roll between us," Ibid., 71.

"Constitutionally unfit for public meetings . . ." Colman, *Elizabeth Cady Stanton*, 33.

"It's interesting that thou should put it that way . . ." Ibid.

"Friends, I suggest . . ." Dorothy Sterling, *Lucretia Mott* (New York: Feminist Press, 1999), 83.

"We shall all be glad . . ." Ibid., 84.

"Ridiculous to call it a World Convention . . ." Jennifer Fisher Bryant, *Lucretia Mott: A Guiding Light* (Grand Rapids, MI: Eerdmans, 1996), 8.

"The ladies' portion of the hall," Colman, *Elizabeth Cady Stanton*, 33.

"After battling so many long years . . ." Stanton, *Eighty Years and More*, 81.

"Humiliation and chagrin," Ward and Burns, *Not for Ourselves Alone*, 30.

"It struck me as very remarkable . . ." Ibid.

"Mrs. Mott was to me . . ." Ibid.

"Independence of the husband and wife . . ." Colman, *Elizabeth Cady Stanton*, 34.

"I sought every opportunity . . ." Ward and Burns, *Not for Ourselves Alone*, 30.

"Felt a newborn sense of dignity and freedom," Colman, *Elizabeth Cady Stanton*, 34.

"Seemed like a being from some larger planet," Doris Weatherford, *A History of the American Suffragist Movement* (New York: MTM, 2005), 22.

"As Mrs. Mott and I walked home . . ." Stanton, *Eighty Years and More*, 82–83.

CHAPTER 2
"All men and women are created equal":
Seneca Falls Convention, 1848

"Lucretia Mott . . ." Sterling, *Lucretia Mott*, 122.

"Dose," Colman, *Elizabeth Cady Stanton*, 36.

"I trusted neither men nor books . . ." Stanton, *Eighty Years and More*, 120–21.

"I had never lived . . ." Colman, *Elizabeth Cady Stanton*, 37.

"All sorts and sizes of meetings . . ." Ibid.

"You believe in woman's capacity . . ." Ibid., 38.

"To keep a house and grounds in good order," Kerrie Logan Hollihan, *Rightfully Ours: How Women Won the Vote* (Chicago: Chicago Review Press, 2012), 20.

"Fully understood the practical difficulties" Colman, *Elizabeth Cady Stanton*, 39.

"I poured out . . . the torrent . . ." Ward and Burns, *Not for Ourselves Alone*, 38.

"Discuss the social, civil and religious . . ." Ann Bausum, *With Courage and*

Cloth: Winning the Fight for a Woman's Right to Vote (Washington, DC: National Geographic, 2004), 18.

"Woman's Rights Convention . . ." Judy Monroe, *The Nineteenth Amendment: Women's Right to Vote* (New York: Enslow, 1998), 9–10.

"All men are created . . . ," Monroe, *The Nineteenth Amendment*, 10.

"Resolved, that it is the duty . . ." Bausum, *With Courage and Cloth*, 18.

"Thou will make us ridiculous . . ." Flexner and Fitzpatrick, *Century of Struggle*, 70.

"Farce," Ward and Burns, *Not for Ourselves Alone*, 40.

"Henry sides with my friends . . ." Jean H. Baker, *Sisters: The Lives of America's Suffragists* (New York: Hill and Wang, 2005), 115.

"The convention will not be as large . . ." Flexner and Fitzpatrick, *Century of Struggle*, 70.

"Felt as helpless and hopeless . . ." Janice E. Ruth and Evelyn Sinclair, *Women of the Suffrage Movement: Women Who Dare* (Petaluma, CA: Pomegranate Communications, 2006), 7.

"I should feel exceedingly diffident . . ." Flexner and Fitzpatrick, *Century of Struggle*, 71.

"We are assembled . . ." Michael Burgan, *The 19th Amendment* (Minneapolis: Compass Point, 2006), 15.

"The power to choose rules . . ." Monroe, *The Nineteenth Amendment*, 12.

"Strange as it my seem . . ." Ward and Burns, *Not for Ourselves Alone*, 41.

"All that distinguishes man . . ." Ibid.

CHAPTER 3
"The right is ours":
Creating a National Suffrage Movement

"The Hen Convention," Eleanor Clift, *Founding Sisters and the Nineteenth Amendment* (Hoboken, NJ: John Wiley, 2003), 13.

"Divorced wives . . ." Ibid.

"A woman is nobody . . ." Ward and Burns, *Not for Ourselves Alone*, 42.

"All the journals from Maine to Texas . . ." Stanton, *Eighty Years and More*, 149.

"So pronounced was the popular voice . . ." Hollihan, *Rightfully Ours*, 26.

"Set the ball in motion," Monroe, *The Nineteenth Amendment*, 13.

"If I had had the slightest . . ." Stanton, *Eighty Years and More*, 149.

"Almost to the condition . . ." Clift, *Founding Sisters*, 15.

"Foolish conduct," Colman, *Elizabeth Cady Stanton*, 49.

"Act in a public capacity," Ibid.

"It will start women thinking . . ." Ward and Burns, *Not for Ourselves Alone*, 42.

"What are we next to do?" Colman, *Elizabeth Cady Stanton*, 49.

"The right is ours . . ." Ibid., 50.

"Sunflower," Ward and Burns, *Not for Ourselves Alone*, 42.

"It will be a glorious day . . ." Colman, *Elizabeth Cady Stanton*, 51.

"Depend upon it . . ." Ibid., 52.

"Not a man was allowed to sit . . ." Weatherford, *History*, 39.

"The legal theory is . . ." Ibid., 40.

"With the air of a queen . . ." Ibid., 50.

"An abolition affair," Ibid.

"Don't let her speak," Ibid., 51.

"Every ear in the house . . ." Ibid.

"Well, children . . ." "Sojourner's Words and Music," Sojourner Truth Memorial, www.sojournertruthmemorial.org/sojourner-truth/her-words/.

"More than one of us with streaming eyes . . ." Weatherford, *History*, 52.

"Some of you have got the spirit . . ." Clift, *Founding Sisters*, 29.

"There she stood . . ." Colman, *Elizabeth Cady Stanton*, 59.

"Intense attraction," Ibid., 60.

"All that is needed . . ." Ibid., 54.

"The sisters were not invited . . ." Ibid., 61.

"I will gladly do all in my power . . ." Ibid.

"Anything from my pen . . ." Ibid.

"Ready to stand alone," Ibid., 62.

"Write to please any one . . ." Ibid.

"A hybrid species, half man and half woman," Ibid., 63.

"I am at length the happy mother . . ." Elisabeth Griffith, *In Her Own Right: The Life of Elizabeth Cady Stanton* (New York: Oxford University Press, 1984), 78.

"Wholly absorbed in a narrow . . ." Colman, *Elizabeth Cady Stanton*, 66.

"Like a captive set free . . ." Ibid., 74.

"Whether their lady friends . . ." Clift, *Founding Sisters*, 20.

"Woman can never develop . . ." Ibid.

"People would stare . . ." Weatherford, *History*, 56.

"I feel no more like a man . . ." Hollihan, *Rightfully Ours*, 25.

"Then you in your agony . . ." Colman, *Elizabeth Cady Stanton*, 65.

"Did not compensate . . ." Ibid., 75.

"The cup of ridicule . . ." Ibid.

"Would modestly permit women . . ." Ibid., 66.

"Do you see at last?" Clift, *Founding Sisters*, 24.

"At last, I see." Ibid.

"You ask me if I am not . . ." Ward and Burns, *Not for Ourselves Alone*, 72.

CHAPTER 4

"In thought and sympathy we were one": A Feminist Friendship

"Why the profession of teacher . . ." Colman, *Elizabeth Cady Stanton*, 69.

"Mr. President . . ." Ibid.

"It seems to me you fail . . ." Ibid.

"Did you ever see . . ." Ibid., 70.

"Grief and indignation," Ibid., 69.

"Woman must have a purse . . ." Ibid., 71.

"I find there is no use . . ." Ibid., 72.

"Most atrocious," Ibid.

"A new code of laws," Ibid., 73.

"A great event," Ibid., 72.

"Unsex every female . . ." Ibid., 74.

"Thus aided, they are enabled . . ." Ward and Burns, *Not for Ourselves Alone*, 75.

"The husband may wear petticoats . . ." Clift, *Founding Sisters*, 33.

"Like flakes of snow," Ibid., 32–33.

"Moved to tears," Griffith, *In Her Own Right*, 82.

"Your first lecture . . ." Ibid., 84.

"I passed through a terrible scourging . . ." Colman, *Elizabeth Cady Stanton*, 73.

"My whole soul . . ." Ibid., 75.

"Were as free," Ibid., 80.

"Not willing that I should write . . ." Ibid., 80.

"Can't thou take thy . . ." Ibid., 76.

"Come here and I will do . . ." Griffith, *In Her Own Right*, 94.

"I forged the thunderbolts . . ." Ibid., 74.

"In thought and sympathy . . ." Clift, *Founding Sisters*, 22–23.

"I'm sure no man could have . . ." Lynn Sherr, *Failure Is Impossible: Susan B. Anthony in Her Own Words* (New York: Times Books, 1995), 6.

"I never felt I could give up . . ." Ibid., 14.

"I thank God every day . . ." Sally G. McMillen, *Lucy Stone: An Unapologetic Life* (New York: Oxford University Press, 2015), 109.

"There was only one will . . ." Hollihan, *Rightfully Ours*, 2.

"It keeps off the sparks," McMillen, *Lucy Stone*, 11.

"Birdlike," Ibid., 77.

"Seeds of truth," Ibid., 82.

"Love me if you can . . ." Baker, *Sisters*, 13.

"I would not have my wife . . ." Ibid., 22.

"I do so love you . . ." Ibid., 23.

"Oh dear! I am sorry it is a girl . . ." Ibid., 1.

"A wife should no more take her husband's name . . ." Clift, *Founding Sisters*, 35.

"Married to Harry Blackwell," Ibid.

"Very happy, that the terrible ordeal . . ." Colman, *Elizabeth Cady Stanton*, 82.

"Imagine me, day in and day out . . ." Ibid.

"For the love of me . . ." Ibid.

"What an infernal set of fools . . ." Ibid., 82–83.

"The lecturing corps," Baker, *Sisters*, 63.

"A reformatory Amazon," Ibid.

"An ungainly hermaphrodite . . ." Ibid.

"I glory in your perseverance . . ." Colman, *Elizabeth Cady Stanton*, 84.

"Ah me!!! Alas!! . . ." Ibid., 85.

"You need expect nothing . . ." Ibid.

"Seemed to take up every particle . . ." Griffith, *In Her Own Right*, 97.

"Where are you? . . ." Colman, *Elizabeth Cady Stanton*, 86–87.

"Upon her bending . . ." Ibid., 88.

"Sacred right," Ibid., 89.

"Set the convention on fire," Ibid.

"Nothing more than legalized prostitution . . ." Ward and Burns, *Not for Ourselves Alone*, 92.

"He is a man and can not put himself . . ." Colman, *Elizabeth Cady Stanton*, 91.

"The desire to please those we admire . . ." Ibid., 90.

"You are not married . . ." Ibid.

"The child belongs by law . . ." Ibid., 92.

"Let us urge you at once . . ." Ibid., 93.

"Don't you know the law of Massachusetts . . ." Ibid., 93–94.

"My child, I think you have done . . ." Ibid., 94.

"No Compromise with Slavery," Ward and Burns, *Not for Ourselves Alone*, 97.

"I have not yet seen one good reason . . ." Colman, *Elizabeth Cady Stanton*, 96.

"All alike say 'Have no convention at this crisis!' . . ." Griffith, *In Her Own Right*, 110.

"We have indulged freely in criticism . . ." Colman, *Elizabeth Cady Stanton*, 97.

CHAPTER 5
"You must be true alike to the women and the negroes": Division in the Suffrage Movement

"Washed every window in the house . . ." Colman, *Elizabeth Cady Stanton*, 98.

"Public work," Ibid., 99.

"To forever blot out slavery . . ." Ibid., 98.

"The country was never so badly . . ." Flexner and Fitzpatrick, *Century of Struggle*, 103.

"The Loyal Women of the Nation," Ibid., 104.

"At this hour the best word . . ." Flexner and Fitzpatrick, *Century of Struggle*, 104.

"There can never be a true peace . . ." Weatherford, *History*, 85.

"There are ladies here . . ." Ibid.

"I rejoice exceedingly . . ." Ibid.

"[The Founding Fathers] said nothing . . ." Ibid., 86.

"One to another . . ." Ibid.

"Many women spoke ably . . ." Ibid.

"Go to the rich, the poor . . ." Colman, *Elizabeth Cady Stanton*, 102.

"These petitions are signed . . ." Ibid., 104.

"When the war-cry was heard . . ." Weatherford, *History*, 91.

"We can no longer . . ." Colman, *Elizabeth Cady Stanton*, 107.

"Feebleness unfitted her . . ." Weatherford, *History*, 89.

"As Abraham Lincoln said . . ." Ward and Burns, *Not for Ourselves Alone*,
     103.

"The aristocracy of sex," Ibid.

"The gate is shut, wholly," Colman, *Elizabeth Cady Stanton*, 108.

"Extend the right of suffrage . . ." Ibid.

"Would have been a wet blanket . . ." Ibid.

"When your granddaughters . . ." Ibid.

"Negro's hour was decidedly . . . " Ibid.

"If that word 'male' be inserted . . ." Ibid., 106.

"I think such a mixture . . ." Ibid.

"Woman's cause is in deep water . . ." Ibid.

"I would sooner cut off . . ." Ward and Burns, *Not for Ourselves Alone*, 104.

"An outrage against women," Baker, *Sisters*, 71.

"If I am responsible for my deeds . . ." Weatherford, *History*, 92.

"You give us a nominal freedom . . ." Ibid.

"I repudiate the idea of expediency . . ." Ibid., 92–93.

"Hold your claims . . ." Ibid., 105.

"Stood with the black man . . ." Ibid.

"Depend on no further help . . ." Ibid.

"When you propose to elevate . . ." Baker, *Sisters*, 71.

"Carried petitions all through . . ." Weatherford, *History*, 94.

"Met a dignified, quaker looking lady . . ." Ibid., 96.

"Reading matter is so very scarce . . ." Ibid.

"There was scarcely . . ." Weatherford, *History*, 97.

"Come to Kansas . . ." Colman, *Elizabeth Cady Stanton*, 120.

"Carry Negro suffrage," Wheeler, *One Woman, One Vote*, 67–68.

"I will give it to you," Flexner and Fitzpatrick, *Century of Struggle*, 144.

"It seems to me . . ." Ward and Burns, *Not for Ourselves Alone*, 110.

"So long as Mr. Train speaks . . ." Wheeler, *One Woman, One Vote*, 68.

"All there is about [Train] . . ." Ibid.

"Men, Their Rights, and Nothing More . . ." Baker, *Sisters*, 72.

"Weekly, not weakly," Ibid.

"Educated suffrage, irrespective . . ." Lori D. Ginzberg, *Elizabeth Cady
     Stanton: An American Life* (New York: Hill and Wang, 2009), 162.

"Venerated," "submitted to her . . ." Weatherford, *History*, 99.

"The morning of the election came . . ." Ibid., 102

"No one thought of trying to buy up . . ." Ibid., 103.

"Not for what it is . . ." Baker, *Sisters*, 72.

"I cannot forgive . . ." Ibid.

"All wise women . . ." Weatherford, *History*, 107.

"I can not shoulder the responsibility . . ." Ibid., 108–9.

"If you will not give the whole loaf . . ." Ibid., 109.

"Shall American statesmen . . ." Lois Beachy Underhill, *The Woman Who Ran for President: The Many Lives of Victoria Woodhull* (Bridgehampton, NY: Bridge Works, 1995), 53–54.

"I must say that I do not see . . ." Ward and Burns, *Not for Ourselves Alone*, 119.

"Is that not all true about black women? Ibid.

"Yes, yes, yes . . ." Ibid.

"Let me tell you that . . ." Ibid.

"If Mr. Douglass had noticed . . ." Ibid.

"It will change . . ." Ibid., 120.

"Mrs. Stanton will, of course, advocate . . ." Ibid.

"Did not believe in allowing . . ." Wheeler, *One Woman, One Vote*, 70.

"There had been so much trouble . . ." Weatherford, *History*, 109.

"I think we need two . . ." Ward and Burns, *Not for Ourselves Alone*, 122–23.

"I hope that you will see . . ." Ibid., 123.

"Saint Lucy," Baker, *Sisters*, 71.

"When I gave away *The Revolution* . . ." Weatherford, *History*, 112.

"My pride for women . . ." Ward and Burns, *Not for Ourselves Alone*, 134.

"Like signing [her] own death warrant," Ibid., 133.

"I feel a great calm sadness . . ." Ibid.

"You know when I drop . . ." Ibid.

CHAPTER 6

"Madam, you are not a citizen": Victoria Woodhull Speaks to Congress

"Worked like a slave," Miriam Brody, *Victoria Woodhull: Free Spirit for Women's Rights* (New York: Oxford University Press, 2003), 12.

"Whipped like a convict," Ibid., 13.

"The Bewitching Brokers," Kate Havelin, *Victoria Woodhull: Fearless Feminist* (Minneapolis: Twenty-First Century Books, 2007), 9.

"Future Presidentess," Brody, *Victoria Woodhull*, 57.

"While others argued . . ." Havelin, *Victoria Woodhull*, 36.

"Women constitute . . ." Underhill, *Woman Who Ran*, 102.

"All persons born or naturalized . . ." Havelin, *Victoria Woodhull*, 43.

"A race comprises all the people . . ." Wheeler, *One Woman, One Vote*, 89.

"In as good style . . ." Brody, *Victoria Woodhull*, 67.

"All the past efforts . . ." Underhill, *Woman Who Ran*, 104.

"Madam, you are not a citizen," Havelin, *Victoria Woodhull*, 43.

"Members of the state," Colman, *Elizabeth Cady Stanton*, 139.

"To secure the natural rights . . ." Wheeler, *One Woman, One Vote*, 90.

"Clearly recognizes the right to vote," Ibid.

"Have another Train affair . . ." Ibid., 74.

"We mean treason . . ." Ward and Burns, *Not for Ourselves Alone*, 140.

"I have asked for equality . . ." Baker, *Sisters*, 127.

"A grand, brave woman . . ." Colman, *Elizabeth Cady Stanton*, 140–41.

"Dr. Woodhull being sick . . ." Havelin, *Victoria Woodhull*, 50.

"Yes, I am a free lover . . ." Wheeler, *One Woman, One Vote*, 91.

"Unlimited freedom of divorce . . ." Brody, *Victoria Woodhull*, 81.

"We have had women . . ." Ward and Burns, *Not for Ourselves Alone*, 140.

"*Only* for the elective franchise . . ." Wheeler, *One Woman, One Vote*, 74.

"I do not believe in any . . ." Ward and Burns, *Not for Ourselves Alone*, 141.

"Mere sail-hoister," Ibid.

"There was never such a foolish muddle . . ." Ibid.

"The time for words has passed . . . " Underhill, *Woman Who Ran*, 4.

"Preach against free love . . ." Ward and Burns, *Not for Ourselves Alone*, 141.

"The Beecher-Tilton Scandal . . ." Underhill, *Woman Who Ran*, 221.

"I have not a shadow of doubt . . ." Havelin, *Victoria Woodhull*, 74.

"'Free love' (whatever it may mean) . . ." Wheeler, *One Woman, One Vote*, 76.

"Current free-love storm," Ibid.

CHAPTER 7
"I have been & gone & done it!!":
Susan B. Anthony Votes for President

"Register Now," N. E. H. Hull, *The Woman Who Dared to Vote: The Trial of Susan B. Anthony* (Lawrence: University Press of Kansas, 2012), 60.

"Seize their rights to go to the polls . . ." Colman, *Elizabeth Cady Stanton*, 147.

"Sue each of [them] personally . . ." Hull, *Woman Who Dared*, page 61.

"I know I can win . . ." Ibid.

"Do you know the penalty . . ." Doug Linder, "The Trial of Susan B. Anthony for Illegal Voting," http://law2.umkc.edu/faculty/projects/ftrials/anthony/sbaaccount.html.

"Citizenship no more carries the right . . ." Ibid.

"What do you say, Marsh?" Hull, *Woman Who Dared*, 63.

"Well, I have been & gone . . ." Ward and Burns, *Not for Ourselves Alone*, 142.

"I sent word to him . . ." Linder, "Trial of Susan B. Anthony."

"What for?" Hull, *Woman Who Dared*, 69.

"Knowingly, wrongfully . . ." Flexner and Fitzpatrick, *Century of Struggle*, 159.

"I am traveling at the expense . . ." Sherr, *Failure Is Impossible*, 108.

"Did you have any doubt . . ." Hull, *Woman Who Dared*, 78.

"You've lost your chance . . ." Linder, "Trial of Susan B. Anthony."

"I could not see a lady . . ." Ibid.

"Is It a Crime for a Citizen of the United States to Vote?" Ibid.

"Friends and Fellow-Citizens . . ." Ibid.

"It was we, the people . . ." Sherr, *Failure Is Impossible*, 110.

"I have just closed a canvass . . ." Ibid., 109.

"The United States on Trial . . ." Ibid.

"A small-brained, pale-faced . . ." Ibid.

"Whatever Miss Anthony's intentions . . ." Linder, "Trial of Susan B. Anthony."

"She is not competent as a witness," Ibid.

"If the same act had been done . . ." Ibid.

"The Fourteenth Amendment gives no right . . ." Ibid.

"Upon this evidence I suppose . . ." Ibid.

"That is a direction no court has power . . ." Sherr, *Failure Is Impossible*, 115.

"Yes, your honor, I have many things to say . . ." Ibid.

"The Court cannot listen . . ." Ibid.

"May it please your honor, I am not arguing . . ." Ibid., 115–16.

"The Court cannot allow . . ." Ibid., 116.

"But your honor will not deny me . . ." Ibid.

"The prisoner must sit down . . ." Ibid.

"All of my prosecutors . . ." Ibid.

"The Court must insist . . ." Ibid.

"Yes, your honor, but by forms . . ." Ibid.

"The Court orders the prisoner to sit down . . ." Ibid., 117.

"When I was brought before your honor . . ." Ibid.

"The prisoner will stand up," Ibid.

"The sentence of the Court . . ." Ibid.

"May it please your honor, I will never pay . . ." Ibid.

"Madam, the Court will not order you committed . . ." Ibid.

"The greatest judicial outrage . . ." Ward and Burns, *Not for Ourselves Alone*, 148.

"Could I have spoken . . ." Linder, "Trial of Susan B. Anthony."

"If it is a mere question . . ." Ibid.

"I stand before you as a convicted criminal," Baker, *Sisters*, 84.

"There never was a trial . . ." Wheeler, *One Woman, One Vote*, 94.

"Membership in a nation . . ." Ward and Burns, *Not for Ourselves Alone*, 149.

CHAPTER 8
"We ask justice, we ask equality": Forward, Step by Step

"Taxation without representation . . ." Ward and Burns, *Not for Ourselves Alone*, 149.

"One half of the citizens . . ." Colman, *Elizabeth Cady Stanton*, 158.

"We protest against this government . . ." Elizabeth Cady Stanton et al., *History of Woman Suffrage, Vol. 3, 1876–1885* (Rochester, NY: Charles Mann, 1886), 4.

"As an historical part of the proceedings . . ." Ibid.

"Run this government for one hundred years . . ." Ibid.

"We propose to celebrate . . ." Ibid.

"Mr. Vice President, we present . . ." Monroe, *The Nineteenth Amendment*, 34.

"Woman has shown equal devotion . . ." Ward and Burns, *Not for Ourselves Alone*, 152–153.

"Men have been faithful in noting . . ." Ibid.

"A perfect prison," Ibid., 154.

"I love to make history . . ." Ibid.

"The right of citizens . . ." Ibid, 155.

"It was with difficulty that . . ." Flexner and Fitzpatrick, *Century of Struggle*, 166.

"The members of Congress always knew . . ." Ward and Burns, *Not for Ourselves Alone*, 156.

"All right, boys . . ." Ibid.

"Surely Mrs. Stanton . . ." Ibid., 159–60.

"The new science of marriage," Ibid., 160.

"Don't you think that the best thing . . ." Ibid.

"I do not believe . . ." Ibid., 161.

"To speak for woman's ballot . . ." Clift, *Founding Sisters*, 66.

"Dazzled by the promise . . ." Ward and Burns, *Not for Ourselves Alone*, 173.

"Love came to me . . ." Philip S. Foner and Yuval Taylor, eds., *Frederick Douglass: Selected Speeches and Writings* (Chicago: Lawrence Hill Books, 1999), 693.

"Complicate or compromise," Colman, *Elizabeth Cady Stanton*, 177.

"I do hope you won't put your foot . . ." Ward and Burns, *Not for Ourselves Alone*, 178.

"The elders were not keen . . ." Ibid., 179.

"When the division was made . . ." Ibid., 183.

"Robust proportion," Ibid., 156.

"That such mental powers," Ibid., 183.

"We are sowing winter wheat . . ." Ibid., 188.

"The best thing I have ever written," Ibid., 189.

"The point I wish plainly . . ." Colman, *Elizabeth Cady Stanton*, 193.

"To Elizabeth Cady Stanton . . ." Ibid., 193–94.

"Church and state . . ." Ibid., 201.

"How can woman's position . . ." Elizabeth Cady Stanton, *The Woman's Bible*, foreword by Maureen Fitzgerald (Boston: Northeastern University Press, 1993), 11.

"Teaches that woman brought sin . . ." Ward and Burns, *Not for Ourselves Alone*, 200.

"So God created man . . ." Ibid.

"If language has any meaning . . ." Stanton, *The Woman's Bible*, 14–15.

"Women have just as good . . ." Colman, *Elizabeth Cady Stanton*, 201.

"Stop hitting poor old St. Paul . . ." Ward and Burns, *Not for Ourselves Alone*, 203.

"This association is non-sectarian . . ." Ibid.

"This resolution . . . will be a vote . . ." Ibid., 203–4

"Much as I desire the suffrage . . ." Ibid., 204.

"Instead of my resigning . . ." Ibid.

"Miss Anthony has one idea . . ." Ibid., 205.

"I fear . . . you may imagine . . ." Colman, *Elizabeth Cady Stanton*, 181.

"A higher sphere, apart from public life," Susan Goodier, *No Votes for Women: The New York State Anti-Suffrage Movement* (Chicago: University of Illinois Press, 2013), 21.

"Marriage is a sacred unity . . ." Elizabeth Cady Stanton et al., *History of Woman Suffrage*, 102.

"Insignificant minority," Colman, *Elizabeth Cady Stanton*, 197.

"Unfitted for the ballot," Ibid.

"Manly," Goodier, *No Votes for Women*, 17.

"Entirely ignored the principle . . ." Ibid., 21.

"These women, who constitute the active members . . ." Anne Myra Benjamin, *Women Against Equality: The Anti-Suffrage Movement in the United States from 1895 to 1920* (Lulu Publishing Services, 2014), 9.

"Massachusetts was the home . . ." Ibid., 10.

"Exaggerated strength," Ibid., 11.

CHAPTER 9
"Failure is impossible!": The Next Generation

"I am not retiring . . ." Sherr, *Failure Is Impossible*, 319.

"The hardships of the last half-century . . ." Colman, *Elizabeth Cady Stanton*, 214.

"Seem to know nothing of . . ." Ibid.

"One's effort must begin . . ." Flexner and Fitzpatrick, *Century of Struggle*, 231.

"In Mrs. Catt, you have my ideal leader . . ." Ward and Burns, *Not for Ourselves Alone*, 205.

"Your president, if you please . . ." Sherr, *Failure Is Impossible*, 321.

"Give it now . . ." Colman, *Elizabeth Cady Stanton*, 215.

"They let the girls in . . ." Ibid., 216.

"We have grown a little apart . . ." Ward and Burns, *Not for Ourselves Alone*, 207.

"Shall I see you again?" Ibid.

"We little dreamed . . ." Ibid., 207–8.

"I placed a table for her . . ." Ibid., 208.

"Mother passed away . . ." Ibid.

"I cannot express myself at all . . ." Ibid.

"The days when the struggle . . ." Colman, *Elizabeth Cady Stanton*, 220.

"To see poor Miss Anthony . . ." Ward and Burns, *Not for Ourselves Alone*, 208.

"It is an awful hush . . ." Ibid.

"I should like to be in my ordinary dress . . ." Ibid.

"Once I was the most hated and reviled . . ." Ibid., 210.

"We have waited . . ." Colman, *Elizabeth Cady Stanton*, 221.

"I shall not be able to come . . ." Ward and Burns, *Not for Ourselves Alone*, 210.

"Hearty good wishes," Ward and Burns, *Not for Ourselves Alone*, 211.

"I wish the men would do something . . ." Sherr, *Failure Is Impossible*, 324.

"There have been also others . . ." Ibid.

"Just think . . ." Ward and Burns, *Not for Ourselves Alone*, 212.

"She suddenly began to utter . . ." Baker, *Sisters*, 92.

"They are still passing before me . . ." Ward and Burns, *Not for Ourselves Alone*, 212.

"The world is profoundly stirred . . ." Sherr, *Failure Is Impossible*, 326.

CHAPTER 10
"Votes for Women": The Second Wave of Suffragists

"There did not seem to be . . ." Bausum, *With Courage and Cloth*, 28.

"As for the suffrage movement . . ." Ibid.

"The infinite patience . . ." Ward and Burns, *Not for Ourselves Alone*, 221.

"I dressed as a working girl . . ." J. D. Zahniser and Amelia Fry, *Alice Paul: Claiming Power* (New York: Oxford University Press, 2014), 48.

"I got my own food . . ." Ibid., 49.

"I thought all my family . . ." Ibid., 1.

"Dear Mamma . . ." Ibid., 71.

"Towards Equality . . ." Christine Lunardini, *Alice Paul: Equality for Women* (Boulder: Westview Press, 2013), 31.

"I attach no particular sanctity . . ." Ibid., 32.

"It seems indeed a far cry . . ." Ibid.

"They seemed in those early days . . ." Bausum, *With Courage and Cloth*, 32.

"Deeds, Not Words," Zahniser and Fry, *Alice Paul*, 66.

"It's totally unsuitable for women . . ." Katherine H. Adams and Michael L. Keene, *Alice Paul and the American Suffrage Campaign* (Urbana: University of Illinois Press, 2008), 80.

"Our right to the Avenue," Mary Walton, *A Woman's Crusade: Alice Paul and the Battle for the Ballot* (New York: Palgrave Macmillan, 2010), 56.

"If the police protection . . ." Ibid., 55.

"We are endeavoring to make the procession . . ." Ibid., 58.

"She's no bigger than a wisp . . ." Ibid., 113–14.

"When you ask her a question . . ." Ibid., 60.

"But she did not do it for me . . ." Ibid., 61.

"Will surely be offensive . . ." Zahniser and Fry, *Alice Paul*, 136.

"Under the suffragette flag . . ." Walton, *Woman's Crusade*, 65.

"The idea that any of the women . . ." Ibid., 67.

CHAPTER 11

"How long must women wait for liberty?": Parades and Protests

"Will refuse to participate . . ." Walton, *Woman's Crusade*, 64.

"Predisposed to side with . . ." Ibid.

"To say nothing whatever about the question," Ibid.

"The suffrage movement stands . . ." Ibid.

"A southern minority . . ." Ibid.

"We have application . . ." Ibid.

"To keep [their] delegation . . ." Paula J. Giddings, *Ida: A Sword Among Lions* (New York: Amistad, 2008), 515.

"We should like to have Mrs. Barnett . . ." Ibid., 516.

"We have come down . . ." Wheeler, *One Woman, One Vote*, 269.

"If the Illinois women do not take a stand . . ." Giddings, *Ida*, 516.

"It is time for Illinois . . ." Ibid.

"I shall not march . . ." Wheeler, *One Woman, One Vote*, 269.

"If I were a colored woman . . ." Ibid.

"There is a difference . . ." Ibid.

"Let anyone say anything . . ." Giddings, *Ida*, 517.

"Suddenly from the crowd . . ." Ibid.

"Horrible howling mob," Walton, *Woman's Crusade*, 74.

"Practically fought their way . . ." Ibid., 78.

"Why don't you go home . . ." Baker, *Sisters*, 185.

"They seemed to be doing . . ." Walton, *Woman's Crusade*, 74–75.

"Just stood by and laughed," Ibid.

"I can do nothing . . ." Ibid, 76.

"There would be nothing like this . . ." Ibid.

"Active and determined . . ." Ibid.

"Where are the people?" Ibid., 74.

"As you ride today . . ." Adams and Keene, 92–93.

"This mistreatment by the police . . ." Walton, *Woman's Crusade*, 79.

"Women were spat upon . . ." Hollihan, *Rightfully Ours*, 97–98.

"Never was I so ashamed . . ." Walton, *Woman's Crusade*, 78.

"[The police] would have taken better . . ." Bausum, *With Courage and Cloth*, 15.

"We exhausted every possible means . . ." Adams and Keene, *Alice Paul*, 97.

"I did my duty," Zahniser and Fry, *Alice Paul*, 162.

"Splendid work," Walton, *Woman's Crusade*, 79.

"While it may seem to you . . ." Ibid.

"An uninterrupted series of indoor . . ." Weatherford, *History*, 198.

"Red-hot, never-ceasing campaign," Bausum, *With Courage and Cloth*, 35.

"I have not come to ask you . . ." Weatherford, *History*, 208.

"Mr. President, how long must women wait . . ." Adams and Keene, *Alice Paul*, 113.

"May the coming year . . ." Ibid., 121.

"Mr. President, what . . ." Walton, *Woman's Crusade*, 143.

"Suffragists bother Wilson," Ibid., 144.

CHAPTER 12
"Power belongs to good": The Silent Sentinels

"How long must women . . ." Bausum, *With Courage and Cloth*, 39.

"Stand on either side of the two gates . . ." Walton, *Woman's Crusade*, 148.

"We always tried to make . . ." Linda J. Lumsden, *Rampant Women: Suffragists and the Right of Assembly* (Knoxville: University of Tennessee Press, 1997), 147.

"Excuse me, Mr. President . . ." Adams and Keene, *Alice Paul*, 162.

"We can't organize bigger processions . . ." Ibid., 159.

"Principle is sure to win," Ibid., 158.

"Visualize the movement . . ." Ibid., 162.

"I know some people . . ." Walton, *Woman's Crusade*, 89.

"I am living . . ." Ibid., 153.

"I wish to make a protest . . ." Ibid., 150.

"Before Alice Paul . . ." Adams and Keene, *Alice Paul*, 163.

"During the eighteen years . . ." Ibid., 166–67.

"The right of self-government . . ." Ibid., 164.

"Democracy should begin . . ." Ibid., 165.

"Resistance to tyranny . . ." Ibid., 164.

"In our hands . . ." Ibid., 164–65.

"Lincoln stood for . . ." Walton, *Woman's Crusade*, 152.

"No one can feel worse . . ." Bausum, *With Courage and Cloth*, 49.

"Unwise and unprofitable . . ." Ibid.

"Good ladies, why all this rudeness?" Adams and Keene, *Alice Paul*, 165.

"Refrain from giving . . ." Ibid., 167.

"We thought it would be . . ." Walton, *Woman's Crusade*, 163.

"Women were the peace-loving . . ." Ibid.

"I may be the first woman member . . ." "Jeannette Rankin," History, Art & Archives, United States House of Representatives, http://history.house.gov/People/Listing/R/RANKIN,-Jeannette-(R000055)/

"I want to stand . . ." Walton, *Woman's Crusade*, 163.

"A dagger in the hands . . ." "Jeannette Rankin," History, Art & Archives.

"Our decision to reestablish picketing . . ." Zahniser and Fry, *Alice Paul*, 264.

"In war time a mild . . ." Adams and Keene, *Alice Paul*, 169.

"Serves the highest interest . . ." Bausum, *With Courage and Cloth*, 41.

"Little less than criminal," Adams and Keene, *Alice Paul*, 171.

"Foolish, childish methods . . ." Ibid.

"I am an American . . ." Zahniser and Fry, *Alice Paul*, 267.

"An unwarranted discourtesy . . ." Ibid., 266.

"The world must be made safe . . ." Adams and Keene, *Alice Paul*, 175.

"It was really a big turning point . . ." Ibid.

"To the Russian envoys . . ." Ibid., 175–76.

"Traitors!" Walton, *Woman's Crusade*, 172.

"Why don't you take . . ." Ibid.

"You are helping Germany," Ibid.

"Come on, boys . . ." Ibid.

"The responsibility . . ." Adams and Keene, *Alice Paul*, 176.

"We have picketed . . ." Bausum, *With Courage and Cloth*, 42.

"Why? Has picketing . . ." Baker, *Sisters*, 216.

"If you do persist . . ." *Adams and Keene*, Alice Paul, 178.

"Well, I think that we feel . . ." Ibid.

"Causing a crowd to gather . . ." Bausum, *With Courage and Cloth*, 42–43.

"The right of the people . . ." Adams and Keene, *Alice Paul*, 179.

"Obstructing the highways . . ." Ibid.

"Not a dollar . . ." Clift, *Founding Sisters*, 131.

"Just governments derive their power . . ." Adams and Keene, *Alice Paul*, 181.

"Liberty, Equality, Fraternity . . ." Ibid., 182.

"We ask not pardon . . ." Ibid., 185.

"Kaiser Wilson . . ." Ibid., 187.

"Mr. President, how long must women be denied . . ." Ibid., 189.

"The time has come . . ." Ibid., 190.

"Dear Mother . . ." Bausum, *With Courage and Cloth*, 47.

CHAPTER 13

"This ordeal was the most terrible torture"
Hungering for Justice

"The beans, hominy, rice . . ." Adams and Keene, *Alice Paul*, 199.

"Obstructing sidewalk traffic," Ibid., 191.

"Was full of rats . . ." Ibid., 199.

"I think this riotous . . ." Clift, *Founding Sisters*, 152.

"Dr. Gannon . . . forced the tube . . ." Adams and Keene, *Alice Paul*, 201.

"Yesterday was a bad day . . ." Ibid.

"It hurts nose and throat . . ." Ibid.

"There were two windows . . ." Ibid., 203.

"This ordeal was the most terrible . . ." Ibid.

"Please talk . . ." Clift, *Founding Sisters*, 147.

"You'll sit here all night . . ." Walton, *Woman's Crusade*, 197.

"He has stiff white hair . . ." Ibid.

"Mr. Whittaker, I am authorized . . ." Ibid., 198.

"Like a dressmaker's dummy," Ibid.

"I felt that I was . . ." Ibid.

"Night of Terror," Adams and Keene, *Alice Paul*, 205.

"The dungeon I was in . . ." Walton, *Woman's Crusade*, 198.

"I'll come with you . . ." Ibid., 199.

"Damned Suffrager! . . ." Clift, *Founding Sisters*, 151.

"Are you going to give your name . . ." Walton, *Woman's Crusade*, 199.

"I kept those . . ." Adams and Keene, *Alice Paul*, 210.

"Determined to deprive [her] of air," Zahniser and Fry, *Alice Paul*, 294.

"Was refusing food . . ." "Miss Alice Paul on Hunger Strike," *New York Times*, November 7, 1917.

"We are put out of jail . . ." Baker, *Sisters*, 220.

"Frankly and earnestly," Adams and Keene, *Alice Paul*, 213.

"This war [World War I] could not have been fought . . ." Woodrow Wilson's address to the US Senate, September 30, 1918, S. Doc. No. 65-7330, at 3.

"We have made partners . . ." Burgan, *The 19th Amendment*, 35.

"Watchfires for Freedom," Zahniser and Fry, *Alice Paul*, 311.

"All the words . . ." Walton, *Woman's Crusade*, 230.

"We had a sort of perpetual flame . . ." Adams and Keene, *Alice Paul*, 234.

"Congregating in the park," Ibid., 221.

"Holding a meeting . . ." Ibid., 223.

"Building a bonfire on a public highway," Bausum, *With Courage and Cloth*, 67.

"Little figure," Adams and Keene, *Alice Paul*, 236.

"We burn not the effigy . . ." Ibid., 237.

"Women who have taken part . . ." Zahniser and Fry, *Alice Paul*, 316.
"The right of citizens . . ." Clift, *Founding Sisters*, 178.

CHAPTER 14
"Don't forget to be a good boy": The Battle for Ratification

"I honor women too highly . . ." Monroe, *The Nineteenth Amendment*, 71.
"A Vote for Federal Suffrage . . ." Wheeler, *One Woman, One Vote*, 344.
"Fad," Ibid., 335.
"Tennessee occupies . . ." Weatherford, *History*, 242.
"National woman's suffrage . . ." Wheeler, *One Woman, One Vote*, 345.
"We now have 35½ states . . ." Bausum, *With Courage and Cloth*, 76.
"To the last ditch . . ." Ibid.
"The bitterest, bare-fisted . . ." Wheeler, *One Woman, One Vote*, 338.
"Never in the history . . ." Weatherford, *History*, 242.
"Even if we win . . ." Clift, *Founding Sisters*, 196.
"Sorry, Joe . . ." Ibid., 197.
"There is one more thing . . ." Wheeler, *One Woman, One Vote*, 346.
"Hurrah and vote for Suffrage," "Letter to Harry Burn from Mother,"
    Knox County Public Library, Calvin M. McClung Historical
    Collection, http://cmdc.knoxlib.org/cdm/compoundobject/collection/
    p265301coll8/id/699/rec/2.
"Traitor to manhood's honor . . ." Wheeler, *One Woman, One Vote*, 347.
"First, because I believe in full suffrage . . ." Monroe, *The Nineteenth
    Amendment*, 76.
"It was a logical attitude . . ." Clift, *Founding Sisters*, 204–5.
"Were called up every half hour . . ." Wheeler, *One Woman, One Vote*, 347.
"Quite tragic . . ." Walton, *Woman's Crusade*, 244.
"I deem it one of the greatest honors . . ." Monroe, *The Nineteenth
    Amendment*, 77–78.
"To get the word male out . . ." Ward and Burns, *Not for Ourselves Alone*,
    218.
"I'm too old . . ." "Charlotte Woodward," National Park Service, http://
    www.nps.gov/wori/learn/historyculture/charlotte-woodward.htm.
"A great and noble woman," Ibid.
"Free and equal citizens," Lumsden, *Rampant Women*, 67.
"Equality of rights under the law . . ." Clift, *Founding Sisters*, 209.

ACKNOWLEDGMENTS

"The history of the past is but one long struggle upward to equality."
—*Elizabeth Cady Stanton*

I offer thanks to those who helped me prepare this history, specifically: the team at Algonquin, including Sarah Alpert, Jacquelynn Burke, Brunson Hoole, Trevor Ingerson, Elizabeth Johnson, Eileen Lawrence, Ashley Mason, and Laura Williams; the writing community at the Vermont College of Fine Arts; Sarah Davies of the Greenhouse Literary Agency; and, of course, Elise Howard—editor, feminist, and lifelong friend.

INDEX

Page numbers in italics refer to photos or illustrations and their captions.